When

the Devil

Came

Down

to Dixie

When
the Devil
Came
Down
to Dixie

Ben Butler in New Orleans

CHESTER G. HEARN

Louisiana State University Press   *Baton Rouge and London*

Copyright © 1997 by Chester G. Hearn
All rights reserved
Manufactured in the United States of America
First printing

06 05 04 03 02 01 00 99 98 97   5 4 3 2 1

Designer: Michele Myatt Quinn
Typefaces: Bodoni, Goudy
Typesetter: Impressions Book and Journal Services, Inc.
Printer and binder: Thomson-Shore, Inc.

Frontispiece courtesy U.S. Army Military History Institute.

Library of Congress Cataloging-in-Publication Data
Hearn, Chester G.
      When the devil came down to Dixie : Ben Butler in New Orleans /
   Chester G. Hearn
          p.   cm.
      Includes bibliographical references and index.
      ISBN 0-8071-2180-0 (alk. paper)
      1. Butler, Benjamin F. (Benjamin Franklin), 1818–1893.
   2. Generals—United States—Biography.   3. United States. Army—
   Biography.   4. New Orleans (La.)—History—Civil War, 1861–1865.
   I. Title.
   E467.1.B87H43 1997
   973.7'092—dc21
   [B]   97-16092
                                                              CIP

To Ann, Chet, and Dana,
the family that keeps me going,
and to the beloved memory of Wendy

CONTENTS

ILLUSTRATIONS

ACKNOWLEDGMENTS

Ideas for books often come from writing other books, and *When the Devil Came Down to Dixie: Ben Butler in New Orleans* is no exception. The major general never distinguished himself as one of the Civil War's brilliant strategists, but examining his military career and its impact on soldiers, sailors, politicians, and the South deepened my curiosity about him. After writing *The Capture of New Orleans, 1862* and *Admiral David Dixon Porter: The Civil War Years,* I began to sift through more of Butler's correspondence and discovered a smart, multifaceted man who could stir up more trouble in less time than a skunk at a wedding reception.

Butler's eight-month regime at New Orleans came at the midpoint of his career. The mere mention of his name still produces groans and grimaces—and occasionally an amused smile—from folks who live in the city today. Most contemporary historians have passed over this phase of Butler's career, missing a part of the general's life that is far more interesting than most of his military bungles and much of his life.

Scattered here and there are an abundance of documents and accounts pertaining to Butler's life. Sifting through them produced enough source material to write a book much longer, but I wanted to analyze the general's administration to determine whether, as New Orleanians claimed, he nurtured corruption and became rich, or whether, as many of his biographers claimed, he was merely a victim of his detractors and doing his job.

I relied on many people to complete this book. I wish to offer a special thanks to Judy Bolton and Rob Outland at Louisiana State University for providing many accounts from the university's two libraries.

Mary White assisted me in collecting letters from sources in New Orleans, as did Mark Cave at the Williams Research Center, who provided letters from the Historic New Orleans Collection. Leon C. Miller made available to me the large collection of correspondence at the Howard-Tilton Memorial Library, Tulane University, and Brenda B. Square provided several reels of microfilm containing Butler correspondence from Tulane's Amistad Research Center. Kathryn Page at the Louisiana State Museum in New Orleans opened thirteen large record groups containing letters and manuscripts written during the months of Butler's administration.

Jeanell Myers at the East Baton Rouge Parish Library offered some excellent recommendations on sources, and Regina M. LaBiche at the Louisiana Historical Center in Lafayette provided help in securing several well-researched accounts from *Louisiana History*. I am also indebted to James Hutson at the Library of Congress and to Michael Musick at the National Archives for their assistance in locating letters of Butler and many of his associates.

I am always indebted to the small library in Milton, Pennsylvania, where Susan Brandau and Mary Harrison work assiduously at gathering microfilm, documents, and primary source material from all over the country. Evelyn Burns, at the James V. Brown Library in Williamsport, Pennsylvania, makes an extra effort—because she knows I write—to find manuscripts and primary sources long out of print. I once received a note from her with the caustic comment "I normally don't look for printed matter older than myself," but I deeply appreciate her exertions on my behalf because it reduces my travel and leaves more time for writing.

To those whom I have forgotten I apologize, because material I received from places like the Essex Institute, Harvard University, and the New York Public Library have been in my possession for quite some time, and I long ago lost the names of the kind people who helped me.

I have never written about a subject more fascinating than Ben Butler, and the effort became not work but entertainment.

When

the Devil

Came

Down

to Dixie

Introduction

MAJOR GENERAL BENJAMIN F. BUTLER's military occupation of New Orleans has been a subject of controversy for many years—and for some persons, may always be. There was neither a trial to prove allegations of corruption, nor medals or awards presented for outstanding civic service. All that remained of Butler's eight months' rule is a staggering stack of correspondence, a few scattered and often controversial biographies, and no clear answers. Writing in 1918, William Dana Orcutt said, "It is a tribute to the personality of any man to have so impressed himself upon his generation that the mere mention of his name twenty-five years after his death revives the animosities of his period and stimulates antagonistic comment on the part of a later generation which has known him only by hearsay." After the passage of another eighty years, not much has changed.[1]

To understand the underpinnings of Butler's personality, one must first understand his profession. As a sharp criminal lawyer before the war, he spent many years profiting legitimately from his association with felons and other unsavory characters. A smart defense lawyer knows his way around the law better than a prosecutor and quickly learns how to avoid creating incriminating evidence. If such an individual wishes to build personal wealth using unethical practices, he needs to create a small, loyal, and layered network to funnel transactions without implicating the instigator. An extremely clever man would narrow the insiders to a few men he could trust—men who could not implicate him without first implicating themselves. Butler

---

1. William Dana Orcutt, "Ben Butler and the 'Stolen Spoons,'" *North American Review*, CCVII (January, 1918), 66.

had such an organization, and it consisted of his brother, Andrew, his brother-in-law, Fisher Hildreth, an agent in Boston, Richard S. Fay, Jr., and to varying degrees, a few members of his personal military staff. Butler also knew how to create and use a political machine, so all the ingredients for a grand conspiracy became well established before the general reached New Orleans.

As a military man, Butler had no training in strategy or tactics, and prior to occupying New Orleans he had never accompanied his men on the field of any fighting. He visibly enjoyed power, resented anyone who questioned his authority, and delighted in reducing opponents to a state of ineffectiveness. He obtained his general's stars through political influence—something quite common in the Civil War. He had friends in the White House, notably Simon Cameron, Edwin M. Stanton, Salmon P. Chase, and Montgomery Blair. He also had enemies, among them William H. Seward. At New Orleans he championed the poor, because they admired him, and made every effort to humble the rich, because they abhorred him. This led to damaging disagreements with Seward, who had the ear of Abraham Lincoln.

When Butler reached Louisiana, his personality and training came with him, and in the military occupation of New Orleans he relied on methods that had been obsolete for many decades.[2] William Watson, a visiting Englishman, admitted to seeing Butler only once, but the exposure left a lasting impression:

> To the Custom-house he was driven daily in a splendid carriage, surrounded by a numerous mounted body guard, and with more pomp and display than I have ever seen accorded to a European monarch. He then sat in imperial dignity in his judgment seat . . . bedecked with all the feathers and tinsel that could be crowded into a major-general's uniform . . . and pronounced sentences according to his undisputed will on the numerous unfortunate wights who were daily brought before him. To see such autocratic power vested in such a man, and the lives and liberties of so many thousands in his hand, and subject to his whim and caprice, seemed to me to be strangely anomalous in a nation which

2. John Rose Ficklin, "History of Reconstruction in Louisiana," *Johns Hopkins University Studies in Historical and Political Science*, XXVII (1940), 33.

had so long borne the name of being the great seal and home of human liberties.[3]

Butler held to his own theory of martial law, shaping it as defined by Sir Arthur Wellesly, later the Duke of Wellington, who wrote, "The will of the Comdg. General [is] exercised according to . . . natural equity." But what, Butler might have wondered, was meant by "natural equity"? In terms of early-nineteenth-century thought, it meant that civil government may exist in subordination to martial law if consistent with the objectives of the commanding general. If civil government did not meet those objectives, it could be abolished. Butler accepted that definition and eviscerated city hall. By doing so, he eliminated the underground voice of the wealthy and forced their exposure. If he could silence his enemies, he could have his way. One group he could not muffle were the numerous and bothersome foreign consuls who ultimately shortened his tenure by their barrage of complaints to their respective ministers seated in Washington.[4]

One of the unexplained curiosities of Butler's administration was the disappearance of a number of his official records, including a book of "Letters-Sent," a "Special Order Book," and, perhaps more incriminating, a "Special Permit Memorandum Book." Had his replacement, Major General Nathaniel P. Banks, received them, he would not have destroyed them, but they were never recovered. John D. Winters, who studied the Civil War in Louisiana, suspected Butler of "removing evidence that might be used against him at some future time," and this would be especially true of permits where applicants paid a fee to obtain a privilege. There are gaps in Butler's own five-volume *Private and Official Correspondence*, but some of the "Letters-Sent" and the "Special Orders" seem to be there, suggesting that the general did delete or destroy incriminating correspondence before making it public.[5]

During his administration in Louisiana, Butler paid very little

3. William Watson, *Life in the Confederate Army, Being the Observations and Experiences of an Alien in the South During the American Civil War* (New York, 1888), 407.

4. Jessie Ames Marshall, comp., *Private and Official Correspondence of Gen. Benjamin F. Butler During the Period of the Civil War* (5 vols.; Norwood, Mass., 1917), IV, 579, hereinafter cited as *Butler Correspondence*.

5. John D. Winters, *The Civil War in Louisiana* (Baton Rouge, 1979), 148.

attention to army regulations, and because of the remoteness of his communications with Washington, he made his own rules as he went. Secessionists among the upper class bitterly resented him. They fought him and suffered, because Butler knew how to use his power. The elite and the literate, accustomed to having their way, attempted to use their wealth and influence to destroy the general and force his recall. Their sordid characterizations of Butler's regime became legendary. Some of their claims, but not all, were true. The huge, illiterate majority—the poorer classes of blacks and whites—would have starved had Butler not fed and employed them, and thousands may have died had his sanitation policies not cleansed the city of disease. For many years after the war the poor continued to praise him, but all the admirable aspects of Butler's administration were clouded by constant accusations of rampant corruption.[6]

Despite the rumors, most northerners—even those who did not like him personally—approved of Butler's heavy-handed tactics. When the war ended, Admiral David Glasgow Farragut, a man who seldom aired his opinions publicly, said, "They may say what they please about General Butler, but he was the right man in the right place in New Orleans." Not everyone agreed, but Farragut had had a taste of civilian belligerence before Butler arrived and knew the city would not be easily tamed. "It is a strange thought that I am here among my relatives," Farragut had written home shortly after the surrender, "and yet not one has dared to say 'I am happy to see you.'" Referring not to Butler but to the mob who controlled the streets, Farragut added, "There is a reign of terror in this doomed city."[7]

Late in December, 1863, Butler departed from New Orleans, his future uncertain. Weeks passed into months. He remained politically active, captivated by the growing number of influential Republicans who spoke of his chances for the presidency. The notion appealed to the general. Enemies recognized the legitimacy of the threat and spoke

---

6. Howard P. Nash, Jr., *Stormy Petrel: The Life and Times of General Benjamin F. Butler, 1818–1893* (Rutherford, N.J., 1969), 172–73.

7. E. J. Sherman to Butler, October 10, 1891, in Benjamin F. Butler Papers, Library of Congress; Loyall Farragut, *The Life of David Glasgow Farragut: First Admiral of the U.S. Navy* (New York, 1879), 262.

loudly against the general's record of corruption. Butler searched for methods to improve his image, and by a stroke of good fortune James Parton, the nation's foremost biographer, offered his services. Delighted, Butler invited the author to his home and gave him access to the many files of documents comprising his life's work. Parton, who wrote with great energy, completed *General Butler in New Orleans* in the autumn of 1863, and it immediately became a huge success. Nobody could splash a coat of whitewash over Butler's administration in New Orleans better than Parton, but the book provided many valuable insights into the general's personality and suspiciously included material one would have expected to find in the missing official documents.[8]

General Butler never distinguished himself as a military commander. Reviewing his performance in Louisiana, one might say he never had the chance. Sent there with about fifteen thousand men, Butler received no reinforcements from the North, but Secretary of War Stanton expected him to garrison Ship Island, fortify and guard the lower Mississippi, provide a protective screen above New Orleans, dispatch part of his force to support Farragut's attack on Vicksburg, seize and hold Baton Rouge, and expand his holdings into southwestern Louisiana. On many occasions Butler was left with fewer troops in the city than the number of former Confederate soldiers mingling among the public.[9]

The general loved controversy and brought most of his troubles on himself. He was a fascinating study of inconsistencies—a remarkable man infused with a politician's appetite for wealth and power and a sincere empathy for the poor. He began his political career as a Democrat and became a Lincoln Republican during the war. Shifting with the tides of power, he joined the Radical Republicans, served in Con-

---

8. *Butler Correspondence*, II, 582, III, 150; Parton to Butler, April 10, 1863, in Butler Papers, LC; James Parton, *General Butler in New Orleans* (Boston, 1863), 615; Milton Flower, *James Parton: The Father of Modern Biography* (Durham, 1951), 64–72. All of Parton's correspondence with Butler can be found in the James Parton Papers, Harvard University Library, Cambridge, Mass.

9. *Report of the Joint Committee on the Conduct of the War*, 37th Cong., 3rd Sess. (3 vols.; Washington, D.C., 1863), III, 354, 356–57; Parton, *General Butler*, 298–99.

gress from 1866 to 1875, and took a leading role in the unsuccessful impeachment of Andrew Johnson. As a Greenbacker, he returned to Congress in 1878, reunited with the Democrats in 1880, and two years later satisfied a lifetime goal when elected governor of Massachusetts. In 1884 the Greenbackers joined with the Anti-Monopoly party and made him their candidate for the presidency, a post he had cherished since the midpoint of the Civil War, but he attracted little national support.[10]

Butler died on January 11, 1893, an immensely wealthy man whose estate topped $7 million. Nobody has ever been able to explain how Butler, who came from simple means and spent the bulk of his career alternating between law and politics, amassed so huge a fortune. Some said he stole it—a popular theory espoused by southerners and north-erners alike—though no one could prove it. Most sources admit that Butler was too clever to leave incriminating evidence where it could be found. It is hard to believe that a man of his skills, surrounded by corruption, remained unblemished. His psyche contained enough of the elements of a shrewd felon to substantiate the claims of his accusers—but did he deserve their accusations?[11]

Some southern historians who have studied Butler's military rule have declared it "no worse, and probably not as bad as that of Recon-structionists of later years," but the general was a harsh administrator plying his skills with consummate vigor. Refined ladies called him "Beast," nobody called him honest. Was it all legend, or did a founda-tion exist to support the attacks on his character?[12]

10. Patricia L. Faust, ed., *Historical Times Illustrated: Encyclopedia of the Civil War* (New York, 1986), 98–99; *Dictionary of American Biography*, III, 357–59.

11. New York *Tribune*, January 12, 1893, quoted in Robert S. Holzman, *Stormy Ben Butler* (New York, 1954), 245; *Dictionary of American Biography*, III, 358.

12. Howard Palmer Johnson, "New Orleans Under General Butler," *Louisiana Historical Quarterly*, XXIV (April, 1941), 532.

I

The Early Years

BENJAMIN FRANKLIN BUTLER came into the world on the afternoon of November 5, 1818, in the town of Deerfield, New Hampshire. His mother, Charlotte Ellison Butler, looked with dismay at the sickly, unattractive child who, many in the South, some forty-four years later, would call "the Beast." At the moment, however, Mrs. Butler had other problems. She had just received news that her husband, John, had succumbed to yellow fever in the Caribbean, and nasty neighbors were spreading rumors that the privateering captain had been hanged for piracy. Left with three children—six-year-old Charlotte, three-year-old Andrew Jackson, and the infant Ben—Mrs. Butler bid her scurrilous neighbors good-bye, boarded Andrew with relatives, and moved to the farm of her in-laws near Nottingham.[1]

By the time Ben reached the age of four, his mother began to probe for her son's potential. Her elder son, Andrew, whose robust body radiated good health, bore no resemblance to young Ben, who remained weak, puny, and indolent. Disfigured by a drooping eyelid and a severe case of strabism, Ben soon realized he looked different from other boys his age, and people practicing their own form of phrenology naturally assumed that the lad possessed latent disorders that would manifest themselves as he matured. His mother, however, remained optimistic, and adhering to her strict Calvinistic beliefs, she sent her son to a school in Nottingham Square to learn to read the Bible. At the age of six, Ben quickly mastered reading, and while his mother coached

---

1. Benjamin F. Butler, *Autobiography and Personal Reminiscences of Major General Benjamin F. Butler: Butler's Book* (Boston, 1892), 41–44, hereinafter cited as *Butler's Book*.

him on memorizing verses of the New Testament, Ben consumed his idle hours reading Robert Louis Stevenson's adventure stories. "My reading," Butler recalled, "was almost continuous, scarcely anything but eating and sleeping intervening. To force me out of doors to take required exercise, [my mother] was obliged to send me on errands, and make me get up the cows from the pasture . . . about a mile away. . . . The nearest boy lived a mile from us, and as he had his own duties to attend to, I saw very little of him."[2]

The boy assimilated knowledge so rapidly that when he reached the age of nine, his mother, anxious to expand his education, pooled the family's resources and enrolled him at Exeter Academy to prepare for college. His youth and peculiar appearance did not attract close friendships among his older classmates, and Ben spent the term in social isolation. Despite his diminutive size and frail body, he quickly became a seasoned fighter, and when an older student called him "a little cockeyed devil," Ben clubbed the boy with a stick. He soon developed a better way of countering insults—by haranguing his adversaries with a baffling choice of words that left them stupefied and speechless.[3]

While Ben divided his time at Exeter between books and bullies, a wealthy clergyman built a boardinghouse next to the First Calvinist Baptist Church in Lowell, Massachusetts, and asked Mrs. Butler to move from Nottingham to manage it. When she did, Ben finished the winter term at Exeter, slipped into his heaviest clothes, packed up his books, and slogged down the muddy road from New Hampshire to his mother's new home in Lowell. According to Marcus M. Pomeroy, one of Butler's early biographers, by the time the boy reached the ripe old age of ten, he was "known as the dirtiest, sauciest, lyingest child on the road. . . . He was tricky and wanton, serving in youth as a warning to other boys. No boy in the country could lie like Ben Butler." There is no record of whether the academy registered any grief over the lad's departure, but his classmates were glad to see him leave.[4]

2. *Ibid.*, 45–51. Strabism, or strabismus, is a visual disorder marked by the inability to direct both eyes on the same object and is commonly called cross-eye.

3. T. A. Bland, *Life of Benjamin F. Butler* (Boston, 1879), 8; *Butler Correspondence*, V, 137.

4. *Butler Correspondence*, V, 52; Marcus M. Pomeroy, *Life and Public Services of*

Ben found the growing industrial center of Lowell much different from his former home. Knitting mills dominated the town, and young factory girls filled Charlotte Butler's boardinghouse. They worked fourteen hours a day, six days a week. Ben sympathized with their long hours and listened patiently to their exhaustive complaining. When the girls went to work, he occupied his time in more nefarious ways. According to Pomeroy, the lad had already launched a career of larceny, and "his mother was called on at last to settle for articles taken from the trunks and wagons of her guests, and thus lost the profits of her business."[5]

Nonetheless, Mrs. Butler wanted the best for her bright little boy, and after consulting with her friend the clergyman, she decided that her son should go to the Baptist college at Waterville, Maine, and study for the ministry. Ben preferred a military career and argued that he should go to West Point. In the interim the pastor at the First Baptist Church scandalized the town by marrying a divorced woman. The troubled couple sought refuge in Mrs. Butler's boardinghouse until the town drove them away. When the pastor turned up dead, the public accused the wife of his murder. The incident soured Ben on any further consideration of the ministry, but like it or not, he went to Waterville. Remembering the clergyman who had urged him to become a preacher, Butler later wrote, "He was a very good man, but had very little insight into human nature, or at least into the nature of the boy for whom he was dealing." Whether Butler, at the age of sixteen, would become a typical example of "human nature" remained to be seen.[6]

One of Butler's earliest setbacks in life was his inability to obtain an appointment to West Point. Mrs. Butler applied to Congressman Caleb Cushing, knowing that if Ben went to West Point she would be spared the cost of educating her son at Waterville. She gathered letters of reference from friends and clergy, but it did no good. When

Benjamin F. Butler, Major-General in the Army and Leader of the Republican Party (New York, 1868), 8.

5. Hans Louis Trefousse, *Ben Butler: The South Called Him Beast* (New York, 1957), 18–19; Pomeroy, *Life and Public Services of Butler*, 9; Bland, *Life of Butler*, 12.

6. *Butler's Book*, 57–58; Charles Crowley, *History of Lowell* (Boston, 1868), 111. The college at Waterville eventually became Colby College.

Cushing replied that his congressional allotment had gone to another lad, Ben discovered the importance of political influence. Whether he would have been accepted at West Point is another matter. Physically, Ben Butler remained frail and sickly in appearance, although he had a fair complexion and reddish brown hair. His forehead lay abnormally flat against his head and this accentuated the peculiarly distinctive features of his face. Deeply chagrined by the rejection, Butler developed antipathy for West Pointers, and lacking family connections himself, he also developed a deep dislike for men of wealth who used their influence to manipulate others. Being more than passively conscious of the privileges that came with power, Ben added these lessons to his extracurricular education. Had he been admitted to West Point, it may have changed the outcome of many of his bungled campaigns during the Civil War.[7]

While attending Lowell High School, Butler had spent much of his free time mulling through the library in a local lawyer's office and reading whatever he could find, but without, he claimed, "any thought to becoming a lawyer." His attitude toward a legal career began to change after he entered the college at Waterville, where excessive emphasis on religious study, monetary fines for failure to attend chapel, and academic deductions for failing to attend sermons weakened his faith. The college's practices rankled Butler, and during his junior year at Waterville he developed a following among students who sided with him on religious issues but lacked the courage to speak out. He petitioned the administration asking that he and his followers be permitted to withdraw from chapel, but in his argument he made the mistake of challenging the school's most sacred principles. Rebuked before the entire student body, he became a martyr to his friends but barely escaped suspension for his impudence.[8]

Butler's flirtation with expulsion bothered him little, and instead of changing his irreverent ways he immersed himself in chemistry, physics, and philosophy, heatedly debating anyone who disagreed with his conclusions. In the midst of this, his junior year, he became

7. Holzman, *Stormy Ben Butler*, 7; Butler to Parton, January 15, 26, February 10, 1866, in Parton Papers.

8. *Butler's Book*, 56, 58–63; Parton, *General Butler*, 19–22.

attracted to another debate—a civil case being argued by Jeremiah Mason, one of the foremost lawyers of the day. Fascinated by the trial, he followed it with all the excitement of a boy about to steal his first kiss, and when it ended in a spectacular finish, Butler had found his niche—to study law.[9]

Having cast his sights on a legal career, he could barely wait to complete his senior year and get away from the suppressive atmosphere of Waterville. At his graduation in August, 1838, he expected to be noticed and appeared at the ceremony attired in an expensive and outlandish new suit. On accepting his diploma, he complained once more of the college's shabby policy of deducting from his academic standing for alleged ecclesiastical indiscretions. After speaking his mind, Butler departed, perhaps wondering if his complaints would work well in a civil suit against the school. He owed the college a small amount of money, and there is no record that he ever paid it.[10]

His arrival home shocked his mother. At ninety-seven pounds he looked consumptive, and Mrs. Butler shipped him off on a sea voyage to recuperate. Ben packed a crate of books, intending to begin his study of law at sea, but the captain stowed them in the hold and sent the lad ashore to buy a set of heavy clothing. Ben wanted something ornamented, something to distinguish himself from the others, and when he returned to the vessel with a ribboned hat, an embroidered jacket, and pantaloons "fit for the stage," the captain eyed the outfit and grumbled, "You look like a monkey."[11]

The four-month cruise restored Butler's health, and by the time he returned to Lowell his personality had been shaped for life. Never would he allow himself to be intimidated, and he would fight any person or institution that tried. He had grown to appreciate the value of politics as a means to achieving power and influence, and he believed a career in law provided the access. Inside his psyche the inclination to become a military man remained strong, though he continued to despise West Pointers. Conscious of his gift of intelligence, coupled with crafty if not larcenous proclivities, Butler aspired

9. *Butler's Book*, 63–64.
10. *Ibid.*, 69; Cooke to Butler, September 11, 1839, in Butler Papers, LC.
11. *Butler's Book*, 69–70.

to gain wealth and prestige, an ambition not uncommon for men of his age in America.[12]

The study of law in the 1830s required that an aspiring attorney clerk in the office of an established lawyer for three years, or until the employer could vouch for his understudy's fitness. Butler joined the office of William Smith, Esquire, who owned the largest library in Lowell and also practiced from a second office in Boston. Smith operated a real estate business and was often away, leaving Ben in the office to absorb Blackstone, Kent, constitutional law, and numerous treatises on pleading. For two years he did little but read, eat, and sleep, except when he had the opportunity to attend court or serve processes on one of Smith's delinquent tenants. Although he was spurned for past transgressions by much of Lowell's society, Butler made a favorable impression upon Judge Joseph Locke, who presided over the local police court. Locke, who wielded influence in state government, took an interest in young lawyers. Sensing opportunity, Ben shrewdly ingratiated himself with the judge and soon became the recipient of invaluable help.[13]

After only two years of study, Butler, in September, 1840, applied to Judge Charles Henry Warren of the court of common pleas for admission to the bar. Warren was not accustomed to being approached by clerks who had not completed the prescribed three-year reading term, but he had observed Ben in court that day and believed he could send the fellow back to his books by questioning him on the facts of the case just decided. Ben answered all of Warren's questions correctly, but in closing said to the judge, "I thought your honor ruled incorrectly." Somewhat astonished, Warren replied, "What reason, Mr. Butler, have you for that?" Ben explained that he had gone back to the office after the decision, studied the case further, and found a precedent in *English Common Law Reports*. Warren asked Ben to get the book, and the next day he recalled the parties and reversed himself. The revised verdict was sustained by the Massachusetts Supreme Court, and Butler, at the age of twenty-one, became a lawyer.[14]

12. *Ibid.*, 70–71.

13. *Ibid.*, 71–73; Smith to Butler, November 22, 1839, in Butler Papers, LC.

14. *Butler's Book*, 74–77. The case in question appears in *Reed* v. *Batchelder*, 1 Metcalf Massachusetts (1840), 559.

During his tenure as a clerk, Butler earned money in Dracut, Massachusetts, by teaching twenty-one students in a school containing mostly boys who had been expelled from other institutions. In the first few weeks he lost half of the rascals, commenting that "no one of them had gone away without a thrashing, the remembrance of which would last him a lifetime." Within three months the enrollment increased to twenty-six, many of them girls, and since he received his pay on the basis of head count, he considered the thrashings justified. For Butler, punishment acquired new meaning, especially if it netted a profit.[15]

Dracut, however, contained more than a school—it was the home of Dr. Israel Hildreth, a wealthy physician, whose daughter Sarah was rapidly becoming a cultured and intellectual actress. When Sarah's brother brought Butler to the house and introduced him, Ben resolved, with the same singular determination that became one of his lifelong traits, to make her his wife. In an age when men married younger women, Ben did not mind that Sarah was two years older than he. Her radiant beauty, love of Shakespeare, and long dark brown braids bedazzled the peculiar paramour with the drooping eyelid and the wandering pupils. In April, 1843, Butler traveled to Cincinnati, where Sarah was starring, and the two became engaged. One year later, May 16, 1844, they married in Lowell's St. Anne's Church. They made an odd couple—the proverbial beauty and the beast—but Ben's wit and constant devotion delighted his wife. During the next four years Butler became an established lawyer, a property owner, and a man of means. Of all the storms he weathered in his hectic political life, even his numerous political enemies agreed that his domestic life was solid, durable, and happy. The couple raised their children in Lowell; Paul, born in 1845, died five years later, but Blanche, born in 1847, the second Paul, born in 1854, and Ben Israel, born in 1856, made up the family.[16]

Butler believed that no lawyer should meddle in politics until he made some money, because politics provided poor compensation. In 1844 he did meddle. After it became apparent that Martin Van Buren

15. *Butler's Book*, 73.

16. *Ibid.*, 78–79; Parton, *General Butler*, 35; Balch to Butler, March 3, 1879, in Butler Papers, LC; Holzman, *Stormy Ben Butler*, 19.

could not win the presidency, he supported James K. Polk, a dark horse standard-bearer for the Democratic party. In stumping for Polk, Butler attacked such giants as Henry Clay. He quickly learned the value of accumulating political allies. After Polk's inauguration, Butler went to Washington and collected his reward—admission to the bar of the Supreme Court. The experience confirmed what Butler already believed: in the political game of quid pro quo, you do nothing without expecting something in return, and if you get less than you anticipated, you find a way to get even.[17]

At the time of his marriage Butler had already begun to acquire the reputation of a "bold, astute and not too scrupulous practitioner," but his first clients were factory girls who scraped together a few dollars to press charges against the employment practices of the Lowell mills, now numbering about thirty. Owners colluded and created a blacklist. No girl could quit one mill and get a job at another without a "pass" from the former. When the girls considered striking for shorter hours, Butler advised against it, suggesting they retain him to appeal on their behalf to the state legislature. He believed it was easier to change the law than the habits of profit-motivated businessmen, so he launched his first political action, arguing for a ten-hour day for all manufacturing operations conducted in the state. Mill owners rebelled, claiming a cutback in hours would cripple their ability to compete. "Let Massachusetts set the example," Butler argued, but the Whigs in power protected the mill owners, and when foreigners willing to work any number of hours migrated to Lowell, they jeopardized the jobs of the farm girls and his efforts failed.[18]

Butler's tenacity carried the crusade for the ten-hour workday into the 1850s. By then he had become a well-established Democrat with a reputation for being a sharp defense lawyer who mingled with thugs and petty thieves, but Butler enjoyed shocking people as long as he made money doing it. In the process of successfully defending felons, Butler gained enormous experience in discovering how to outwit plaintiffs and prosecutors. He also discovered the power of coalitions, and

17. Trefousse, *Ben Butler*, 31.
18. *Butler's Book*, 77, 89–92; New York *Post*, January 11, 1893, quoted in Holzman, *Stormy Ben Butler*, 11–12; Bland, *Life of Butler*, 14.

in 1849 Butler the Democrat joined forces with the emerging Free-Soil party to garner support for the ten-hour workday. This entailed salting the state legislature with Free-Soil candidates, and on election day, November 10, 1851, the town of Lowell cast eight thousand votes in a district of eight hundred registered voters, thereby giving the coalition a majority in the house. When the error was discovered the Whigs demanded a revote. Lowell mill owners posted notices that read: "Whoever, employed by this corporation, votes the Ben Butler ten-hour ticket on Monday next, will be discharged."[19]

The notice frightened many of the ticket's supporters away, but Butler remained resolute and accepted an invitation to speak at a meeting at city hall two days before the second vote. Mill owners expected riots and threatened to call out the militia. Butler had covered that base also. In 1839 he had joined the Lowell City Guard and was now its colonel. There would be no militia, and when he arrived at the hall to speak, it was so packed he could not get to the rostrum. The crowd in the rear hoisted him over their heads and rolled him over the audience until he landed on the platform. Disheveled but laughing, Butler delivered a speech that energized the voters. The next day the mill owners repudiated their notices, and shortly thereafter the legislature passed a compromise bill calling for a workday of eleven and one-quarter hours. Butler's hometown newspaper, the Lowell *Courier*, did not approve of his actions, and the editor vented his anger by writing:

BEN BUTLER

This notorious demagogue and political scoundrel, having swilled three or four glasses of liquor, spread himself at whole length in the City Hall last night. . . . The only wonder is that a character so foolish, so groveling and obscene, can for a moment be admitted into decent society anywhere out of the pale of prostitutes and debauches.[20]

Butler loved a fight and decided to have a little fun by seeking an indictment against the publisher. Judge Ebenezer Hoar, a Whig and

19. *Butler's Book*, 92–93, 98–100; Nash, *Stormy Petrel*, 38–47.
20. *Butler's Book*, 101–107, 123–24; Bland, *Life of Butler*, 21.

supporter of the mill owners, ruled that the Ben Butler named in the editorial was not Benjamin F. Butler and disallowed the suit. Butler eventually got even with Hoar, as he did with many of his perceived enemies, but the victory in the state legislature gave him visibility as an emerging politician and a friend of labor. Workingmen would have no other lawyer, and Butler cleverly played one group against the other. He told mill owners, "If I am not for you, I shall be against you; and you can take your choice." The mills discovered it was far less expensive to engage Butler than to fight his workers' suits, and the biggest beneficiary of this arrangement was, of course, Ben Butler.[21]

Butler's suit against John H. Warland, the editor of the Lowell *Courier*, extended into the 1850s. Butler baited the situation when he suggested that the editor's facial disfigurement resulted from "illicit dealings" in Mexico—not that the accuser was incapable of illicit misdealing himself. Warland flew into a rage and hired a friend to compose nasty verses in the same vein about Butler. Their publication in the newspaper gave Butler precisely what he wanted. He sued Warland for libel and won. Winning made an impression on Butler, but in the future he adopted a slightly different practice, preferring to attack his detractors outside the courts. At the time, he could not have imagined how many enemies he would accumulate during his lifetime, but there is little evidence to suggest he ever cared.[22]

Butler not only learned the law, he used it, and where voids existed, he capitalized on them. Having a wily disposition, he took pleasure in discovering defects in the law that enabled him to win cases. His adversaries referred to his methods as legal chicanery. When a known burglar was caught in the act of stealing a key to a Lowell shop, the owner turned him over to the city marshal. After the marshal learned who had taken the case, he confronted Butler and said, "If you get him off, I will throw up my commission." The case against the burglar appeared to be indefensible, and an elderly member of the bar said,

---

21. *Butler's Book*, 108–109; Bland, *Life of Butler*, 13; Nash, *Stormy Petrel*, 44. Years later, Hoar became attorney general under Ulysses S. Grant and Butler induced the Senate to reject him as justice of the Supreme Court; when Hoar's brother ran against Butler for the House of Representatives in 1876, Butler won (Holzman, *Stormy Ben Butler*, 14).

22. Boston *Globe*, January 11, 1893, quoted in Holzman, *Stormy Ben Butler*, 20.

"Butler, why do you take such cases, when you know you are sure to be beaten?" Butler replied, "It's a custom I have." When the trial began, Butler argued that larceny is the taking of personal property, and because the key was in the door, it was not personal property but "real estate, and taking real estate is not larceny. I move the court to direct a verdict of acquittal." Baffled, the district attorney dropped the charge, but soon afterwards the state legislature passed a law expanding the definition of larceny.[23]

Butler also had a sense of humor, and when Lowell passed an ordinance ordering all dogs on the street to be muzzled, the young attorney took his pet for a walk with a muzzle tied to its tail. As the ordinance did not specify on what part of the dog the muzzle was to be placed, the statute became a joke.[24]

In a suit against a mill brought by a factory girl for unpaid wages, Butler looked about to attach a piece of company property worth about the same amount as the money owed his client. He attached the mill's waterwheel, without which the mill could not run. His unorthodox methods of winning cases bewildered the opposition, many of whom could never decide whether to hate the man or to admire him. Judges, for the most part, respected Butler for his ability without personally liking him as an individual. Many years later Judge Josiah G. Abbott of Boston summed up the opinions of his peers when he said, "In one faculty Butler was never excelled, that was the keeping out and getting in of evidence."[25]

As the young lawyer's reputation grew, so did his caseload, and in 1849 he obtained a partner and opened an office in Boston, leaving a second partner in Lowell. Although frail as a youth, he now worked all day in Boston and until midnight in Lowell. Giving credence to Butler's energy, Moorfield Storey, a nineteenth-century biographer, claimed that during this period Ben tried four times as many cases as any other Massachusetts lawyer. When still in his thirties, he held his own in court when opposed by such respected legal giants as Daniel Webster, Caleb Cushing, William M. Evarts, and Rufus Choate. By the beginning of the Civil War, his law practice netted more than

23. *Butler's Book*, 987–88.
24. Boston *Globe*, January 12, 1893, quoted in Holzman, *Stormy Ben Butler*, 15.
25. *Ibid.*, 16; Parton, *General Butler*, 25.

eighteen thousand dollars a year, the most lucrative in New England. Butler also invested wisely, lived lavishly, and in 1843 began to build Belvedere, his imposing home on the banks of the Merrimack in Lowell.[26]

For all of the 1850s Butler remained a Democrat, gaining political prominence as each year passed. As a delegate to the Worchester Convention in 1850, he supported the South by endorsing the Compromise of 1850 and the Fugitive Slave Law. A year later he helped form the coalition of Democrats and Free-Soilers that ousted the Whigs. This led to his election to the Massachusetts legislature in 1852, but it also led to a crossroad in his political career. Butler wanted a seat in Congress, and his support of Franklin Pierce—another dark horse—for president scared away the national wing of the Democratic party in Massachusetts. They distrusted him and deposed Fisher Hildreth, his brother-in-law, from the office of sheriff in Middlesex County. For the next few months Butler remained in a political quagmire, but by supporting Pierce he eventually obtained a postmastership for his brother-in-law.[27]

Aware of the large Catholic population of Massachusetts, Butler looked after their interests and won their support, and in March, 1853, this enabled him to attend the Constitutional Convention as a delegate on the coalition ticket. Butler once again rubbed elbows with the leaders of the Democratic party, men like Senator Charles Sumner and Congressman Nathaniel P. Banks, who asked him for favors in exchange for theirs. Butler understood the system and worked it advantageously, attending the Democratic National Convention in 1856. Two years later he won a seat in the Massachusetts senate—the only

26. Parton, *General Butler*, 34–35; Moorfield Storey, *The Record of Benjamin F. Butler* (Boston, 1883), 23.

27. Roy Frank Nichols, *The Democratic Machine, 1850–1854* (2 vols.; New York, 1923), II, 81, 133–34; Butler to Cushing, May 2, 1853, in Caleb Cushing Papers, LC; Cass to Butler, December 21, Sumner to Butler, December 22, 1853, in Butler Papers, LC; Butler to Sumner, December 19, 1853, in Charles Sumner Papers, Harvard University Library, Cambridge, Mass. The Democratic Convention of 1852 contained two delegates named Benjamin F. Butler, the other coming from New York. During this period, some historians have confused one Butler with the other, and the same mistake was made by some of the citizens of New Orleans—but only for a short time. See note 50 in chapter 4.

Democrat to do so. Butler's star was in the ascendant, but not even he knew where it might lead.[28]

In 1859 Butler took his seat in the Massachusetts senate and quickly became one of the dominant members of the legislature, but this was not enough to satisfy his quest for political power. In September he accepted the Democratic nomination for governor, hoping to oust Henry J. Gardner, the Know-Nothing governor who had attempted to disband the state militia. Colonel Butler had a personal stake in the regiment, and in 1855, when Gardner issued orders to dissolve the militia, Butler refused to obey them, calling the act illegal. He dared the governor to order a court-martial and threatened to try the case in court. Knowing Butler's knack for winning suits, Gardner reorganized the Lowell unit under a different district, thereby depriving the colonel of his command. Butler, however, would not be outflanked by a political enemy. He waited for the restructured Massachusetts Volunteer Militia to choose new officers, who in turn would elect the regimental and brigade officers. When the process finally reached the stage of electing the brigadier general, Butler won and enjoyed the gratification of receiving his commission from none other than Governor Gardner. Not content with beating Gardner at his own game, Butler vowed revenge and made a determined effort to overthrow him at the polls. Running his campaign on the platform of tariffs and slavery, Butler, the Democrat, lost a close election to Banks, who was now a Republican, but he privately celebrated when Gardner and his Know-Nothings fell from power.[29]

Butler wore many hats, and it was amazing that he wore them all so well—a state senator, a gubernatorial candidate, a brigadier general of militia, and a busy trial lawyer all at the same time. During the 1850s he also acquired a substantial amount of stock in Middlesex Mills at depressed prices. As a director he led the company's successful reorganization and pocketed a tidy profit. A lesser person than Butler would have worn himself to a frazzle trying to keep his life organized, but Ben

28. *Butler's Book*, 110–23; Cushing to Butler, November 20, 1851, Banks to Butler, March 16, 1853, Sumner to Butler, December 22, 1853, in Butler Papers, LC; Cowley, *A History of Lowell*, 159; Nash, *Stormy Petrel*, 45–54. Soon after 1856, Sumner and Banks became Republicans.

29. *Butler's Book*, 124–26; Nash, *Stormy Petrel*, 29–30.

neither faltered nor missed an opportunity. Whatever he did, however, he did for himself, and at the close of 1859 nobody in New Orleans paid much attention to the wily lawyer-general in Massachusetts who on the one hand talked about protective tariffs for revenue and endorsed the Dred Scott decision with its obvious sanction of slavery in the territories. On the other hand he supported Stephen A. Douglas from Illinois on the matter of popular sovereignty, thereby straddling many of the issues dividing Republicans and Democrats.[30]

In June, 1860, Charleston, South Carolina, sprouting with secessionists, became the site of the Democratic National Convention. Massachusetts Democrats had split, sending Erasmus Beach to the convention as a Douglas delegate and Butler as a John C. Breckinridge delegate. By the time the convention came to order, northern Democrats felt that Breckinridge would not attract votes and appealed to Butler to back Douglas. Butler disliked certain aspects of Douglas' platform and abstained. After seven unsuccessful votes by the delegates to nominate Douglas, Butler astonished the convention by switching his support to Jefferson Davis of Mississippi, whom he presented as being the best appeasement candidate for maintaining unity between the North and South. On his way to Charleston, Butler had stopped in Washington, talked at length with Davis, and mistakenly formed the opinion that the future president of the Confederacy was at heart a Unionist. Having convinced himself of Davis' fidelity, Butler voted for him on the next fifty ballots.[31]

With the convention reaching new levels of disharmony, delegates from seven southern states walked out after refusing to accept a popular-sovereignty plank in the party platform. The northern delegation withdrew and on June 18 reconvened at Baltimore's Front Street Theater to nominate Douglas. The convention split again, the bolting delegates retiring to the Maryland Institute in Baltimore to cast their ballots for Breckinridge. By supporting Breckinridge, Butler lost his credibility when he refused to adhere to the Democratic party of Mas-

30. Cowley, *History of Lowell*, 53; Trefousse, *Ben Butler*, 52.

31. *Butler's Book*, 134–40; Butler to Chapman, August 22, 1889, in Butler Papers, LC; William B. Hesseltine, *Lincoln and the War Governors* (New York, 1948), 83; Parton, *General Butler*, 28; Bland, *Life of Butler*, 27–30. Butler claimed he voted for Davis fifty-seven times, but he voted only fifty.

sachusetts' eleventh-hour demand that he support Douglas. The debate became so heated that Butler engaged a Boston prizefighter to escort him to and from the convention. With two Democrats, Douglas and Breckinridge, now sharing the ticket, Butler returned home to hisses, hoots, and jeers. His party called him a "traitor" and no longer a Democrat. His behavior at the convention almost defied explanation, but biographer T. A. Bland, who researched Butler's motives for supporting Breckinridge, found that early in the convention Butler had spoken with southern leaders in an effort to discourage them from seceding, receiving in exchange for his support promises of high office, honors, and cash. Covert deal-making was not inconsistent with Butler's methods for acquiring power and wealth. Alexander Stephens, who later became the Confederacy's vice president, looked at Butler's motives differently, crediting the cagey delegate with attempting to block the election of Lincoln by forcing the final decision into the House of Representatives, where a coalition of Democrats and moderates might yet win the presidency for Breckinridge.[32]

Back in Massachusetts, the faltering Breckinridge Democrats in 1860 named Butler as their choice for governor. With public opinion against him, he could not win and polled a meager 4 percent of the vote. His sympathizers in the South warned of their intentions to secede and invited Butler to "come down and live with us; we will take care of you; we want such men as you are." Butler replied that he could not, "because it is treason to the country, and the North will fight to prevent it." His southern friends scoffed at the idea. A few months later, however, Butler accepted the invitation to "come down and live" in the South, but under entirely different circumstances. When he came, he brought thousands of soldiers dressed in blue. Southerners soon realized their mistake and did not want him anymore.[33]

The rift growing within a nation on the brink of bloody transition did not seem to bother the citizens in faraway Louisiana quite as much as it did her southern sisters. Nor in early 1860 could anyone in New

32. Storey, *Record of Butler*, 7; Bland, *Life of Butler*, 34; Nash, *Stormy Petrel*, 64–65; Trefousse, *Ben Butler*, 56–57; Alexander H. Stephens, *A Constitutional View of the Late War Between the States* (2 vols.; Philadelphia, 1868), II, 276.

33. *Butler's Book*, 149–50.

Orleans predict that some cockeyed lawyer by the name of Butler would invade their town with fifteen thousand blue-coated Yankees and impose great misery upon their lives. A close acquaintance described Butler as a person having the "ability to change in an instant from a well-mannered, affectionate gentleman to an insolent, brazen bully. . . . Butler was at once passionately loved and passionately hated. He was a man who left few people indifferent." The description probably fit Butler about as well as his best suit of clothes.[34]

It might have been well for New Orleanians to have given more study to this man called Butler. They may have fought harder to save their city.

34. Trefousse, *Ben Butler*, 49.

2

Butler Goes to War

IN THE AUTUMN OF 1860 Abraham Lincoln won the presidential election, and Ben Butler pondered his options. Out of favor with his party, he went to Washington to confer with friends. While he was there, South Carolina seceded from the Union and a body of southern commissioners turned up in Washington to speak with James Buchanan, the lame-duck Democrat in the White House. Butler, with his dander up over secession, converged on Buchanan and demanded that the emissaries be arrested by the United States marshal and indicted for treason. As an experienced criminal lawyer, Butler offered to assist in the trial without—of all things—a fee. He promoted the concept that all convicted traitors should be hanged, and to the relief of the commissioners, Buchanan declined to accept Butler's recommendations.[1]

Disgusted with Buchanan's timidity, Butler sought his friend Jefferson Davis, the purported Unionist senator and the man he had risked his political career to make president. Davis disappointed him by declaring his first duty was to Mississippi, which was then in the process of seceding. "I never afterwards saw him," Butler wrote, "which was a good piece of fortune for him; for if we had met while I was in command of the . . . army, he would have been saved a great deal of the discomfort which he suffered by being confined in prison." Butler did not intend his statement to be construed as a gesture of benevolence.[2]

After his conversation with Davis and other southern secessionists,

1. *Butler's Book*, 151–56.
2. *Ibid.*, 159.

Butler returned to Massachusetts and warned Governor John A. Andrew that the militia may have to be activated during the winter. Seeing an opportunity to turn a quick profit from what might become a very short war, Butler convinced the governor to float an appropriation to purchase heavy clothing for the troops. When the money became available, Middlesex Mills, where Butler held considerable stock, produced the cloth. In 1862 stockholders pocketed a dividend of 31 percent, enjoying equal or better returns throughout the war.[3]

When seven southern states separated from the Union, Butler vowed to take an active part in reunifying the country, even if it meant leaving his practice to go to war. After voting fifty times for Jefferson Davis during the Democratic convention, he had some soul searching to do regarding his political life. Having attached himself to the discredited radical wing of the party, he had rendered himself politically impotent, and the only office of public trust he still occupied was that of brigadier general in the Massachusetts militia. He began to mend his fences with Republican governor Andrew by offering to lead the troops if called to duty and warned they may be needed in Washington on March 4, the day of Lincoln's inauguration. Butler's overtures toward Andrew, a staunch abolitionist, coincided with the governor's own concerns, and much to the surprise of many of his old enemies, Butler supported all of the war preparations being espoused by Republicans. Andrew doubted whether Butler could be trusted, but he needed the lawyer's residual influence with the Democrats to pass his legislative initiatives.[4]

Lincoln's inauguration transpired without the trouble predicted by Butler, and in Washington five weeks of inactivity followed, compelling the Massachusetts legislature to repeal its emergency appropriations. The members adjourned on April 11 and went back to their districts. Four days later news of the bombardment of Fort Sumter reached Boston and Lincoln asked for 75,000 troops. Secretary of War Simon Cameron sent Andrew an urgent request for 1,500 militiamen, and the governor hurriedly recalled the legislature.

3. *Butler Correspondence*, I, 10; Parton, *General Butler*, 66; Storey, *Record of Butler*, 4.

4. *Butler Correspondence*, I, 6–14; *Butler's Book*, 161; Schouler to Butler, August 3, 1870, in Butler Papers, LC.

Butler was trying a case in Boston when he learned that the 6th Regiment of his brigade had been summoned to Faneuil Hall. He postponed the trial and departed for Lowell. Using as a wedge his past relationship with Secretary of War Cameron, who was once a Democrat and now the leader of Pennsylvania Republicans, Butler dispatched a wire: "You have called for a brigade of Massachusetts troops; why not call for a brigadier-general and staff? I have some hope of being detailed." The strategy worked. Overnight a requisition for a brigade with a brigadier general landed on Andrew's desk. There were other obstacles to hurdle, senior generals being one, but Butler had an inside track. He knew the legislature would have to find the money to finance the brigade's expedition to Washington, so on the morning of April 16 he called on the president of Boston's Bank of Mutual Redemption, James G. Carney, and arranged a loan of fifty thousand dollars. Then he stopped at Andrew's office and found the governor and the commonwealth's treasurer deliberating over the problem of raising money to finance the transfer of troops to the nation's capital. He presented Carney's letter of commitment, thereby sealing his own appointment as the brigade's commanding general.[5]

As a brigadier general, Butler had no military experience, but he now commanded six thousand militia and regarded himself as competent and important, eclipsing such notable commanders as General in Chief Winfield Scott. The lavish pomp and ceremony prior to the departure of the brigade from Boston fed Butler's hunger for recognition and attention. Even more peculiar was the impression of unity displayed by Butler when he stood with Governor Andrew and a number of political enemies during a review of the troops. The command, however, split when the 3rd and 6th Massachusetts departed by steamer for Baltimore by way of Fort Monroe, and the 8th Massachusetts entrained for Washington with Butler.[6]

Ben's brother, Andrew, happened to be home on a visit from California, where he had spent the past eleven years in the gold rush, and the general quickly commissioned him colonel and made him a staff

---

5. *Butler's Book*, 168, 170–73; Parton, *General Butler*, 68–69; *Butler Correspondence*, I, 15–16.

6. *Butler's Book*, 127; *Butler Correspondence*, I, 15–16; Bland, *Life of Butler*, 37.

officer. Andrew, who thought wars were fought with pickax handles, had no more military experience than his younger brother, but he stood an impressive "six feet two in his stockings and weighed one hundred and eighty pounds." Ben, now forty-two, possessed none of his brother's physical features. Short in stature, he had become fleshy and rotund with thin, chicken-like legs, and the droop of his normal eyelid was rapidly descending to the level of the other. The pair made great companions, but the depth of the relationship would not become apparent until mid-1862, after Federal troops occupied New Orleans.[7]

On the trip to Washington, Butler stopped at New York for a round of cheers, and again at Philadelphia for another celebration. Complications, however, began to occur when the 6th Massachusetts landed at Baltimore and were attacked by a mob. The troops fired into the crowd, killing or wounding several hostiles. With bridges damaged and communications with Washington interrupted, Butler decided not to go through Baltimore. He hired a steamer at Philadelphia, sailed up Chesapeake Bay, and disembarked at Annapolis, Maryland's capital and the home of the United States Naval Academy. From there he made arrangements to hurry part of his command to Washington.[8]

Butler remained at Annapolis, where he had defied Governor Thomas H. Hicks by landing troops on Maryland's soil. Asked what he intended to do, Butler replied, "I have no orders. I am carrying on the war now on my own hook; I cut loose from my orders when I left Philadelphia." But when a slave insurrection threatened in Baltimore, Butler offered Hicks the use of Massachusetts troops to put down the revolt. Governor Andrew, an abolitionist, could not restrain his temper when he learned that Butler had diverted troops and offered them to aid a governor who had refused to allow the regiment to land. Now, Andrew grimly wrote, "[you] help rebels who stand with arms in their

---

7. *Butler's Book*, 190; Bland, *Life of Butler*, 37.

8. *Butler's Book*, 174–76; Bland, *Life of Butler*, 37; *Butler Correspondence*, I, 16–17, 23; Parton, *General Butler*, 70–98; Thompson to Cameron, April 23, 1861, in *Official Records of the Union and Confederate Armies, War of the Rebellion* (128 vols.; Washington, D.C., 1987), II, 596–97, hereinafter cited as ORA, with all citations to Series I unless specified otherwise. For an account of Butler's march to Washington, see Trefousse, *Ben Butler*, 65–75.

hands, obstructing [your] progress toward the city of Washington." Whether the mob be black or white, Butler replied, "It was simply a question of good faith and honesty of purpose."[9]

Nobody could stir up trouble in less time than Ben Butler. When Colonel Marshall Lefferts, who was also rushing a regiment to Washington, appeared off Annapolis with the 7th New York, Butler attempted to exercise his rank and merge the command into his own. Lefferts rebelled, and when the New Yorkers set out for Washington with the 8th Massachusetts, they were happy to leave the quarrelsome militia general behind at Annapolis.[10]

Butler missed the excitement of marching into the capital, but he continued to act independently and created his own kind of chaos. On April 24, Lincoln, now anxious to placate offended Marylanders, dispatched messengers to Annapolis with instructions for Butler to stay there and keep the road to Washington open. The following day General Scott sent written instructions, ordering Butler to establish headquarters there. Lincoln may have had ulterior reasons for not wanting the troublesome political general at the capital, and on April 27 Scott created the Department of Annapolis, which covered twenty miles on both sides of the railroad running between the general's headquarters and Washington, naming Butler its commander. Lincoln expected Butler to become conciliatory to the needs of Governor Hicks, who had called a special meeting of the state legislature. The governor preferred to keep his legislators away from the Massachusetts militia and moved the seat of government to Frederick. With Hicks gone, a temporary calm settled over Annapolis, and Butler sent for his family.[11]

Butler soon tired of guarding the railroad and on May 1 journeyed to Washington to suggest to Scott an advance on Manassas Junction.

9. *Butler's Book*, 169, 192, 194; Andrew to Butler, April 25, Butler to Andrew, May 9, 1861, in *Butler Correspondence*, I, 37; Holzman, *Stormy Ben Butler*, 31.

10. *Butler Correspondence*, I, 18; William Swinton, *History of the Seventh Regiment, National Guard, State of New York, During the War of the Rebellion* (New York, 1870), 53–60.

11. Lincoln's Order No. 3, April 24, 1861, in Butler Papers, LC; Scott to Butler, April 25, General Orders No. 12, April 27, 1861, ORA, II, 600, 607; *Butler Correspondence*, I, 52.

Scott—old, feeble, and suffering from gout—was still alert enough to know that Virginia's ordinance of secession had not been ratified and ordered Butler back to Annapolis. Three days later Butler returned to Washington, this time to see Lincoln, and learned that plans were secretly afoot to occupy Baltimore and recover the Gosport Navy Yard. Scott gave Butler a minor role by ordering him to occupy Relay House, a key junction about nine miles west of Baltimore where the Baltimore and Ohio Railroad switched from its east-west track to the spur running to Washington. Two days later Butler seized the junction and requested further instructions.[12]

Butler moved his base of operations to Relay House and, while waiting for word from Scott, cast a malicious eye toward Baltimore and sent Captain Peter Haggerty into town disguised as an organ grinder and fitted out with a live monkey. This appealed to Butler's sense of intrigue. Haggerty returned to report no hostile troops in the city, but he learned of several tons of gunpowder hidden in a building on Calhoun Street and ostensibly placed there for the use of the enemy. Since Baltimore fell within what the general now considered part of his department, and since Massachusetts troops had been killed there, he decided to bypass Scott's authority and generate a little publicity. On May 13 he loaded a thousand troops on a train, feinted his intentions by traveling a short distance away from Baltimore, and then, in a driving rainstorm, cut the telegraph lines, reversed the engine, and rumbled back to the city. Before Baltimore knew what had happened, Butler occupied Federal Hill. The general seated himself comfortably in a local beer garden and issued a proclamation "enforcing respect and obedience to the laws" of Maryland and the United States. To add substance to his words, he arrested several prominent men, confiscated arms, and threatened to hang Ross Winans, an elderly millionaire who had advocated Maryland's secession. A year later he would pen another proclamation, but the citizens of New Orleans would not react with the same submissiveness as Marylanders.[13]

Butler's unexpected occupation of Baltimore, followed by his unau-

12. *Butler's Book*, 222–23; *Butler Correspondence*, I, 64–65; Scott to Patterson, May 4, Butler to Scott, May 6, 1861, ORA, II, 619–20, 623–24.

13. *Butler Correspondence*, I, 80; *Butler's Book*, 226–34; Butler's Proclamation, May 14, 1861, ORA, II, 30–32; Parton, *General Butler*, 110–15; Bland, *Life of Butler*, 41.

thorized proclamation, horrified Lincoln and Scott, both of whom had been tiptoeing around the delicate issue of Maryland's status. If the state seceded, Washington would become enclosed within the Confederacy and the Union government would be compelled to move. Reverdy Johnson, an old enemy of Butler, rushed to Washington and appealed to Lincoln for Winans' release. To Butler's chagrin, Lincoln complied, and the angry general suggested that Winans must have bribed somebody in order to obtain his parole.[14]

Never having any use for militia generals, Scott raged at his subordinate's impudence, but Butler's occupation of Baltimore played so well in the press that Lincoln constrained Scott from taking action. Aware also that Butler had been influential in mobilizing the war Democrats, Lincoln counseled Scott to wire Butler instructing him to issue no more proclamations and suggested that the general be delicately removed from Baltimore and placed in command of Fort Monroe, where there would be less opportunity for him to make trouble. In a further appeal to the war Democrats, however, Lincoln invited Butler to the White House and made the mistake of elevating him to the grade of major general, thereby making him one of the highest-ranking officers in the army under Scott. As proof of Butler's enormous popularity, after he reached Washington a huge crowd assembled outside his hotel to cheer him, and the general, never timid about speaking, delivered a speech that infused the crowd with patriotism. Scott, however, was not as forgiving as Lincoln, and after a turbulent interview with the general, Butler threatened to resign. Scott said he should, but Lincoln, Cameron, and Treasury Secretary Chase smoothed over the quarrel and promised Butler a larger department. Gratified by the pledge, Butler departed for Fort Monroe, bringing with him his staff of cronies, his brother Andrew, and a better understanding of how to manipulate Lincoln.[15]

---

14. *Butler's Book*, 232; Carl Sandburg, *Abraham Lincoln: The War Years* (4 vols.; New York, 1939), I, 275–76.

15. Scott to Butler, May 14, 15, 18, 1861, ORA, II, 28, 640–41; Cameron to Sprague, May 15, 1861, *ibid.*, Ser. 3, I, 207; *Butler Correspondence*, I, 95–97, III, 66–70, 85; *Butler's Book*, 237–42; Parton, *General Butler*, 117; Horowitz, "Ben Butler and the Negro: 'Miracles Are Occurring,'" *Journal of Louisiana History*, XVII (Spring, 1976), 165.

On May 22 the general marched into Fort Monroe and, having no desire to be associated with a mere fort, advised Scott that he had assumed command of the Department of Virginia. Fort Monroe, although strategically placed at the tip of the Virginia peninsula, was no more than an eighty-acre field enclosed by a low stone-and-brick wall mounting old naval guns that swept the waters of Hampton Roads, where the James River spills into Chesapeake Bay. Because the fort had been built to protect the sea face, no guns covered the landward side, and for a large garrison, there was insufficient water. The site contained barracks, hospitals, a chapel, parade grounds, gardens, and a comfortable mansion for the post commander, Colonel Justin Dimick, whose residence Butler commandeered to house his own family.[16]

Scott, already scorched once by Butler's independent campaigning, promised the major general 7,500 troops but cautioned him to "submit your plans and ask instructions from higher authority" before initiating risky ventures and to "communicate with me often and fully on all matters important to the service." Butler held no fear of reprisal from the seventy-five-year-old Scott, who was partially disabled from an old wound, forever soaking his gouty feet in a tub of water, and incapable of taking the field. Having no cavalry assigned for reconnaissance, Butler sent brother Andrew to Baltimore with requisitions for horses. Unwise in the ways of horse thieves, Andrew found that the general's horses had been sent to Washington, and he returned to Fort Monroe empty-handed. Andrew Butler would not make this mistake again. By the time he reached New Orleans, he had learned enough from his younger brother to give lessons to felons.[17]

The general's network of conspirators reached back to Lowell, where brother-in-law Fisher A. Hildreth handled the brigade's invoices. The process worked as smoothly as a well-oiled engine. J. F. Whipple, a New York hatmaker, offered to sell Butler six thousand caps. The general agreed to the sale if Whipple would revert to the command's quartermaster "ten per cent to divide around." Astonished by the demand, Whipple withdrew his offer but learned later from another supplier

16. Scott to Butler, May 18, Butler to Scott, May 22, 24, 1862, ORA, II, 640–41, 643, 648–49; *Butler's Book*, 246; Faust, ed., *Historical Times Illustrated*, 276.

17. Scott to Butler, May 18, 1861, ORA, II, 641; *Butler's Book*, 243–44, 266–67.

that standard practice at Butler's headquarters was for the quartermaster to buy whatever he wanted and pass the invoices through Hildreth, who would then bill the army at *his* prices.[18]

In addition to brother Andrew, Butler's affiliates included Lieutenant George H. Butler, nephew and aide-de-camp to the general. Colonel Joseph B. Carr, commanding the 2nd New York Volunteers, recalled being accosted by George one evening and told, "Colonel, Uncle Ben wants you and is going to give you hell." Puzzled, Carr asked, "Who is Uncle Ben?" "Why, General Butler," the lieutenant replied, adding that the issue concerned an act of vandalism by Carr's New Yorkers. Carr, unimpressed by the summons, muttered a few words of disrespect. Young George thought that was alright and said, "I like to see men who are not afraid of Uncle Ben."[19]

Isolating "Uncle Ben" at Fort Monroe kept him away from Marylanders but exposed him to the property of Virginians. Two days after Butler's arrival a sentinel captured three runaways creeping along the perimeter fence and took them into custody. This prompted Major John B. Cary of the Virginia Artillery to call upon Butler and inquire what the general intended to do with Colonel Charles K. Mallory's slaves. Butler said he had put them to work on the fort. Astonished, Cary demanded their return in compliance with fugitive slave laws. Butler, anxious to practice a little law, reminded the major that Virginia had just passed an ordinance of secession and replied, "I am under no constitutional obligations to a foreign country, which Virginia now claims to be."

Cary countered, arguing, "But you say we cannot secede, and so you cannot consistently detain the Negroes."

"But you say you have seceded," Butler declared, "so you cannot consistently claim them. I shall hold them as contraband of war. You were using them against the Government: I propose to use them in favor of it. If, however, Colonel Mallory will come in and take the

18. Holzman, *Stormy Ben Butler*, 39–40.

19. Joseph B. Carr, "Operations of 1861 About Fort Monroe," in Robert U. Johnson and Clarence C. Buel, eds., *Battles and Leaders of the Civil War* (4 vols.; New York, 1884–88), II, 146, hereinafter cited as *B&L*. Carr became a major general and commanded a division in the Army of the Potomac.

oath of allegiance to the United States, he shall have his Negroes."[20]

At first, Lincoln was not sure what to make of Butler's unilateral policy of emancipation. The Republican party quickly endorsed it, though it came from a Democrat, and the term *contraband* caught the public's imagination and became an overnight appellation for runaway slaves. The press heaped praise on Butler, and even General Scott, who distrusted his subordinate, agreed with the remark, referring to it as "Butler's fugitive slave law." After a conference between a troubled Lincoln and his divided cabinet, Secretary of War Cameron wrote Butler, "Your action in respect to the negroes who came into your lines from the service of the rebels is approved." The confiscation, however, stirred the political pot, and it was not until August 6, some two weeks after the Battle of First Bull Run, that Lincoln allowed an act to be passed legalizing Butler's "contraband" order.[21]

Butler sopped up attention like a sponge, but isolated as he was from the mainstream of the conflict, he felt unduly restrained by Scott, who plainly did not want the political general to succeed. Butler seldom listened to advice, and because his past actions had appealed to the public, he gave little notice to cautions coming from his friends in the cabinet. When rumors began to radiate from the fort that Butler would soon be in Richmond, Postmaster Montgomery Blair urged him to be patient until somebody superseded Scott. With so small a force Butler knew he could not capture Richmond, but through private sources— and not through Washington—he obtained maps of the Confederate capital and shielded his intentions from the War Department. To get far up the peninsula, however, he would have to move his brigade through Big Bethel, a small church near a bridge located about thirteen miles below Yorktown where a small Confederate force maintained an outpost.[22]

Confederates had fortified Big Bethel with a howitzer and 1,400

20. *Butler's Book*, 256–58; Deane to Butler, March 14, 1891, in Butler Papers, LC; Bland, *Life of Butler*, 50.

21. Burton J. Hendricks, *Lincoln's War Cabinet* (Boston, 1946), 229; *Butler Correspondence*, I, 116–17, 119, 121–22; Cameron to Butler, May 30, 1861, *ORA*, Ser. 2, I, 754–55; Folger to Chase, June 15, 1861, in Salmon P. Chase Papers, LC.

22. Scott to Butler, May 18, 1861, *ORA*, II, 640–41; *Butler Correspondence*, I, 127–30; George Fort Milton, *The Age of Hate* (New York, 1930), 26.

troops, and Butler believed he could capture the small garrison and open the way for a larger force to attack Richmond. To the general's way of thinking, a surprise attack of 3,500 blueclads supported by artillery could easily overwhelm the small detachment of Rebels. He assigned the mission to Brigadier General Ebenezer W. Pierce, who in turn organized a pincer movement utilizing the regiments of Colonel Frederick Townsend's 3rd New York and Colonel John E. Bendix's 7th New York. Before daybreak on June 10, the two green militia units started out on different roads, and when they reached the point of juncture, they mistook each other for the enemy and opened fire. Butler attributed the disaster to mismanagement by officers "being very much scared" and so inexperienced that they failed to send out skirmishers to probe for pockets of the enemy. The debacle ended in the blueclads being stampeded back to the fort, and the setback nearly cost Butler confirmation of his two stars, which passed the Senate by only two votes. Butler never took the field and blamed the disaster on its commander, writing that "if Pierce had given the order to sit down and take lunch, the enemy would have run away . . . because they would have supposed we had come to stay."[23]

Sniffing the atmosphere for Washington's reaction to the Big Bethel affair, Butler heard nothing from the White House but was conscious of the South's jubilation over such an easy victory. After the Union defeat at Bull Run, Scott stripped four regiments from Butler's command. Even Lincoln began to question the wisdom of leaving a person of Butler's military incapacities in charge of field operations, and on August 11 he directed Scott to reinstate seventy-two-year-old Major General John E. Wool to active duty and relieve Butler.[24]

The Massachusetts general remained at Fort Monroe waiting for reassignment, and Wool, puzzled by his presence, placed him in charge of all the troops outside the fort. Since these were few in number, Butler wrote his friends in Washington, who were as perplexed as Lincoln

23. Carr, "Operations of 1861 About Fort Monroe," *B&L*, II, 148–51; Butler's Report, June 16, 1861, *ORA*, II, 80–81; *Butler's Book*, 269–70; Parton, *General Butler*, 153.

24. *Butler's Book*, 277, 279–80; Parton, *General Butler*, 175–76; Lincoln to Scott, August 7, 1861, in Roy P. Basler, ed., *The Collected Works of Abraham Lincoln* (9 vols.; New Brunswick, N.J., 1953), IV, 478; Scott to Wool, August 8, Butler to Scott, August 11, Wool's General Orders No. 1, August 17, 1861, *ORA*, IV, 600, 601.

in deciding how best to assuage their own peculiar creation. Blair lobbied privately that Cameron be ousted and Butler elevated to secretary of war. Cameron, who was falling out of favor, suggested placing Butler in some capacity where he could use his popular skills as a "standard bearer" for the Union cause. In the meantime, the navy hatched a scheme to capture Cape Hatteras and applied to the army for troops. Being too old for strenuous operations, Wool scraped together nine hundred soldiers and, with Scott's blessing, yielded his command of the operation to Butler.[25]

Determined to erase the odium of Big Bethel, Butler departed from Fort Monroe on August 26 to cooperate with Flag Officer Silas H. Stringham's squadron in an assault on two sand forts guarding the entrance to North Carolina's Pamlico Sound. As this was the first joint operation of the war, Lincoln and his cabinet took great interest in the expedition.

On August 28 Stringham's squadron opened with its guns, circling off the two forts as the first wave of 315 soldiers and 55 marines rowed through heavy breakers. The surfboats swamped and the men struggled ashore on an island north of Fort Clark. With powder wet and not a cracker among them, they impaled a few wild sheep with their swords, roasted the meat on bayonets, and warmed the leftovers for the following morning's breakfast. One company rowed to the mainland, strolled up the beach, and discovered Fort Clark abandoned, the defenders having withdrawn to sturdier Fort Hatteras. Stringham concentrated his fire on the larger earthwork, but Fort Hatteras held out another night. Flag Officer Samuel Barron, the senior Confederate officer present, offered to surrender providing he was permitted to depart with his command. Butler, viewing the operation from the deck of the USS *Harriet Lane*, refused, demanding "full capitulation," and to force his demands by intimidation he "demonstrated" with his transports, grounding both in range of Barron's guns. Stringham, however, continued to shell Fort Hatteras, and Barron finally submitted to Butler's terms. Though the accuracy of the squadron's fire was deplorable, the

---

25. Hendricks, *Lincoln's War Cabinet*, 391; Special Orders No. 9, August 21, 1861, ORA, IV, 602; Welles to Stringham, August 9, 1861, *Official Records of the Union and Confederate Navies, War of the Rebellion* (30 vols.; Washington, D.C., 1987), 69–70, hereinafter cited as ORN, with all citations to Series I unless otherwise indicated.

navy made the victory possible. Butler, however, took the lion's share of the credit, claiming the capture of both forts, 715 prisoners, thirty-one old guns, and a huge inventory of muskets and supplies. To celebrate, he entered Fort Hatteras on the morning of August 29, seized the keys to the magazine, and ordered a major general's salute fired in honor of *his* victory.[26]

Credit, however, devolved upon the person who first delivered the good news to the White House, and while Stringham dallied off Pamlico Sound, Butler steamed back to Fort Monroe. Wool, delighted with Butler's version of the victory, sent him to Washington for further instructions. Butler beat Stringham to the capital by bribing a locomotive engineer to make the trip without his usual train of cars. Arriving late at night, he hurried to the home of Montgomery Blair, located directly across from the White House. He found the postmaster general in the study with an old acquaintance from Lowell, Gustavus Vasa Fox, the newly appointed assistant secretary of the navy. Butler related the splendid news of the victory, and despite the hour, Blair suggested a trip to the White House.[27]

With Butler in tow, Blair and Fox crossed the street and for fifteen minutes hammered on the door of the executive mansion before rousing the sleepy watchman. Lincoln appeared in his nightgown and slippers, looking even taller than he did in public, and when Fox announced the victory, Lincoln grabbed the pudgy five-foot naval assistant around the shoulders and whirled him about the room in the strangest victory dance ever witnessed by Butler. Later, Fox received a letter from John P. Bankhead, a lieutenant on the USS *Susquehanna*, who wrote, "We have a joke down here on the two late commanders of the 'Hatteras' expedition—That after the fight they had a foot race North to see who should get there first and get the most credit. Butler beat Stringham.—Had they both remained, we might have had the

---

26. Butler's Report, August 30, 1861, ORA, IV, 581–86; Stringham's Report, September 2, 1861, ORN, VI, 120–23; *Butler Correspondence*, I, 227–28; Fletcher Pratt, *Ordeal by Fire* (New York, 1935), 68; Parton, *General Butler*, 178; Rowena Reed, *Combined Operations of the Civil War* (Lincoln, Nebr., 1993), 11–13.

27. Wool to Scott, September 2, 1861, ORA, IV, 580–81; *Butler's Book*, 285–86. Fox was appointed assistant secretary of the navy on September 4, 1861; see Basler, ed., *Collected Works of Abraham Lincoln*, IV, 507.

whole coast in our possession." Nonetheless, the capture of Cape Hatteras provided the first naval success worth mention, but more importantly for Butler, it was the first successful joint operation of the war, giving Lincoln and the war cabinet the mistaken impression that on future expeditions, Butler could be trusted to work in harmony with the navy.[28]

When the cabinet met in the morning, Butler repeated his achievements. He was forgiven for disobeying his orders to sink sand-filled tugs in the inlet, and everyone agreed that Cape Hatteras should be garrisoned and held. Before the day ended, Butler had expunged the infamy of Big Bethel and reestablished his image as the hero of the public. Wool still retained sway over the Department of Virginia, and Butler was still a major general without a command. Instead of putting Lincoln in a compromising situation, Butler offered a solution. If Scott would not give him a command, he would go back to Massachusetts and raise one. Lincoln liked the idea, and noting that Butler had been on active duty since mid-April, said, "You have a right to go home, General, for a little rest, but study out another job for yourself."[29]

Butler went home to plot his next move. Crowds praised him at every stop along the way, but no demonstration greeted him with more enthusiasm than that of the joyous citizens of Lowell. He enjoyed the flattery. Swarmed by members of both sexes, "I think I at last came to know what hero worship meant," he recalled. During the first weeks of September, no future of any general seemed brighter, and Butler found it difficult to move about Lowell without a military escort to shield him from his fans. He had won the support of both Democrats and Radical Republicans. Now all he needed were the men to help him finish the war.[30]

28. *Butler's Book*, 287–88; Robert Means Thompson and Richard Wainwright, eds., *Confidential Correspondence of Gustavus Vasa Fox* (2 vols.; New York, 1938), I, 385, hereinafter cited as *Fox Correspondence*.

29. Wool to Cameron, September 3, 1861, *ORA*, IV, 604; Draft of Order to Butler, September 10, Lincoln to New England Governors, September 12, 1861, in Basler, ed., *Collected Works of Abraham Lincoln*, IV, 515, 518.

30. *Butler's Book*, 294; Crowley, *History of Lowell*, 180–81; Trefousse, *Ben Butler*, 86–87.

Had the president studied Butler's performance at Hatteras, he might not have been so willing to risk the general's questionable military skills on an important expedition secretly under study at the executive level in the Navy Department—a course that would bring Ben Butler to the magnificent southern city of New Orleans.

3

To Be a Lieutenant General

ON JULY 27, 1861, LINCOLN placed Major General George B. McClellan in charge of the army defeated at First Bull Run, and "Little Mac" quickly reshaped the shattered command into the Army of the Potomac. On November 1, Lincoln announced Winfield Scott's long-expected retirement and elevated McClellan to commanding general. With Scott gone and Little Mac, a Democrat, leading the revitalized Union army, Butler, who had grown weary waiting for an assignment, traveled to Washington for another of his friendly visits with the president.[1]

Although he had been authorized by Lincoln to raise six regiments, Butler found recruiting in his home state obstructed by Republicans who, he claimed, formed units only out of "scalawags, State prison birds, and other vagabonds." Democrats, Butler declared, would not join these units because they had no confidence in the "politics" of the units. The general's difficulty in raising six regiments had nothing to do with Republicans. Every unit he recruited would go to the army at large, and what Butler wanted was his own command. In the autumn of 1861 recruiting had lapsed right along with the leisurely pace of the war, and this worried Lincoln. Butler promised to raise as many as ten thousand troops from Democrats if Lincoln would agree to establish and place him in command of the Department of New England. Butler added a sweetener, suggesting that he would be able to swing their votes in the next election. Lincoln liked the idea and

1. General Orders No. 1, August 20, General Orders No. 94, November 1, 1861, ORA, V, 575, 639; Lincoln to McClellan, November 1, 1861, in Basler, ed., *Collected Works of Abraham Lincoln*, V, 9–10; *Butler's Book*, 295.

asked Butler to draft an order for his signature. The president carefully made the order contingent upon acceptance by the six New England governors, but all approved the directive and Lincoln signed it.[2]

Butler returned to Boston with an order from Cameron "to fit out and prepare such troops in New England . . . for the purpose [of making] an expedition along the Eastern Shore of Virginia." The general, anticipating an independent command, immersed himself in the task of raising his own army, and Cameron put no limits on its size. Lincoln created a small problem the day he made Butler a major general, who now ranked McClellan, and if Butler remained with his recruits it would be difficult to assimilate the New Englanders into the Army of the Potomac—at least at this stage of the war. To Cameron, it made sense for Butler to support McClellan by occupying Virginia's eastern shore because the War Department expected Little Mac to march south via Manassas and Fredericksburg and not by way of Virginia's peninsula.[3]

In September and October of 1861, nobody in Washington gave any serious thought to launching an expedition to New Orleans—certainly not Butler. At the time, the quarrelsome general was fighting with Governor Andrew over who had the lawful prerogatives of organizing, commissioning, and commanding Massachusetts volunteers answering Butler's call for "special service." Lincoln muddied the waters slightly by placing all recruiting officers under the authority of the governors, but he did not rescind Butler's orders. When Andrew refused to allow Butler to commission officers in the new regiments, the general transferred his appointees to standing regiments, secured their commissions, and transferred them back. Andrew countered by declaring that all troops raised by Butler in Massachusetts would not be entitled to aid granted by the legislature to families of the enlistees. Butler responded with a countermove, promising to provide for families "from my private means" in the same amount. He then went the

2. Lincoln to Governors, and Andrew *et al.* to Cameron and Lincoln, September 11, ORA, Ser. 3, I, 498, 499; *Butler's Book*, 295–98; *Butler Correspondence*, I, 219–24, 238, 245; Draft of Order to Butler, September 10, Lincoln to New England Governors, September 12, 1861, in Basler, ed., *Collected Works of Abraham Lincoln*, IV, 515, 518.

3. Cameron Directive, September 12, 1861, ORA, Ser. 3, I, 817.

extra step of obtaining the War Department's approval to offer a bounty to every new recruit. "The governor could not get any such inducement," Butler victoriously declared. At this stage of the general's recruiting effort, the White House had not disclosed any reason for giving Butler preferential treatment, nor had it assured Andrew that Butler's enlistments would count toward Massachusetts' levy.[4]

The feud between the general and Governor Andrew finally descended on Lincoln. Reaching the end of his well-known patience, the president complained, "I am getting mad with the governor and Butler both." Andrew then traveled to Washington to complain about Butler in person. Lincoln already had a solution under consideration, but one he could not share with the governor. Instead, he promised action, placating Andrew with some of his homespun humor: "General Butler is cross-eyed; I guess he don't see things the way other people do."[5]

In early November two unrelated events changed Butler's future and the fortunes of New Orleans. With seventeen wooden warships and twelve thousand men, Flag Officer Samuel F. DuPont entered Port Royal Sound and captured the two earthworks guarding the entrance, thereby invalidating the old axiom that wooden vessels could not pass heavy fortifications without paying a costly toll in vessels and men. A few days later, November 12, Commander David Dixon Porter returned from the Gulf of Mexico and stopped at the Navy Department with a unique idea for capturing New Orleans. Porter had recently spent several months on blockade duty off the mouth of the Mississippi River. He was also familiar with the lower stretch of the river between the Gulf and New Orleans. For a squadron of wooden warships to ascend the river to the Crescent City, they must first pass two heavily armed bastions, Fort Jackson and Fort St. Philip, located about seventeen miles up the main stem of the river and some seventy miles by water below New Orleans. Porter believed that the forts

4. *Butler's Book*, 309–10; James L. Bowen, *Massachusetts in the War, 1861–1865* (Springfield, Mass., 1889), 38–40; Parton, *General Butler*, 183–87; Hesseltine, *Lincoln and the War Governors*, 189.

5. Hesseltine, *Lincoln and the War Governors*, 190–91; Butler's feud with Governor Andrew can also be found in A. Howard Meneely, *The War Department, 1861: A Study in Mobilization and Administration* (New York, 1928), 213–21.

could be disabled in forty-eight hours if submitted to a smothering bombardment of 13-inch mortars mounted on twenty-one modified schooners. This would enable a squadron of wooden gunboats to run the gauntlet with minimal damage, steam to New Orleans, and hold the town under siege.[6]

Ailing seventy-one-year-old Major General David E. Twiggs, commanding the District of Louisiana, understood the vulnerability of New Orleans but lacked the energy and resources to get much done. Surrounded by water, the city was connected to the mainland by a narrow strip of land running between Lake Pontchartrain and the river. Not only was New Orleans approachable by several water routes, it became especially difficult to defend when the river was high, exposing it to naval attack, thereby enabling the heavy guns of warships to bear directly upon the town or, by breaking levees, completely inundate it. Twiggs assessed the difficulties, but during his short, ineffective administration, he did little to correct them. Governor Thomas O. Moore, noting Twiggs's deficiencies, expressed his alarm to President Davis, asking that New Orleans, "the most important [city] to be preserved of any in the Confederacy, and our coast, the most exposed on all the States, be no longer neglected." By the time Twiggs asked to be relieved, precious time had been lost.[7]

The Union Navy Department had already opened secret discussions concerning New Orleans, but passing Forts Jackson and St. Philip gave strategists grave concern because of the combined firepower of the two sturdy bastions. If the Union lost its fleet in the river, Secretary of the Navy Gideon Welles would be without the vessels he needed to maintain the Gulf blockade. Furthermore, the loss would be devastating in a war already growing unpopular in the North. DuPont's victory coupled with Porter's suggestions brightened Welles's

6. DuPont to Welles, November 8, 1861, *ORN*, XII, 262–66; Daniel Ammen, "DuPont and the Port Royal Expedition," *B&L*, I, 671–91; David Dixon Porter, *Incidents and Anecdotes of the Civil War* (New York, 1885), 64–66; Chester G. Hearn, *Admiral David Dixon Porter: The Civil War Years* (Annapolis, 1996), 70–71.

7. Twiggs to Walker, June 18, July 9, 30, August 14, Benjamin and Conrad to Davis, September 27, Twiggs to Benjamin, October 5, Walker to Twiggs, July 17, 1861, *ORA*, LIII, 699, 707, 722, 726–27, 744, 748, 713; Moore to Davis, September 20, 1861, *ibid.*, VI, 740.

view that an expedition to New Orleans could succeed if properly supported by ships and infantry. Assistant Secretary Fox concurred, and the pair escorted Porter to the White House to share his proposal with the president.[8]

Lincoln warmed to the idea, so on the night of November 15, Welles, Fox, Porter, and the president rode to the home of General McClellan to discuss the plan. Little Mac cautioned against the attack, doubting whether wooden vessels could survive the fire from Fort Jackson. If they did, McClellan warned, they would then have to pass Fort St. Philip in disabled condition. When Porter explained his thoughts on using a flotilla of mortar schooners to level the forts beforehand, McClellan approved the concept and declared the mortars "absolutely essential." The general hesitated, however, when asked for troops—he had been piling every recruit he could collar into the Army of the Potomac—but because of the special nature of Butler's command, McClellan agreed to send the New England regiments with the expedition providing the Massachusetts general went with them. Little Mac did not want his efforts to build an army distracted by the presence of Butler, his fellow Democrat, and when the meeting ended, all five men agreed to keep the enterprise secret. Welles cautioned against leaks in the Navy Department, ordering Fox and Porter to not even use the words "New Orleans" in any reference whatsoever.[9]

Butler knew nothing of the mission and continued to collect recruits for an unspecified campaign against Virginia's eastern shore. Because of tight security and no further mention of the enterprise, McClellan put the expedition out of his mind and all but forgot it. Porter began collecting twenty-one schooners and fitting them with mortars while the Navy Department cast about to find seven steam-driven gunboats to tow the sailing vessels up the Mississippi. In the meantime, Welles

---

8. Gideon Welles, "Admiral Farragut and New Orleans, with an Account of the Origin and the First Three Naval Expeditions of the War," *The Galaxy: An Illustrated Magazine of Entertaining Reading*, XII (November, 1871), 677; Montgomery Blair, "Opening the Mississippi," *The United Service: A Monthly Review of Military and Naval Affairs*, IV (January, 1881), 38.

9. Welles, "Admiral Farragut and New Orleans," 677–78; Chester G. Hearn, *The Capture of New Orleans, 1862* (Baton Rouge, 1995), 100; Hearn, *Admiral Porter*, 73.

scanned his list of captains for a flag officer—someone with the experience and fortitude of Lord Nelson—a person willing to accept responsibility for an expedition having an uncertain chance of success. New Orleans was the largest, grandest, and wealthiest city in the South, and to send a squadron of seventeen wooden warships, a mortar flotilla that had to be towed, and a scant fifteen thousand raw, untested infantry under the incompetent generalship of Butler could become a recipe for disaster.

In his search for a flag officer, Welles discarded thirty-six candidates on the Navy Register's captains' list before his finger touched the name of David Glasgow Farragut, a sailor whom he barely knew but faintly remembered from the Mexican War. Welles did not have much information about Farragut other than that the captain was sixty years of age, was in good health, and had "a good but not conspicuous record." Among his peers Farragut had an excellent reputation and, at least in Welles's mind, unquestioned fidelity to the North. Another important consideration for Welles involved the special relationship that existed between Farragut and Porter—they were foster brothers, Farragut having been taken into the Porter family at the age of eight. If Porter could test his foster brother's interest and enthusiasm for the expedition before Welles committed to naming a flag officer, it would keep Farragut, who was in New York, away from the Navy Department and minimize the risk of the mission leaking to the public.[10]

Sending Porter, a junior commander, to interview Farragut, a senior captain, would have been extremely awkward had the two men not shared a brotherly relationship. Porter, being every bit as ambitious as Butler, could not have chosen a person more likely to help with his career than Farragut. Porter's account of the interview in his "Private Journal" described the meeting as one of intrigue and guarded questioning. For Porter to have rejected his foster brother as the best man to lead the expedition would have been unlikely. Farragut could have declined the mission because he had relatives in New Orleans, but he favored it. On Porter's recommendation, Welles invited Farragut to

10. Farragut, *Life of David Glasgow Farragut*, 9–11, 204–205; Gideon Welles, *The Diary of Gideon Welles*, ed. John T. Morse (3 vols.; Boston, 1911), II, 116–17, 134–35; Welles, "Admiral Farragut and New Orleans," 681–82; Hearn, *Capture of New Orleans*, 101.

Washington late in December, and after sending him through a round of interviews with Fox and Blair, he spoke with the captain directly. Convinced that Farragut not only believed in the viability of the expedition but was determined to make it successful, Welles named him flag officer. In an effort to maintain secrecy, he did not issue Farragut's orders until January 9, 1862, naming him commander of the West Gulf Blockading Squadron but making no mention of New Orleans.[11]

In the meantime, Butler continued to recruit, drill, and assemble his newly formed regiments while waiting for orders. McClellan, having heard nothing further about New Orleans, cast a longing eye at Butler's unassigned New England regiments. Feeling pressure from Little Mac to commandeer the Massachusetts recruits, Lincoln decided to move part of Butler's command away from the eastern theater. On November 21, Brigadier General John W. Phelps, "a tall, saturnine, gloomy, angry-eyed sallow man, soldier-like, too," departed on the steamer *Constitution* for Ship Island with nineteen hundred New Englanders—the 9th Connecticut, the 26th Massachusetts, and the 5th Massachusetts Light Battery. Because Lincoln could not trust either Cameron or Butler to keep the reason for the expedition out of the press, he intimated that Ship Island was to be occupied for a possible invasion of Texas.[12]

A glistening strip of white windswept sand about eight miles long and less than a mile wide, Ship Island lay fifteen miles off the coastal town of Biloxi, Mississippi. Barren except for gulls, fleas, a solitary fishing shack, a dilapidated brick fort, and a clump of pine trees, the island made an ideal base for operations against either Mobile Bay, fifty miles to the east, or New Orleans, seventy-five miles to the west by way of Lake Pontchartrain. A burned-out shell of a lighthouse on the eastern end of the island had been left by departing Rebels as a

11. David D. Porter, "Private Journal of Occurrences During the Great War of the Rebellion, 1860–1865," 81, in David Dixon Porter Papers, LC, hereinafter cited as Porter, "Journal of Occurrences," all references being to vol. I; Welles to Farragut, January 9, 1862, ORN, XVIII, 5; Hearn, *Admiral Porter*, 75.

12. Butler's Report, December 2, 1862, ORA, VI, 463–64; Edward Bates, *The Diary of Edward Bates, 1859–1866* (Washington, D.C., 1933), 208; William Howard Russell, *My Diary, North and South* (Boston, 1863), 41.

sole reminder of war. The leeward side of Ship Island provided a natural harbor for vessels seeking shelter from the Gulf's frequent storms, and when Phelps arrived with his regiments on December 3 he found the USS *Massachusetts*, commanded by Captain Melancton Smith, waiting in the harbor to assist his landing. General Phelps expected more transports to arrive with the balance of the command, but Captain Charles Wilkes inadvertently delayed the operation by capturing the British mail steamer *Trent* on the high seas and seizing two Confederate commissioners, James M. Mason and John Slidell.[13]

Butler had already loaded a second transport with two thousand troops when an urgent telegram reached him, reading, "Don't sail; disembark the troops." Bewildered by the order, and perhaps anticipating some nefarious sleight-of-hand by McClellan, Butler set out for Washington. There he learned that England had rattled His Majesty's swords over the *Trent* affair and war threatened on a new front. Lincoln explained that if England entered the war, Butler would have to keep his command in New England to safeguard against the threat of an invasion from Canada. Furthermore, the troops stationed at Ship Island would have to be recalled.[14]

By December 23 the dispute with Great Britain showed signs of settlement, and on January 1 Butler embarked another 2,200 troops on transports in Boston Harbor. Once again they were detained, this time by McClellan, who wanted to divert the troops to Brigadier General William T. Sherman. Once again Butler went to Washington, this time to convince Lincoln and the Joint Committee on the Conduct of the War that McClellan's gross exaggerations of the enemy's strength were without foundation, and that Little Mac was simply holding up the war because of timidity.[15]

Before going to Lincoln, Butler paid McClellan a visit. Midway through the conversation he sensed that behind the scenes McClellan was doing everything in his power to thwart the expedition to Ship

13. Phelps's Report, December 5, 1862, ORA, VI, 465–66; Parton, *General Butler*, 195; *Butler's Book*, 314, Hearn, *Capture of New Orleans*, 128–29.

14. *Butler's Book*, 324; Bland, *Life of Butler*, 64.

15. Thomas to Butler, January 4, 1862, ORA, Ser. 3, I, 777; *Butler Correspondence*, I, 318–19; *Report of the Joint Committee on the Conduct of the War* (1863), I, 75, II, 247–48.

Island. Secretary of War Cameron had just been replaced by Edwin M. Stanton, so on January 19 Butler held a private conversation with the new secretary, an old friend and fellow Democrat. During a lengthy breakfast Butler handed Stanton a memorandum suggesting the formation of the Department of the Gulf; then, after confirming that Lincoln had himself expressed concern over the commanding general's lack of aggressiveness, Butler revisited McClellan and said, "General, shall I call on you before or after I call on the President?" Little Mac replied, "Better call before." Because McClellan's supporters suspected Butler of undermining their champion, they lobbied to have the troublesome New Englander sent as far away as possible.[16]

Butler never went to Washington without stirring up trouble, and this trip was no exception. Nor was it unusual for Butler to get his way when he took the time to garner support for his schemes. Two days after his meeting with Stanton, the secretary countermanded McClellan's orders detaining Butler's expedition. Little Mac vehemently disagreed but acknowledged that "New Orleans . . . should be the object [of attack], rather than Mobile or the coast of Texas." He argued against committing a single man to it, claiming the expedition required "not less than 30,000 men, and it is believed 50,000" to take and hold the Crescent City. McClellan had conveniently forgotten his commitment on November 15 to Lincoln, Welles, Fox, and Porter to provide troops for the New Orleans campaign, partly because none of the foursome had ever mentioned it again.[17]

Since the expedition to Ship Island involved the navy, Butler went to see Fox to discuss his difficulties with McClellan, warning that the general was attempting to stop the expedition. At this time, neither McClellan nor Butler clearly understood that the target was New Orleans and not Mobile or the coast of Texas. Welles still said nothing to Butler and deferred the matter to Farragut, who had no objection to

16. McClellan to Thomas, January 25, 1862, ORA, VI, 678; *Butler's Book*, 333–35; Welles, "Admiral Farragut and New Orleans," 820; Butler to Stanton, January 19, 1862, in Edwin M. Stanton Papers, LC; Lincoln to Cameron, January 11, 1862, in Basler, ed., *Collected Works of Abraham Lincoln*, V, 96–97; T. Harry Williams, *Lincoln and His Generals* (New York, 1952), 50–70.

17. McClellan to Thomas, January 25, 1862, ORA, VI, 678; George C. Gorham, *Life and Public Services of Edwin M. Stanton* (Boston, 1899), 314.

cooperating with the general because he believed the army would play a minor role in the attack and would only be needed for occupation duty. With Butler cleared by the navy, Fox went to Stanton to explain the mission in detail. Stanton enthusiastically endorsed it, overruled McClellan, and sent orders to Butler authorizing the continuation of his command's interrupted voyage to Ship Island. When Butler learned of his true destination, he prepared a third shipment of infantry, and on February 23, 1862, he finally received his marching orders from McClellan.[18]

McClellan disapproved of committing any troops to be used for opening another theater of operations, but he was glad to be rid of the bothersome New Englander who cavorted about the capital telling anyone willing to listen that it would be a simple matter to dislodge the Confederate army occupying Manassas. Lincoln thought so, too, and ordered McClellan to attack the Rebels no later than Washington's birthday. McClellan ignored the order. For the moment, his first priority was dispensing with Butler. Confirming that "the great object to be achieved is the capture and firm retention of New Orleans," McClellan approved Butler's recommendation that the Department of the Gulf consist of all geographical components west of Fort Pickens (Pensacola Bay) that fell under the occupation of Union forces. For this vast area of real estate, Little Mac authorized thirteen New England regiments, three companies of cavalry, and two light batteries—units recruited by Butler. Having promised Stanton he would provide the Department of the Gulf with 15,000 troops, McClellan threw in the 21st Indiana, 4th Wisconsin, and 6th Michigan, bringing Butler's army to 15,255 men. If additional troops were needed, Butler would have to draw them from Key West or Fort Pickens.[19]

The president privately celebrated the departure of Butler because it resolved a problem that had continued to fester between the general

18. *Butler Correspondence*, I, 330–31, 333–34, 335, 345, 349; Welles, "Admiral Farragut in New Orleans," 820; Welles, *Diary*, II, 60–61; McClellan to Butler, February 23, 1862, ORA, VI, 694–95.

19. Lincoln's War Orders, January 27, 31, 1862, ORA, V, 41; Butler to McClellan, February 12, McClellan to Butler, February 23, General Orders No. 20, February 23, 1861, ORA, VI, 686–88, 694–95, 695–96; *Butler Correspondence*, I, 360; T. H. Williams, *Lincoln and His Generals*, 62–65.

and Governor Andrew over recruiting prerogatives. In a restrained message to Andrew on January 11, Lincoln had written, "I will be greatly obliged if you will arrange somehow with General Butler to officer his two un-officered regiments." The governor replied that "if the Federal Government wishes me to organize those men into companies and regiments, and to appoint and commission officers . . . I will undertake it. . . . [B]ut I must frankly say that there are names . . . whom to commission would offend both my sense of honor and of duty." Among those rejected by the governor as uncommissionable was Butler's brother, Andrew. Lincoln solved the problem by dissolving the Department of New England, and when he did, the Massachusetts governor accepted the disputed regiments as part of the state's regularly organized volunteer force and granted commissions to most of Butler's officers, excluding those he found most objectionable. Anxious to be off to the Gulf, Butler accepted the settlement, denying, however, that he ever intended to interfere "with the legitimate authority of Governor Andrew."[20]

For other reasons, Lincoln believed Butler was the right man to send on the expedition. If New Orleans fell, a Democrat would be more acceptable to the conquered city. After all, in the 1860 presidential convention Butler had supported both Jefferson Davis and John C. Breckinridge, the latter now a Confederate general. Lincoln remembered New Orleans as a fun-loving town. His father had fought there under Andrew Jackson during the Battle of New Orleans, but he misjudged Butler by believing that the general shared his sentiments and would revive allegiance to the Union through mild polices of reconstruction.[21]

Because the expedition had been planned and organized by the navy, McClellan cautioned Butler to accept a supportive role. In reference to Forts Jackson and St. Philip, he wrote: "It is expected that the navy can reduce these works. In that case you will, after their capture,

20. Lincoln to Andrew, January 11, 1862, in Basler, ed., *Collected Works of Abraham Lincoln*, V, 96; Andrew to Lincoln, January 11, 1862, ORA, Ser. 3, I, 862; General Orders No. 17, February 20, Stanton to Andrew, February 19, Butler to Stanton, February 20, 1862, *ibid.*, 896, 897; *Butler Correspondence*, I, 330.

21. Dabney, "The Butler Regime in Louisiana," *Louisiana Historical Quarterly*, XXVII (April, 1944), 495; Trefousse, *Ben Butler*, 53–58.

Approaches to New Orleans from Ship Island. From *Autobiography and Personal Reminiscences of Major General Benjamin F. Butler.*

leave a sufficient garrison in them to render them perfectly secure. . . . Should the Navy fail to reduce the works, you will land your forces and siege train, and endeavor to breach the works, silence their guns, and carry them by assault." McClellan was aware that Major General Mansfield Lovell had taken command of New Orleans and improved the defenses on the lower Mississippi, and he warned Butler of other earthen batteries strung along the river and around the city that may have to be assaulted by land forces. He was also aware that New Orleans supported many Unionists, mostly northerners and foreigners, and he believed that while "it may be necessary to place some troops in the city to preserve order," Butler should capitalize on pro-Union sentiment to establish control among the citizens and "keep [his] men out of the city."[22]

Once the New Orleans environs became militarily secure, McClellan ordered, Butler was to continue to support the navy in expeditions against Baton Rouge, Berwick Bay, Galveston, and Mobile. Little Mac, after predicting that New Orleans could not be captured with less than fifty thousand troops, never explained how all this was to be accomplished with only fifteen thousand men. Perhaps he did not care. Before leaving Washington, Butler learned that Brigadier General Randolph B. Marcy, McClellan's father-in-law and chief of staff, had said, "I guess we have found a hole to bury this Yankee elephant in."[23]

Slurs never bothered Butler, especially when he had an opportunity to get even. In a parting meeting with Stanton and Lincoln, Butler stopped to say, "My orders cannot be countermanded after I get to sea, for I am going to take New Orleans or you will never see me again."

In Lincoln's presence, Stanton replied, "Well, you take New Orleans and you shall be a lieutenant-general."

Butler bowed and departed, and on the evening of February 25 he anchored off Fort Monroe. "I stood on the deck of the good steamer *Mississippi* with my wife and some of my staff officers beside me, and

22. McClellan to Butler, February 23, 1861, ORA, VI, 678. Major General Mansfield Lovell replaced Twiggs on October 7, 1861, but he did not arrive at New Orleans until late in the month; see Special Orders No. 173, October 7, 1861, *ibid.*, 643.

23. McClellan to Stanton, January 25, McClellan to Butler, February 23, 1861, *ibid.*, 678, 694–95; *Butler's Book*, 336.

gave orders to 'up anchor for Ship Island.' I had sixteen hundred men on board with me, and the enormous sum of seventy-five dollars in gold in my pocket with which to pay the expenses of the expedition."[24]

Money would never become a problem for Butler. There were large sums of it hidden in New Orleans.

24. *Butler's Book*, 335–36.

4

"Picayune" Butler
Comes to Town

ANYBODY WHO PAUSED TO TAKE notice might wonder why
Butler—no matter where he was or what he did—attracted trouble.
Even the simple voyage to Ship Island on the steamer *Mississippi* turned
into a circus.

On the second day of the cruise, the transport grounded on Frying
Pan Shoals off Cape Fear, North Carolina. The skipper, Captain Fulton, dropped anchor and one of the flukes ripped a hole in the ship's
hull. Rumors spread among the soldiers that Fulton was a southerner
and a saboteur, but the tide had simply ebbed and when the vessel
settled on the bottom it struck the anchor. The USS *Mount Vernon,*
on blockade duty off Cape Fear, worked in close to *Mississippi,* and her
commander, Oliver S. Glisson, sent a hawser to pull off the transport.
When that did not work, Butler lightened the vessel by taking off 250
passengers, Mrs. Butler and her maid among them. The incoming tide
refloated the transport, and with hands manning all the pumps, Butler
got the vessel off the rocks and ordered her into Port Royal for repairs.
With a patch jack-screwed over the hole, he reembarked his infantry
on the morning of March 10 and ordered steam. Fulton moved the
transport by the stern, backed against the shallows, struck the rudder,
parted the tiller ropes, lost steerage, and ran hard against the shore a
half mile from the wharf. That was enough for Butler. He arrested the
captain, ordered a court of inquiry, and took command of the vessel
himself, arriving off Ship Island on March 20.[1]

1. *Butler's Book,* 339–51; Glisson's Report, March 1, 1862, ORN, VI, 674–75;
Itinerary of Joseph Bell, *ibid.,* XVIII, 699–702; Fulton's Court of Inquiry, March 12,
1862, *ibid.,* 702–704; Butler to Fox, March 2, 1862, in *Fox Correspondence,* I, 430–32.

General Phelps, who had been eagerly awaiting the next install-
ment of troops, greeted Butler with a thirteen-gun salute, and the
rumble of artillery alerted the navy that the general had arrived. At
the time, a large number of vessels were at anchor in Mississippi Sound
and riding out a gale that kept the seasick New Englanders confined to
the ship. Butler expected the naval attack to start within a week, and
he did not want to lose the opportunity of being present. Farragut,
however, could not get his heavy vessels over the bar into the river
and brought several of them back to Ship Island to be lightened.[2]

In the early planning of the expedition, Farragut depended upon
surprise, intending to move his vessels into the Mississippi quickly and
run by the forts before the enemy could improve their defenses. If this
could be done with speed, he doubted whether Porter's mortars or
Butler's infantry would be needed to make the passage, thereby con-
serving them to capture the forts and open the river for the delivery
of supplies, especially if New Orleans offered a stubborn resistance.
Expecting the imminent arrival of Butler, Farragut began to send his
squadron into the passes in early March. *Brooklyn* grounded at Pass à
l'Outre and had to steam around the delta to try the bar at Southwest
Pass. The vessel grounded again, but Farragut was at hand with the
USS *Hartford*. With help from the flagship, *Brooklyn* scraped over the
bar and entered the river. Several light-draft gunboats followed,
and the first wave of Farragut's squadron moved up to Head of Passes,
the point some seventeen miles below the forts where the stem of the
river branched into its three main outlets. Confederate scout boats
observed the entry, but Brigadier General Johnson K. Duncan, operating from Fort Jackson headquarters, interpreted the intrusion as a
tightening of the blockade—not a positioning of vessels for an attack
on New Orleans. With part of his force in the river, Farragut sent
Winona, Kineo, and *Kennebec* upriver to screen his activities, but he
kept them below the forts and mostly out of sight.[3]

At New Orleans, General Lovell read the signs about the same. On

2. Thomas Hamilton Murray, *History of the Ninth Regiment, Connecticut Volunteer
Infantry*, "The Irish Regiment" in the War of the Rebellion, 1861–1865 (New Haven,
1903), 72.

3. Farragut to Craven, February 22, Farragut to Welles, March 14, 1862, ORN,
XVIII, 35, 64–65; Welles, "Admiral Farragut in New Orleans," 683; Hearn, *Capture of
New Orleans*, 130, 135.

February 27 he advised Secretary of War Judah P. Benjamin that he regarded "Butler's Ship Island expedition as a harmless menace so far as New Orleans is concerned. A black Republican dynasty will never give an old Breckinridge Democrat like Butler command of any expedition which they had any idea would result in such a glorious success as the capture of New Orleans. He will not have 10,000 men for a demonstration by land upon any of the Gulf cities." The words "harmless menace" might apply to the Ship Island expedition, but the citizens of New Orleans would soon discover that the same two words did not fit General Butler.[4]

At this stage of Farragut's preparations, Secretary of War Benjamin detached troops from Lovell's command and transferred them to Major General Albert Sidney Johnston's army in Tennessee, leaving mostly militia to man the Crescent City's earthworks. Both Benjamin and Davis agreed with Lovell's assessment of the Gulf situation and continued to detach artillery and infantry units as fast as Governor Moore could recruit them. The war upriver had taken a turn for the worse. In February the Union army began its push into Tennessee, capturing Fort Henry, Fort Donelson, and finally Nashville. A week later Lovell began to show concern for the depletion of his force, and his worry escalated as more Union vessels moved into the lower river. On March 9 he warned Benjamin that "this department has been completely stripped of every organized body of troops." Then, ignoring the general's concerns, Secretary of the Navy Stephen R. Mallory added to Lovell's worries by sending the Confederate fleet upriver to check the advance of a second Union flotilla, this one above Island No. 10. Lovell disagreed, writing Benjamin that "the fleet threatening us below is much more formidable than that above, and I object strongly to sending every armed vessel away from New Orleans. . . . This city has been already too much weakened by . . . detachments of all kinds."[5]

Benjamin, baffled by unexpected setbacks, admitted from Richmond, "We grope in the dark here, and this uncertainty renders our counsels undecided and prevents that promptness of action which the

4. Lovell to Benjamin, February 27, 1862, ORA, VI, 832–33.

5. *Ibid.*; Lovell to Benjamin, March 6, 9, 10, 1862, ORA, VI, 841–42, 847, 850.

emergency requires. . . . [W]ithout additional supplies of arms we cannot hold our entire exposed coast and frontier, and we must withdraw from the defense of the whole Gulf except New Orleans." Benjamin may have meant well, but he continued to siphon troops from Lovell's command.[6]

On March 13, while Lovell badgered Richmond for reinforcements, Porter arrived with the mortar schooners and all but two of his seven gunboats. Five days later he led the entire squadron through Pass à l'Outre, anchored them near the Head of Passes, and ordered the "bummers" to strip the schooners for action. Porter was a few days behind Farragut's original schedule, but it made no difference. At the time, Butler had not arrived, and Farragut could not drag the balance of his squadron over the bar.[7]

Of the eighteen warships assigned to Farragut to run the batteries of Forts Jackson and St. Philip, four could not move into the river— *Richmond, Pensacola, Mississippi,* and *Colorado*. With *Colorado's* draft at twenty-three feet, Farragut decided to keep it in the Gulf and concentrate on lightening the other three. He sent all four vessels back to Ship Island, just as Butler hove into sight.[8]

On March 23 the general moved Mrs. Butler, her linen, and her dishware into his new headquarters, a hastily built shack, but the scarcity of lumber compelled the troops to live in tents. For many, it was their first good look at the general, and Captain John W. De Forest of the 12th Connecticut described him as being "not the grossly fat and altogether ugly man who is presented in the illustrated weeklies. He is stoutish but not clumsily so; he squints badly, but his eyes are very clear and bright; his complexion is fair, smooth and delicately flushed; his teeth are white and his smile ingratiating. You need not understand that he is pretty; only that he is better looking than his published portraits." When Butler spoke, De Forest noticed how the general mechanically smiled from time to time "to show his handsome

6. Benjamin to Bragg, February 18, Benjamin to Lovell, February 8, 16, 1862, *ibid.*, 823–24, 827, 828.

7. Porter to Welles, March 13, 18, Farragut to Welles, March 18, 1862, *ORN*, XVIII, 64, 71–72.

8. Farragut to Fox, March 16, Farragut to Welles, March 18, 1862, *ibid.*, 67–68, 71; Hearn, *Capture of New Orleans*, 152–53.

teeth, [and] on the whole he seemed less like a major general than like a politician who was coaxing for votes. The result of the interview was that we got the desired order and departed with a sense of having been flattered."[9]

Although Farragut had fallen behind schedule at the risk of having his plans discovered, Butler needed time to brigade his regiments, whip them into shape, and make preparations for the assault—a matter nobody had taken time to clarify. After designating Generals Thomas Williams, John W. Phelps, and George F. Shepley as brigade commanders, Butler contacted Farragut to determine where and when to send the troops: "I am now ready to put on board ship six regiments and two batteries, and will be able to be in the 'passes' in twelve hours. . . . If the Navy are not to be ready for six to eight days I ought not to sail, as my coal is running short, and I cannot carry more than eight days' for sailing."[10]

Coal seemed to have been a commodity overlooked by everyone except Butler, who had ballasted some of his vessels with anthracite instead of stone. As a businessman, he knew the vessels would have to return to New England in ballast. Expecting the price to advance, he planned to resell the coal and pocket a profit. When Farragut's squadron began to run low on fuel, Butler loaned the navy eight hundred tons shortly after he arrived at Ship Island and kept the warships supplied for about two weeks. Farragut questioned the practice, reminding the general that "army regulations are against it." Butler replied, "I never read the . . . regulations, and what is more I sha'n't, and then I shall not know I am doing anything against them." He later admitted that the transfer caused him embarrassment, "as my accounts are not regular." Butler also underestimated his own needs and ran short, and by the time he departed from the Gulf in December, 1862, he would have many accounts described by some critics as irregular.[11]

Butler was also brooding over the Senate's refusal to confirm his brother, Andrew, as commissary of subsistence and acting quartermas-

---

9. *Butler's Book*, 352; John William De Forest, *A Volunteer's Adventures* (New Haven, 1946), 9.

10. Butler to Farragut, March 30, 1862, ORA, VI, 706; *Butler's Book*, 352.

11. Farragut to Welles, April 8, 1862, ORN, XVIII, 109; *Butler's Book*, 355.

ter, a function he would temporarily perform with no credentials. Without Andrew, however, Farragut would have been forced to abandon steam and use his sails, for it was Butler's brother who ballasted the transports with coal. The general blamed Governor Andrew's influence with the Senate for disenfranchising his brother, and because the general stubbornly resisted appointing someone acceptable to the governor, his command almost exhausted its supplies.[12]

Farragut, with three of his heaviest vessels mired in mud at Southwest Pass, asked Butler to detain his forces a little longer. The soldiers grumbled. They had been confined on Ship Island too long and wanted action, so Butler staged a minor diversionary action against Biloxi and Pass Christian, a poor substitute for combat but enough to give a few troops an opportunity to stretch their legs. The affair started after a young girl had been picked up in a lifeboat with several sailors from an abandoned blockade runner. Learning the child's parents had been taken to the mainland by another boat, Butler detailed a launch to sail her into Biloxi under a flag of truce. The vessel ran aground on the return trip and came under enemy fire. At high tide it floated free and returned unharmed, but as soon as Butler learned of the incident he sent six hundred men of the 9th Connecticut ashore to avenge the insult. "They . . . landed, marched six miles into the country and [broke] up a camp of militia," Captain De Forest recalled. "The enemy . . . fired two rounds without hitting anybody, and then emigrated due north at the top of their speed." The regiment returned, having executed their first mission of the war, "loaded with a whimsical variety of spoil and bubbling over with blatherskite."[13]

Early in April, Butler decided to visit Farragut at Head of Passes and brought with him his engineering officer, Lieutenant Godfrey Weitzel, who had been stationed at the forts for five years before the war. The flag officer had already received a lengthy report from Brigadier General John G. Barnard, who had worked on Fort Jackson and rebuilt Fort St. Philip in the 1850s, but Farragut appreciated the

12. Butler to Thomas, February 13, 21, 1862, ORA, VI, 689, 693; Thomas to Butler, February 6, 1862, in Butler Papers, LC; *Butler's Book*, 356–58.

13. Murray, *History of the Ninth Connecticut*, 72–84; De Forest, *A Volunteer's Adventures*, 8–9; Thomas Williams, "Letters of General Thomas Williams, 1862," *American Historical Review*, XIV (January, 1909), 307–309.

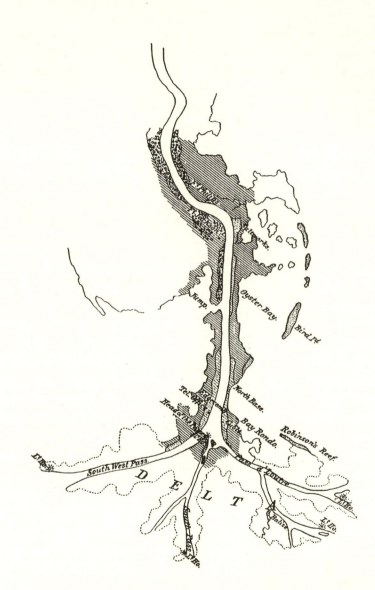

The lower Mississippi and its passes. From *Official Records of the Union and Confederate Navies, War of the Rebellion*, Vol. XVI.

advantage of having at his side an engineer who could answer his questions. Farragut acknowledged the possibility that, if the Confederates had used their time judiciously, his flotilla could be stopped at a chain barrier stretched across the river below Fort Jackson. What the flag officer and the general did not know was that the forts had received a few heavier guns but otherwise remained much as Barnard and Weitzel remembered them.[14]

Of Fort Jackson's seventy-four guns, sixty-four bore on the river, ten on the flanks. Most of the guns were 32-pounders or smaller—only nineteen were larger—and most of them were smoothbores, sacrificing distance and accuracy. Fort St. Philip, seven hundred yards upriver and located at an angle across from Jackson to maximize crossfire, mounted fifty-two guns, much like those in her sister fort. With a combined firepower of more than one hundred guns bearing on a section of the river one-half mile wide and three and one-half miles long, any vessel attempting to pass would be under a hail of fire for as long as thirty minutes.[15]

Lovell, however, had begun to despair. By the latter part of March, with Farragut's fleet at the mouth of the river, the city had become virtually defenseless. Lovell and Moore implored Benjamin and Davis for support, but their appeals were in vain. With the fate of New Orleans resting entirely with the forts, Lovell and the public officials believed they had been deserted in their hour of greatest need. The editor of the New Orleans *Daily Delta* must have been wearing rose-colored glasses when he assured the public that the forts would handily repulse an attack and promised "no fears of a bad result to our side." Then came another blow—the Confederate defeat at Shiloh. A few days later New Orleans watched as the body of General Albert Sidney Johnston passed slowly up St. Charles Street to the beat of muffled drums. "The war," wrote young George Cable, a store clerk, "was coming very near."[16]

14. Barnard's Report, January 28, 1862, ORN, XVIII, 15–24; *Butler's Book*, 365; Charles S. Foltz, *Surgeon of the Seas: The Life of Surgeon General Jonathan M. Foltz* (Indianapolis, 1931), 215; Parton, *General Butler*, 210, 239.

15. Barnard's Report, January 28, Harris to Gerdes, May 4, 1862, ORN, XVIII, 15–24, 393; "The Opposing Forces in the Operations at New Orleans, LA," *B&L*, II, 75; Hearn, *Capture of New Orleans*, 174–76, 273–74.

16. For the correspondence passing between New Orleans and Richmond, see

With Butler's coal and great effort from Porter's gunboats, *Richmond, Pensacola,* and *Mississippi* scraped over the bar at Southwest Pass and on April 7 all three vessels entered the river, bringing to seventeen the number of warships available to run the gauntlet. Farragut advised Butler that he required four or five days to rearm, provision, and coal before he could commence the attack, and he invited the general to come over and watch it. Butler, anxious to be part of the operation, wasted no time accepting. He prepared two brigades for embarkation before leaving Ship Island and then departed, taking the headquarters ship *Saxon* into the river to witness the grand battle between Farragut's sailors and the forts. Butler also needed to have a conversation with the flag officer because his role had not been defined, and it seemed to the general that the army's participation depended too much on Porter's mortar boats reducing the forts. If Porter failed, it had been agreed that Butler would have to attack the works from the rear, but even those plans had not been developed.[17]

As Farragut readied his warships for the attack, Butler remained in harmonious communication with the flag officer, whose fleet now numbered forty-eight wooden vessels—eight heavily armed steam sloops, seventeen steam gunboats, two sailing sloops, and twenty-one mortar schooners that could hurl 215-pound shells two miles. Porter had, at this stage, very little communication with Butler, as he had been upriver preparing his schooners for the bombardment. Under the plan, Porter would concentrate his fire on Fort Jackson and disable its batteries, after which Farragut would run the gauntlet with seventeen of his fastest and most heavily armed vessels. If Farragut got above the forts, Butler would land in Quarantine Bay and assault the lightly defended rear of Fort St. Philip—a miserably swampy area the defenders of the fort never thought to fortify. Weitzel claimed the swamps could be crossed. Before the war he had spent many happy hours poling through the estuaries hunting ducks.[18]

ORA, VI, 864–72, *passim*; New Orleans *Daily Delta*, April 1, 1862; George W. Cable, "New Orleans Before the Capture," *B&L*, II, 18.

17. Farragut to Welles, April 8, 1862, ORN, XVIII, 109; Farragut to Butler, April 7, 1862, ORA, LIII, 521; Murray, *History of the Ninth Connecticut*, 90–95; T. Williams, "Letters," 310; Foltz, *Surgeon of the Seas*, 215.

18. *Butler's Book*, 359–60; Hearn, *Capture of New Orleans*, 270–71, 272–73; "The

Aside from the forts, Farragut had other concerns. Ranging above St. Philip were twelve Confederate gunboats, including the dreaded CSS *Louisiana,* a huge ironclad tied along shore, and the CSS *Manassas,* an ironclad ram that in October had attacked a small squadron of Union vessels and driven them out of the river. Another flotilla of armed steam launches and tugs ranged up the river, and Farragut had no way of knowing what threat they presented. Fire rafts heaped with combustibles, ready to be lit and set adrift once the expected attack began, created another concern.[19]

Much to Porter's chagrin, his mortars demoralized the defenders of Fort Jackson but after six days of shelling failed to disable the bastion. Farragut tired of waiting, especially with Butler pestering him for action, and early on the night of April 23 he put the squadron into battle formation. At three o'clock the next morning, Porter opened on Fort Jackson's batteries, using his entire force of seven gunboats and twenty-one mortars. Farragut's line pushed through the broken chain barrier and immediately came under fire from both forts. Moments later, Union guns answered. Smoke covered the river, obscuring everything from sight. Shot, shell, shrapnel, and canister flew in every direction. Little of it hit a target, and at dawn fourteen Union vessels anchored above the forts at Quarantine. Three of the gunboats— *Itasca, Winona,* and *Kennebec*—failed to make the passage and were forced to turn back and join Porter below the forts. *Varuna* sank near Quarantine, destroyed by the Confederate navy. Farragut paused to assess the damage and sent a detail ashore to cut the telegraph wires to New Orleans.[20]

Butler watched the passage of Farragut's squadron from the deck of *Saxon,* positioned a short distance below the fleet. "The moment Farragut's guns opened fire," he recalled, "the smoke settling down made it impossible to see anything one hundred yards away, except the bright flashes, or hear anything save the continuous roar of cannon."

Opposing Forces in the Operations at New Orleans, LA," *B&L,* II, 74–75; Parton, *General Butler,* 210.

19. Farragut's Prize Cases, May 1, 1872, *ORN,* XVIII, 249. The October attack of CSS *Manassas* is described in Hearn, *Capture of New Orleans,* 81–95.

20. Caldwell to Farragut, Nichols to Farragut, April 30, 1862, Log of *Kennebec, ORN,* XVIII, 225–26, 226–27, 808–809; Hearn, *Capture of New Orleans,* 209–236.

Soon daylight flooded the river with brilliant sunlight. Smoke could be seen far upriver, and wreckage began to float by the Union flotilla anchored below the forts. Time passed, and Butler paced the deck, waiting for word from above. Commander Charles S. Boggs, in the only boat salvaged from the sunken *Varuna*, crossed through the swamps and finally brought word that the squadron was safe and for Butler to commence his landing in the bay.[21]

Not blessed with skippers possessing good seamanship, Butler's flagship became partially disabled, and he had to borrow the USS *Miami* from Porter in order to get out of the river. If somewhere there was a jinx, it may well have been Butler because *Miami*, Porter's lightest-draft steamer, grounded twice at Pass à l'Outre, again detaining the general. Butler was frantically trying to reach Brigadier General Williams, who had been waiting for orders for several days with six thousand troops huddled in transports off Sable Island.[22]

The trip back to the Gulf gave Butler time to send his compliments to Farragut: "Allow me to congratulate you and your command upon the bold, daring, brilliant, and successful passage of the forts by your fleet this morning. A more gallant exploit has never fallen to the lot of man to witness." Butler asked that two gunboats be detained at Quarantine for his use, but underlying all the conviviality lay a moody general who could not claim credit for any part of the navy's remarkable feat. Privately, he condemned Farragut for running off and leaving the forts intact, calling it "an unmilitary proceeding" and nothing more than a "race for the glory of the capture of New Orleans." Farragut may have been less inclined to leave Butler with two gunboats had he known of the general's grousing, but the request made sense and gave sailors an opportunity to bury their dead.[23]

Butler, however, now had an important piece of business to conduct. There was still plenty of glory for the man who captured the two isolated forts, and he commanded the troops. With Porter's flotilla in the river and the army pressing from the rear, the forts would certainly

21. Boggs to Farragut, April 29, 1862, ORN, XVIII, 211; *Butler's Book*, 365–67.

22. Butler's Report, April 29, 1862, ORA, VI, 504; *Butler's Book*, 365, 367; *Butler Correspondence*, I, 426–27.

23. Butler to Farragut, April 24, 1862, ORA, VI, 713; *Butler Correspondence*, I, 422.

have no choice but to surrender to the infantry. The plums were there. All Butler had to do was to move fast enough to fetch them.[24]

The general did not get his men in motion quite as fast as he hoped. After being detained by the grounding of *Miami*, he did not reach Sable Island until April 27, where he lost precious time setting up a temporary headquarters. Embarking the 26th Massachusetts and the 6th Massachusetts Battery on *Miami*, he sent them toward the swamps in the rear of Fort St. Philip. A short distance behind in another transport came companies from the 4th Wisconsin and the 21st Indiana. Six miles from shore *Miami* grounded, and the soldiers transferred their guns and gear to thirty rowboats. Nobody had taken the trouble to sound the bay, and a mile from the steamer the invaders found only two and a half feet of water. Searching ahead, they located a bayou with deeper water and finally reached Manuel's Canal, a mile and a half from their landing site, but a stiff current running "like a mill-race" impeded progress, forcing the men to get into waist-deep water and drag the boats through muck until they reached shore. Once on dry stretches of the swamp, one detachment crossed the river above Fort Jackson and the other began a cross-marsh trek to the rear of Fort St. Philip.[25]

Butler, however, reacted with dismay when he discovered that Farragut had pushed on to New Orleans with his squadron. He had brought scaling ladders to assault fort St. Philip from the rear and expected to find Farragut's vessels in position to lay siege to the forts from above. Missing by a day his opportunity for glory—or perhaps a piece of it—he could have blamed it on the skipper of his flagship or the commander of *Miami*, as both had detained him, but it was mostly the fault of his own shoddy preparations. In the end he blamed it on Porter, who accepted the surrender of both forts on the morning of April 28—twelve hours after the defenders of Fort Jackson mutinied, disappeared into the swamps, and left their officers with no option but to capitulate. Butler had no insight into the demoralizing effect six days of shelling had on the defenders of Fort Jackson. He anticipated a

24. Butler to Farragut, April 24, 1862, ORA, VI, 713; *Butler Correspondence*, I, 426.
25. Butler's Report, April 29, Duncan's Report, April 30, 1862, ORA, VI, 504, 529; *Butler Correspondence*, I, 426.

protracted siege and failed to be present for the surrender. After he learned of Porter's victory, he hurried back to the forts to glean whatever crumbs of credit remained. He found little to sate his appetite. His infantry had captured between 250 and 300 mutineers as they fled through the swamps, and at Porter's bidding, Massachusetts troops under General Phelps, who had been waiting on sailing vessels near the mouth of the river, had been towed by Porter's gunboats up to the forts, but Phelps missed the actual surrender.[26]

Had Butler remained below the forts with Porter instead of chasing up and down the river in search of fame, he might have been on hand to add his signature to the articles of capitulation. Instead, he attempted to embarrass Porter, whom he underestimated by thinking of him as a junior commander who would not argue with a major general. He read Porter's report first, and then, with all the guile of a skillful lawyer, composed his own. He declared that the mortar squadron failed in its mission to reduce the forts, called it "superbly useless," and claimed that both forts were "substantially as defensible as before the bombardment." Butler, after asserting that the surrender of the forts had been induced by his "pickets," chastised Porter for granting better terms than "ought to be given . . . to a rebel officer or soldier." The general demonstrated a mean streak for the enemy—which now seemed to include Porter—even though most of the Confederate soldiers were militia or conscripted foreigners who manifested little enthusiasm for continuing the war.[27]

The general's grievance with Porter had nothing to do with the forts but everything to do with the army being excluded from the surrender. Butler made a mistake by agitating Porter, who was every bit as feisty as the general when it came to matters reflecting on his professional performance. "Butler did it all!!!" Porter raged after reading Butler's scurrilous account. "So I see it reported by that blackguard reporter of the *Herald* . . . who had his nose in everything. . . . If you could have seen the trouble I had getting old Butler and his soldiers up

26. Butler's Report, April 29, Phelps to Strong, April 30, 1862, ORA, VI, 505, 508–509; Duncan's Report, April 30, 1862, ORN, XVIII, 273–74; T. Williams, "Letters," 313–14; De Forest, A *Volunteer's Adventures*, 15; Richard S. West, Jr., "Admiral Farragut and General Butler," U.S. *Naval Institute Proceedings*, no. 640 (June, 1956), 637.

27. Butler's Report, April 29, 1862, ORA, VI, 505; *Butler's Book*, 371–72; Butler to Stanton, June 1, 1862, *Butler Correspondence*, I, 538.

to the Forts, to take charge of them . . . you would laugh at the old fools pretensions. But he actually asserts that it was his presence (30 miles off) which induced the Forts to surrender."[28] The discord begun on the lower Mississippi lasted thirty years, and during Butler's occupation of New Orleans no Union officer became more critical of the general's administration than Porter. Butler, despite the facts, always insisted that the victory was his and his alone.

After agitating Porter, Butler detailed the 26th Massachusetts to garrison the forts and on April 29 sped back upriver to Quarantine, where he stopped to rest before continuing to New Orleans. Once again, the busy general missed a ceremony, this one less official.[29]

On the morning of April 25, the approach of Farragut's fleet threw the town into a panic. "Like an electric shock," reported one diarist, "the news soon spread all over the city." Twelve taps from the fire bell spread the alarm—the signal for the town's militia to report to their commands. Merchants closed their stores, teachers suspended classes, banks made hurried requests to depositors to withdraw their valuables, women hid their silver plate and jewelry, and Confederate currency descended to "a perfect state of chaos," many people discarding it. The rumble of heavy guns a few miles downriver drove people wild. Aside from the militia, the men in town consisted mainly of foreigners, blacks, wealthy businessmen, and the elderly. They broke into the Marine Hospital, which had been converted into a small arms factory, and made off with all the muskets and ammunition. By noon, civil order collapsed.[30]

General Lovell, who had returned from the forts early that morning, detained all steamboats and held the Jackson and Great Northern Railroad in readiness to evacuate troops and government supplies. He barred citizens from transporting private property but permitted

28. Articles of Capitulation, April 28, 1862, *ORN*, XVIII, 438; Porter to Fox, June 2, 1862, in *Fox Correspondence*, II, 113.

29. Butler's Report, April 29, 1862, *ORA*, VI, 505.

30. Briskell's Testimony, April 17, 1863, *ibid.*, 576; "Reminiscent of War-Times: Eventful Days in New Orleans in the Year 1862," *Southern Historical Society Papers*, XXIII, 182–84; James O. Lang, "Gloom Envelops New Orleans: April 24 to May 2, 1862," *Journal of Louisiana History*, I (Summer, 1960), 283–84; Elliott Ashkenazi, ed., *The Civil War Diary of Clara Solomon: Growing Up in New Orleans, 1861–1862* (Baton Rouge, 1995), 344.

them, if they wished to leave, to book passage on steamboats. Laborers, angered by Lovell's abandonment, refused to work, and those willing declined to do so if paid in Confederate notes. By the time Lovell got organized, many of the steamboat crews had deserted. Another detail under the provost marshal seized wagons and began hauling cotton from warehouses and setting it on fire. The town grew surly, articulating a lasting hatred of Lovell. In their view he had been sent there to protect their city, not to burn its wealth. Marion Southwood, a vocal observer, wrote, "We felt how cruelly we had been deceived." Young Clara Solomon echoed the lament, writing, "Never shall I forget the 25th of Apr. 1862. Such expressions of woe as were on the faces of everyone, & such sadness as reigned in every heart." Julia Le Grand put it bluntly: "Lovell, a most worthless creature . . . did little or nothing and the little he did was all wrong. . . . The wretched generals . . . here with our troops, ran away and left them."[31]

Rage expressed its form in many ways. The maddened crowd seized a man whose only crime was that of looking "like a stranger and might be a spy." They located a rope and unceremoniously hanged him from a lamppost on the corner of Magazine and Common Streets. Before he choked to death a patrol from the city's European Brigade cut him down and saved his life. A larger mob, many approaching levels of starvation, brushed aside the militia, broke into warehouses, smashed barrels, and made off with sacks of sugar, bacon, rice, and corn. Once again the European Brigade attempted to disperse the mob, only to find it at work someplace else. Naval officers torched the unfinished Confederate ironclad *Mississippi*, and its builders, Asa and Nelson Tift, fled upriver to Vicksburg, where they were seized by an angry mob and almost lynched.[32]

31. Lovell to Cooper, April 26, 1862, James's Testimony, April 11, Williams' Testimony, April 18, Cooke's Testimony, June 18, 1863, ORA, VI, 510–11, 568–69, 579, 634–35; "Reminiscent of War-Times," 182–84; Cable, "New Orleans Before the Capture," *B&L*, II, 20; Marion Southwood, *"Beauty and Booty": The Watchword of New Orleans* (New York, 1867), 19; Ashkenazi, ed., *Diary of Clara Solomon*, 345; Kate Mason Rowland and M. L. Croxwell, eds., *The Journal of Julia Le Grand, New Orleans, 1862–1863* (Richmond, 1911), 39.

32. Cable, "New Orleans Before the Capture," *B&L*, II, 20; "Reminiscent of War-Time," 183–84; Briskell's Testimony, April 17, 1863, ORA, VI, 576–77; Senlac's Tes-

After pounding Chalmette—fifteen hundred feet of earthworks below the city—the Union fleet threaded its way through burning vessels and at noon arrived off the great city of New Orleans. Farragut's sailors witnessed an unforgettable spectacle—the massive destruction of $10 million in Confederate wealth. Sunken hulks floated down the river, more than eleven thousand bales of cotton lay smoldering on the wharves, fires leapt from sheds filled with tobacco, ships and dry docks lay partially sunk along the levee, coalyards and lumberyards still blazed, and not a Confederate banner was in sight along the riverfront. A New York *Herald* reporter wrote, "The atmosphere was thick with smoke and the air hot with flames. It was a grand but sad sight."[33]

The town looked deserted except for a growing gathering of Unionists who dared to cheer the reappearance of the forbidden national emblem. *Mississippi* ran in close to the wharf, and its band struck up "The Star-Spangled Banner." Some of the crowd cheered and waved their hats, but the celebration lasted only minutes. A troop of Confederate horsemen charged down one of the streets, fired into a gathering of men, women, and children, and hightailed it back to the city. Commander James Alden called the incident "atrocious," a word soon to echo among the suppressed population of the Crescent City—but for different reasons.[34]

Madame Loreta Janeta Velazquez, a secret agent for the Confederacy, stood among the crowd, and after viewing Farragut's fleet she voiced a sullen observation no doubt shared by others: "When I saw these splendid vessels appearing off the levee I began to have a greater respect for the power of the Federal government than I had before, and a greater appreciation of the weakness of the Confederacy."[35]

Farragut sent Captain Theodorus Bailey and Lieutenant George

timony, n.d., *ORN*, Ser. 2, I, 509; Charles W. Read, "Reminiscences of the Confederate States Navy," *Southern Historical Society Papers*, I, 347.

33. John Smith Kendall, *History of New Orleans* (3 vols.; Chicago, 1922), I, 260; New Orleans *Daily Picayune*, April 26, 1862; West, "Admiral Farragut and General Butler," 638.

34. Alden's Journal, Roe's Diary, *ORN*, XVIII, 741, 770.

35. Loreta Janeta Velazquez, *The Woman in Battle: A Narrative of the Exploits, Adventures, and Travels of Madame Loreta Janeta Velazquez, Otherwise Known as Lieutenant Harry T. Buford, Confederate States Army* (Hartford, 1876), 233.

Perkins ashore to demand the surrender of the city. General Lovell, having at his disposal but three thousand militia armed with muskets and shotguns, had withdrawn all his troops from the area, leaving New Orleans under civilian control. This forced Bailey to negotiate with Mayor John T. Monroe, who was not inclined to surrender anything. A mob followed the two naval officers to city hall, shouting, "Shoot them! Kill them! Hang them!" The pair maintained their composure, entered city hall, and demanded the Stars and Stripes be raised over the post office, the customhouse, and the United States mint, and the Louisiana banner be lowered over city hall. Monroe deferred to Lovell, who was summoned under a flag of truce from his hideout in the city. He arrogantly refused to surrender, stating that he had withdrawn and that matters of capitulation must be discussed with the mayor. Bailey and Perkins departed through a side door and reported the situation to Farragut, who wrote the Navy Department, "His Lordship [Lovell] said he would surrender nothing, but at the same time he would retire and leave the mayor embarrassed." The situation remained volatile, and Farragut, while awaiting further word from the mayor, kept an anxious eye downriver for Butler.[36]

Late that night Lovell crept back to the city and met with the mayor. A plot was afoot to board the enemy vessels and carry them by assault. All it would take, the conspirators claimed, would be a thousand men. Lovell considered the plan foolish but agreed to it if volunteers could be raised. Major Samuel L. James promised to seize several steamers for the mission, and Captain St. L. Dupiere said he would have the men at the landing by nine o'clock the following morning. When only 140 volunteers reported, James canceled the mission and entrained the men for Camp Moore.[37]

The mayor firmly believed that as a civil magistrate he could maintain his allegiance to the Confederate government and ignore the invaders. He simply refused to lower the state flag flying over city hall and told Farragut that if he wished to take it down, to do it himself.

36. Lovell's Report, May 22, 1862, Lovell's Testimony, April 10, 1863, *ORA*, VI, 513, 565–66; Frank Moore, ed., *The Rebellion Record* (12 vols.; New York, 1861–68), IV, 522–23.

37. Lovell to Cooper, May 22, James's Testimony, April 11, 1862, *ORA*, VI, 515–16, 568–69.

Having nothing but a few companies of marines scattered throughout the fleet, Farragut paced the deck of *Hartford,* waiting for the army. He could not send sailors or marines ashore without having them threatened by a mob, and earlier efforts to communicate with Monroe had come close to causing riots, forcing Farragut to threaten a bombardment if the town did not settle down and accept his terms. If forced to level the town, he warned the mayor that women and children would have but forty-eight hours to pack their possessions and evacuate. During brief daily negotiations, the marines managed to hoist a flag over the mint, but they stayed away from city hall, where a huge hostile crowd congregated in the streets and threatened to make trouble. Pierre Soulé, a former United States senator and envoy to Spain, acted as intermediary between Farragut and Monroe and judiciously provided security for the Union officers quarreling with the mayor over protocol. Lovell made a brief reappearance and offered to return to the city and fight for it with his entire command, but Monroe declined, convinced that Farragut's threat to level the town was meant to be taken seriously.[38]

Meanwhile, a member of the Crescent Guards, who remained in the city, peered through the veil of smoke still rising from the wharves, and wrote, "The dusky, long, morose, demon-like Yankee steamers . . . lay like evil messengers of woe at our very front." He watched as the boatload of marines marched into the city, raised the Stars and Stripes over the mint, and returned to their vessel. The town turned suddenly hostile, and moments later four men lowered the flag and tore it to shreds. Infused by a fresh surge of patriotism, the crowd marched to the riverfront, led by a woman carrying the Confederate banner. She stood under the guns of Farragut's flagship while a fifer piped "Bonnie Blue Flag" and "Dixie." The crowd expanded and once again hungry mobs began breaking down doors and looting closed stores. Clara Solomon's family began to pack a few belongings. "We intended to

38. Monroe to Farragut, April 26, Farragut to Monroe, April 28, 1862, Log of *Hartford,* Alden's Journal, Roe's Diary, ORN, XVIII, 231–33, 722–24, 741–43, 770–72; Hearn, *Capture of New Orleans,* 237–48; see also Marion A. Baker, "Farragut's Demands for the Surrender of New Orleans," *B&L,* II, 95–99. This was the new state flag, raised on February 21, 1861, and not the old traditional Pelican flag as thought by some.

take but a few clothes," she wrote, "and were willing to make any sacrifice to behold our prided city reduced to ruins rather than it should fall into the hands of the barbarous invaders."[39]

Soon after the marines returned to their ships for morning prayers, the lookout in the maintop of *Pensacola* hollered to the deck, "The flag is down, sir," and fired his howitzer. Sure enough, the Stars and Stripes no longer fluttered over the mint, and when the shell from the howitzer exploded near the group cheering beside the flagstaff, they dispersed. Farragut had threatened to bombard the town if anyone disturbed the national flag, and the men on *Pensacola* jumped to their guns. Fortunately for New Orleans, all the primers had been removed a half hour earlier and Captain Henry W. Morris restrained the gunners from taking action. The culprits who shredded the flag, however, remained unidentified—at least for the moment.[40]

Growing impatient and wondering what had happened to the army, Farragut sent a vessel downriver to find Butler and bring up the infantry. The captain's clerk went ashore at Quarantine and located the general on a hospital cot, sleeping noisily "with his head encased in a red nightcap." The clerk shook Butler awake, telling him to get his troops up to New Orleans. He also mentioned that he was off to Washington with Farragut's dispatches, and if the general had any, he would be happy to carry them. At the mention of dispatches Butler bounded out of his cot and penned a lengthy report to Secretary of War Stanton. In it he wrote: "I find the city under the dominion of the mob. They have insulted our flag—torn it down with indignity. This outrage will be punished in such manner as in my judgment will caution both the perpetrators and abettors of the act, so that they shall fear the stripes if they do not reverence the stars of our banner." Butler's reference was to the flag-shredding incident at the mint. The morning papers had given the desecrater a name—William Mumford, a New Orleans gambler who had dragged the banner through the streets, distributed pieces of it to the mob, and was reported to be wearing one of the scraps as a boutonniere. After joining Farragut on

39. New Orleans *Daily Picayune*, April 27, 1863; "Reminiscent of War-Times," 183; Ashkenazi, ed., *Diary of Clara Solomon*, 347.

40. Farragut to Monroe, April 26, 28, 1862, Roe's Diary, *ORN*, XVIII, 230–31, 232–33, 771.

April 27, Butler vowed to "hang that fellow," but Farragut, who was in a quandary over conditions at New Orleans, replied, "You'll have to catch him first," and urged Butler to go back downriver and bring up his division.[41]

The general had missed little of the excitement, but for a man who prided himself on capitalizing on opportunities by exercising clever timing, he sure experienced bad luck on the lower Mississippi. His one advantage, however, was keeping a flock of reporters nearby. When the forts surrendered, the press attributed it to Porter and Butler, and shortly after the general began his administration of New Orleans, they began to credit him for the success of the entire operation. Not much time passed before Butler viewed Porter as his archenemy, referring to him as "untruthful" and "villainous." Because of his growing dislike of Porter, the general made an extra effort to be friendly toward Farragut. Public recognition of Farragut's great victory came slowly, except in Washington, and at the root of the confusion was Butler's influence with the press.[42]

By April 29 Farragut tired of waiting for the return of Butler and sent 250 marines ashore with two howitzers. They landed at the foot of Canal Street, marched to the customhouse, post office, and mint, lowered Confederate flags, and once again unfurled the Stars and Stripes. This time the Union banner stayed up. Another detachment entered city hall, and Lieutenant Albert Kautz climbed to the roof and lowered the state flag. Because the building was not the property of the Federal government, Farragut left the flagstaff bare. Butler missed the forcible occupation of the town, but Farragut, always generous, attempted to share the credit.[43]

On the trip upriver Butler penned instructions to his command, forbidding "all plundering of public or private property . . . under the

41. Butler's Report, April 29, 1862, *ORA*, VI, 503–506; Albert Kautz, "Incidents of the Occupation of New Orleans," *B&L*, II, 93: *Butler's Book*, 370–71, 376.

42. Charles Lee Lewis, *David Glasgow Farragut: Our First Admiral* (Annapolis, 1943), 76–77; *Butler's Book*, 371.

43. Kautz, "Incidents of the Occupation of New Orleans," *B&L*, II, 91–94. On June 7, after deposing the mayor, Butler raised the Union flag over city hall to the roar of thirty-four guns in Lafayette Square "to give the semblance of submission by a city which never surrendered" (Dabney, "The Butler Regime in Louisiana," 494).

severest penalties." He also ordered that "no officer or soldier will absent himself from his station without arms or alone, under any pretext whatsoever." He held regimental commanders responsible for "strict execution of these orders," but he made no mention of the same rules applying to himself or his staff.[44]

On the evening of May 1, 1862, the general's transports hauled through the fleet to roaring cheers from the sailors. After depositing the 21st Indiana at Algiers, the vessels tied to the city wharf and fourteen hundred blue-cladded infantry filed down the gangway at the foot of Canal Street. They formed at the landing and, with flags flying and regimental bands playing "Yankee Doodle," waited for the general. Prisoners from the forts, with paroles tucked into their tattered clothing, disembarked. The crowd jeered them, threw rocks, and booted them through the streets. Mrs. Butler and the general observed the mayhem from the deck of the transport *Mississippi* as hundreds of people began spilling from the city and congregating on the riverfront. The general expressed his one concern—"None of my troops up to this time had ever received or given a hostile shot."[45]

Farragut, relieved by the arrival of Butler, extended his congratulations to the general by writing: "The intrepidity with which you so soon followed up your success by landing your forces at the Quarantine, through mud and mire and water for miles, and which enabled us to tighten the cords around [Forts Jackson and St. Philip] . . . has also added to my obligations, and I trust that you will now occupy and hold the city without further difficulty other than those incident to a conquered city, disordered by anarchy and the reign of terror which this unfortunate city has passed through." In writing, Farragut gave no thought to the possibility of another reign of terror—this one orchestrated by the recipient of his compliment. "Now with safety," one historian wrote, Farragut could "turn loose of the tiger's tail, since the keeper of the zoo had arrived."[46]

---

44. General Orders No. 15, May 1, 1862, *ORA*, VI, 717.

45. Roe's Diary, *ORN*, XVIII, 771–72; Butler to Stanton, May 8, 1862, *ORA*, VI, 506–508; Parton, *General Butler*, 279. Butler's command consisted of the 30th and 31st Massachusetts, 4th Wisconsin, 6th Michigan, 9th and 10th Connecticut, 21st Indiana, three artillery batteries, and two cavalry companies.

46. Farragut to Butler, May 1, 1862, *ORN*, XVIII, 244; West, "Admiral Farragut and General Butler," 639.

James Parton, the first of Butler's many biographers, described the scene at the moment of debarkation:

A company of the Thirty-first Massachusetts landed on the extensive platform raised above the levee for the convenient loading of cotton, and, forming a line, slowly pressed back the crowd, at the point of the bayonet, until space enough was obtained for the regiments to form. When the Thirty-first had all landed, they marched down the cotton platform to the levee, and along the levee to De Lord street, where they halted. The Fourth Wisconsin . . . then disembarked, after which the procession was formed in the order following:

First, as a pioneer and guide, Lieutenant Henry Weigel . . . aid to the general, who was familiar with the streets of the city . . . now rose from a sick bed to claim the fulfillment of General Butler's promise that he, and he only, should guide the troops to the Customs-House.

Next, the drum-corps of the Thirty-first Massachusetts. Behind these, General Butler and his staff on foot, no horses having yet been landed, a file of the Thirty-first marching on each side of them. Then Captain Everett's battery of artillery, with whom marched Captain Kensel, chief of artillery to the expedition. . . . Next, General Williams and his staff, preceded by the fine band of the Fourth Wisconsin. . . . The same orders were given as on the march into Baltimore: silence; no notice to be taken of mere words; if a shot were fired from a house, halt, arrest inmates, destroy house; if fired upon from the crowd, arrest the man if possible, but not fire into the crowd unless necessary for self-defense, and then not without orders.[47]

Marion Southwood, a lady of the city, watched the procession from the levee, casting her eyes from time to time on the general and his wife. She had a keen interest in the future of her town. "There was a perfect *rush* to see this awful representative of human authority," she wrote. "It was a scene which will not soon be forgotten; all seemed to be fearful that it would be the only chance they might have of seeing 'Picayune Butler.'" The general's reputation had preceded him. As soon as he stepped off the transport to join the march to the custom-house, men, women, and children "went splashing through the mud" to catch sight of him, and "every epithet which could be applied to

47. Parton, *General Butler*, 280–81.

the vilest was heaped upon him. . . . [T]hey knew no language too gross to accost him with . . . and this only ended when he was safely ensconced in the Custom-House." Other observers described the crowd as good-natured—more like spectators viewing a ceremony— and considering the large number of civilians in dire circumstances, those in need would be less inclined to make hostile demonstrations.[48]

Slurs and maledictions were hurled by the mob. One man cried out to the passing soldiers, "You'll never see home again." Another snarled, "Yellow Jack will have you before long." The crowd then took special interest in a dumpy-looking officer with a large bald head, a drooping moustache, squinting cocked eyes, and a rumpled uniform bedecked with gold braid. Someone shouted, "Where is the d——d rascal?" Another replied, "There he goes, G——d d——n him!" and a man craning his neck grumbled, "I see the d——d old villain!" Butler, a little unsteady himself, ordered his men to disregard the insults, fix bayonets, and reply to no taunts. Hisses pouring from open windows became absorbed in the bedlam on the street, but the general, having no ear for music, ignored the shouts and concentrated on keeping in step with the band. "And so they marched," Parton reported, "along the levee to Poydras street; Poydras street to St. Charles street; past the famous hotel, closed and deserted now with five hundred inmates three days before; along St. Charles street to Canal street and the Customs-House—that vast, unfinished, roofless structure, upon which the United States had expended so many millions." The 31st Massachusetts broke down the door, posted guards, lodged themselves on the second floor, and prepared their evening meal. The general and his staff returned to the transport *Mississippi* for the night, passing once again through the throng that followed with more insults. Threats did not bother Butler—they merely amused him.

When the promenade ended, the city showed its softer side. As evening approached the streets fell silent, and the town became "as still as a country hamlet." General Phelps, ignoring Butler's orders to go nowhere alone, walked about the city unattended and unmolested.

48. Southwood, *"Beauty and Booty,"* 41, 43. In Louisiana's colonial days, the picayune was the smallest coin, worth six and a quarter cents. In the 1860s it meant "small, contemptible," and was used in a jocular sense in one of the many minstrel songs of the day (see Dabney, "The Butler Regime in Louisiana," 495, nn. 2, 3).

He spoke to many people, who all greeted him cordially and, despite his uniform, answered his inquiries politely. When he returned to his brigade an officer asked him, "You didn't mention your name, did you, General?" Phelps laughed and replied, "No, no one asked it."[49]

New Orleanians also had a scoffing sense of humor, one that Butler required time to understand. During the afternoon the general had heard "Picayune Butler" shouted by the crowd gathered at the wharf. Thinking it was a song, he asked the band to play it. The musicians had never heard of it for good reason. Picayune Butler was a black barber in New Orleans who had a son named Benjamin F. Butler, and some local jokester had spread it about town that the general was none other than the barber's son. As the story went, Picayune Butler's son emigrated to Liberia, where

> he developed an indisposition for labor and . . . turned his attention to the bar, to prepare for which he repaired to Massachusetts. Having mastered his profession, he acquired a fondness for theological study and became an active local preacher, the course of his early labors leading him to New York, where he attracted the notice of Mr. Jacob Barker, then in the zenith of his fame as financier, and who, discovering the peculiar abilities of the young mulatto, sent him to northern New York to manage a banking institution. There he divided his time between the counting-house and the court-house, the prayer-meeting and the printing office.

If New Orleanians believed the story, they were certain to be disappointed when Butler appeared manifesting none of the features of the barber's son. The sobriquet "Picayune" stuck, however; yet there is no indication that it ever bothered the general.[50]

Ben Butler had come to town. They would see him often—but not as a mulatto—and nothing would ever be the same again.

49. Parton, *General Butler*, 281; Bland, *Life of Butler*, 75.
50. Parton, *General Butler*, 174–75, 279. There was a religiously inclined New Yorker named Benjamin F. Butler who served in the cabinets of Andrew Jackson and Martin Van Buren, but he was white and died in 1858. This coincidence probably escaped most of those in the crowd who had shouted "Picayune" Butler.

5

When the Devil
Came Down to Dixie

WHEN BUTLER TOOK POSSESSION of New Orleans on the
evening of May 1, 1862, he understood little of the town's long history
and made the mistake of believing that all of its citizens espoused the
same rebellious sentiments as the inhabitants of Charleston, South
Carolina. During his ceremonial march to the customhouse, he might
have taken closer notice of the mixed mob that followed him.

Captain De Forest, who formed his Connecticut company along
the levee, observed two of the many sides of the city's populace. First
there were "the roughs, the low women and the ragged urchins" who
continued "to hoot, jeer, swear, and call us evil names." He praised his
company for standing "like statues, without replying by word or look."
The mob became even more excited when word leaked out that the
soldiers had loaded with ball. A red-nosed man, who addressed the
captain personally, declared with many oaths, "We don't want you
here, damn it! You haven't come among friends, not by a damn sight.
We don't want you, d'ye understand? We wouldn't give you a cup of
water." De Forest made no reply, but a ragged Irishman carrying a four-
foot shillelagh did. He pushed his way through the crowd, swinging
the cudgel over his head, meanwhile "damning and . . . God-damning-
to-hell the red-nosed man, who hastily depart[ed] around the nearest
corner. Then the Irishman salutes me in military style," De Forest
recalled, "takes off his shabby hat to the colors and makes them a low
bow." Whatever the march to the customhouse accomplished for Butler, it did little for the regiment from Connecticut. Having no quarters, the soldiers marched back to the wharf, posted sentries, and
passed the night on the dock. The general, accustomed to more

elegant accommodations, moved into the fashionable but empty St. Charles Hotel, and Farragut, glad to shed the vexatious role of watchdog, dispatched seven vessels under Captain Thomas T. Craven to go upriver and force the surrender of Louisiana's capital, Baton Rouge.[1]

If the ragamuffins of New Orleans were divided, the same could be said for some of the rich. Louisiana derived most of its wealth from agriculture, but New Orleans became the greatest and wealthiest city in the Confederacy from its commerce. In the decade prior to the Civil War thousands of northerners migrated to the Crescent City to establish shops, banks, trading houses, small factories, and shipping companies. Free trade attracted scores of Europeans, who cashed in on the city's growth by bringing capital to build warehouses and buy ships to transport the Mississippi River's abundant harvests back to the tables and mills of France and Great Britain. There were no banks in America stronger or with better-protected currency than those in New Orleans. Union occupation did not fit into the plans of a city accustomed to continued growth and rich profits.[2]

In 1860 the population of New Orleans had grown to 168,675, more than four times greater than that of any other southern city. Charleston, South Carolina, at 40,522, and Richmond, Virginia, at 37,910, came in a distant second and third. Aside from New Orleans, Louisiana's towns were small, Baton Rouge at 5,428 being the largest. The economy of the interior depended heavily upon slave labor, which made up 46.8 percent of the state's population of 708,000. In 1860 Louisiana reported 17,646 free blacks, and the majority of them lived in the Crescent City. Unionists owned slaves, and so did blacks. Even foreign consuls held slaves, although such acts were forbidden by their governments. The city boasted thirteen banks with a capital of $24,496,866, deposits of $19,777,812, and $12,115,431 in gold or silver. In 1860 New Orleans was still growing and enormously prosperous.[3]

From early colonial days, the Crescent City had become the most progressive and gayest metropolis in America. Even when war clouds

1. De Forest, *A Volunteer's Adventures*, 18–19; Farragut to Craven, May 3, 1862, ORN, XVIII, 465.

2. Henry Rightor, ed., *Standard History of New Orleans, Louisiana* (Chicago, 1900), 578.

3. E. Merton Coulter, *The Confederate States of America, 1861–1865* (Baton Rouge, 1950), 259, 409, Vol. VII of Coulter, *A History of the South*; Jefferson Davis

threatened, the town did not lose its carefree and effervescent enjoyment of life, and in the fall and winter of the first year of the war the banquets and balls, the opera and theater parties, never stopped. Unconcerned by the feeble efforts of war practiced by Yankees far to the north, the citizens of New Orleans staged their annual Mardi Gras celebration, never thinking that a cross-eyed general by the name of Butler would turn their future upside down three months later.[4]

When Farragut's squadron passed the forts and appeared off the city, New Orleanians felt deceived by their government and abandoned by General Lovell, who had been sent there to protect them. They had raised militia companies and recruited volunteer regiments for the Confederate army, and because the port city functioned as a clearinghouse for all Louisiana units mustered into the service, the populace had watched thousands of soldiers entrain with their muskets, blankets, and artillery to serve with the armies in Virginia and Tennessee. In their local shipyards they had built a small navy, and when Richmond failed to deliver funds to finish the ironclads *Louisiana* and *Mississippi,* the town's Committee of Public Safety raised $100,000 and sent its members all over the South to expedite the acquisition of machinery and guns needed to complete the vessels. But in April, 1862, it all came to nothing. Secretary of the Navy Mallory sent the Confederate fleet upriver, the formidable *Louisiana* could not stem the current and was destroyed at the forts, and the unfinished CSS *Mississippi* was set afire to keep it from falling into enemy hands. By the time Butler reached the city, the townspeople were furious, and if the Confederate government would not fight the Yankees, some of them would.[5]

No city in the South had a greater mix of cultures than New Orleans, and the blend contributed to the town's vigorous growth before the

---

Bragg, *Louisiana in the Confederacy* (Baton Rouge, 1941), 23; Dabney, "The Butler Regime in Louisiana," 488.

4. Winters, *Civil War in Louisiana,* 17; New Orleans *Daily Picayune,* February 11, 28, 1862.

5. Hearn, *Capture of New Orleans,* 28–30, 142–45, 148, 150, 168–69, 188, 239–40; "Historical Militia Data on Louisiana Militia," April 1–20, 1861, p. 35, in Louisiana and Lower Mississippi Valley Collections, Louisiana State University Libraries, Louisiana State University, Baton Rouge.

war. The Spanish and Creole population still represented the elite and dominated the city's social life, but foreigners, including Italians, Germans, Irish, French, Poles, Slavonians, Belgians, Dutch, and British, had established themselves in great numbers, and when the Union blockade began to create mass unemployment, much of the working class enlisted in militia companies organized by nationality. The numerous free blacks caused concern because some whites believed they might incite a slave insurrection, and to discourage it Governor Moore, a large cotton planter and slaveholder, became the first in the South to organize a Native Guard as part of the state's forces. When Farragut's fleet arrived in the river, many of the men who had not enlisted in the Confederate army joined the militia, which by April had grown to about ten thousand members, but when Lovell abandoned the city, he took most of the remaining units with him. By the time Butler marched into town, many of the young men had departed to fight on other fields, leaving the city to the elite, the politicians, women and children, and a bizarre assortment of gamblers, gangsters, shopkeepers, tradesmen, slaves, vagabonds, Unionists, and foreigners who had come to New Orleans to make money—not to make war.[6]

The secession movement in New Orleans had begun on December 21, 1860, the day after news arrived that South Carolina had withdrawn from the Union. A great celebration took place in the building of the Southern Rights Association on Camp Street, followed by an eight-hundred-gun salute to honor South Carolina. A large crowd gathered to hear and cheer speeches, and after several days of enthusiastic celebration, the stage was set for Governor Moore to act.[7]

The aristocracy who ran New Orleans played a large role in Louisiana's secession, and with their wealth and influence they controlled business, politics, and the delegates elected to the secession convention. Of the state's 376,280 free voters, the elite represented a

---

6. Ella Lonn, *Foreigners in the Confederacy* (Chapel Hill, N.C., 1940), 100–14; Roger W. Schugg, *Origins of Class Struggle in Louisiana: A Social History of White Farmers and Laborers During Slavery and After, 1840–1875* (Baton Rouge, 1939), 118–19, 172; Joseph T. Wilson, *The Black Phalanx: A History of the Negro Soldiers of the United States in the Wars of 1775–1812, 1861–'65* (Hartford, 1888), 481–82; Winters, *Civil War in Louisiana*, 73–74.

7. Johnson, "New Orleans Under General Butler," 437.

small percentage. On January 7, 1861, when delegates to the convention were elected, 17,296 votes went to those committed to preserving the Union and 20,448 went to those favoring secession. Although the secessionists held a slight majority, the vote at the convention could have swung in either direction. From political pressure and various forms of coercion, the Unionists deserted their electorate on January 26 and voted for secession, the final vote being 113 to 17. In the final analysis, 5 percent of the voters took New Orleans and Louisiana out of the Union and into war. The decision was widely celebrated in New Orleans, but much of the public suppressed their reservations. By law, the act of secession required ratification by the people, but Governor Moore sidestepped the process. On December 10, 1860, he created a military board, and on March 3, 1861, New Orleans' city council authorized a $1 million bond issue for defense.[8]

When Butler arrived, New Orleans was still the largest city in the South but no longer prosperous. War and the blockade had destroyed trade and brought hunger in its stead. When inflation spiraled out of control, banks discontinued specie payments, and all other forms of currency disintegrated to a point where five-cent streetcar tickets became an acceptable form of exchange. George W. Cable, who watched the decline of his town's economy, wrote, "The current joke was that you could pass the label of an olive-oil bottle [as money], because it was greasy, smelt bad, and bore an autograph." Captain De Forest noticed that "almost the only people visible are shabby roughs and ragged beggars . . . poor Irish and Germans [who] hang about our regiments begging for the refuse of our rations. The town is fairly and squarely on the point of starvation."[9]

With a hungry city on his hands, and one whose people still raged over Lovell's perceived desertion, Butler had a marvelous opportunity to garner the town's support by patiently practicing leniency. Having

8. *Official Journal of the Proceedings of the Convention of the State of Louisiana, 1861* (New Orleans, 1861), 5–20; Schugg, *Origins of Class Struggle in Louisiana,* 163–67; Willie M. Caskey, *Secession and Restoration of Louisiana* (Baton Rouge, 1938), 29–33; Bragg, *Louisiana in the Confederacy,* 59; Harold Sinclair, *The Port of New Orleans* (Garden City, N.Y., 1942), 220–21.

9. Cable, "New Orleans Before the Capture," *B&L,* II, 16–17; De Forest, *A Volunteer's Adventures,* 21; Dabney, "The Butler Regime in Louisiana," 492.

brought only 2,500 troops, he needed the help of the populace. New Orleans had been reduced by war to about 150,000 inhabitants, and despite the city's poverty and the Confederate government's enormous bungling in stripping the state of troops, a great number of people remained loyal to the South. This was especially true of the aristocracy. They had been injured financially by the war, but they retained enough of their wealth that by hoarding they still lived far more comfortably than the vast majority, who had neither jobs nor money to buy food.[10]

Butler's reputation had preceded him, and nobody who had followed the general's career in war or politics felt inclined to extend a warm greeting to the invaders. To the starving population, however, he represented a potential source of subsistence; but there was something about his physical appearance they distinctly disliked. His first few days in New Orleans would set the tone for his administration, and it began on the morning of May 2 when the general's staff entered the St. Charles Hotel and ordered breakfast. When the son of one of the hotel's two absent proprietors refused to serve the food, Major George C. Strong threatened to confiscate the building. "As to . . . giving up the hotel," the son replied, "[my] head would be shot off before [I] could reach the next corner if [I] should do it." Somewhat shakily, the young man explained that "waiters would not dare wait upon them, nor cooks to cook for them, nor porters to carry for them. Moreover," he added, "there were no provisions to be had in the market; [and] he could not see what could be gotten for them beyond army rations." Major Strong, finding negotiations tiresome, told the son quietly but firmly that there was no need to concern himself about giving up the hotel. "In the name of General Butler, they would venture to *take* it," and for that day, the St. Charles Hotel became the headquarters of the Army of the Gulf.[11]

Butler had barely settled into the ladies' parlor when Lieutenant Kautz arrived from the USS *Hartford* with keys to the customhouse. Kautz was better known in the city as the Yankee who pulled down the Louisiana state flag from the staff on city hall. On leaving, the

10. Rowland and Croxwell, eds., *Journal of Julia Le Grand*, 40; Dabney, "The Butler Regime in Louisiana," 492–94.
11. Parton, *General Butler*, 284–85.

young lieutenant turned to the general and said, "I fear you are going to have rather a lawless party to govern, from what I have seen in the past three or four days." Butler replied laconically, "No doubt of that, but I think I understand these people, and can govern them." Kautz departed, less than convinced.[12]

Butler's first act, after commandeering the St. Charles Hotel, was to invite Mayor Monroe to headquarters for a chat. The mayor declined, replying indignantly that he conducted business only at city hall and during office hours. After Colonel Jonas H. French, Butler's emissary, and two Union officers assured His Honor that this stubbornness would only lead to repercussions, the mayor finally condescended and arrived at the hotel with his retinue: Pierre Soulé, who had earlier acted as intermediary between Farragut and the mayor, members of the city council, and the police chief, all "highly respectable gentlemen of the city." A mob of Monroe supporters followed the procession to the hotel and milled about outside while the conferees retired to the ladies' parlor—located at a corner of the hotel on the first floor. Rumor reached the street that Soulé would not accept the hand of the general, and a new wave of patriotism swept through the crowd.[13]

Outside, the crowd became furious when they learned that Butler had taken over the hotel. Inside, negotiations failed to get under way because the mob surrounding the hotel created such a roar that no one could concentrate. Butler tried again, but Lieutenant J. C. Kinsman broke into the meeting and reported that Judge Somers, a Union man who had once been recorder of the city, was at the hotel requesting protection. Butler told him to take the headquarters guard and move the man to the customhouse for protection. Butler watched from the window as the guard escorted Somers to a carriage, but the judge stood nearly six and a half feet tall and was instantly recognized. The mob gathered about the carriage "hooting, yelling, cursing; new hundreds rushing in from every street, for all the men in the city were idle." Several times the carriage came to a stop, and Kinsman, pistol in hand, ordered the driver to push through the crowd. Halfway to the

12. Kautz, "Incidents of the Occupation of New Orleans," *B&L*, II, 94.

13. *Butler's Book*, 374; Parton, *General Butler*, 285; Rowland and Croxwell, eds., *Journal of Julia Le Grand*, 46. Pierre Soulé was a well-mannered gentleman and too polished a diplomat to refuse a handshake.

customhouse he came upon a streetcar blocking the road with a single man on board who was waving his arms and urging the mob to capture the carriage.

Kinsman turned to the guard and shouted, "Bring out that man!"

Two soldiers entered the vehicle, "collared the lunatic," pulled him out and placed him under guard, where he "continued to yell and gesticulate in the most frantic manner."

"Stop your noise," thundered the lieutenant.

"I won't," said the man. "My tongue is my own."

"Sergeant, lower your bayonet. If a sound comes out of that man's mouth, run him through!"

By the time Kinsman reached the customhouse, he had arrested several men and held them under guard. Leaving the judge in the care of the 31st Massachusetts, the lieutenant started back to the hotel, only to be followed like Pied Piper by a heavily reinforced crowd.[14]

Having vented some energy on the carriage, the mob caught its breath on the trip back to the hotel and erupted in another burst of shouting. General Williams brought up a regiment, wedged it between the hotel and the hooting public, and sent an aide into the ladies' parlor to warn Butler that the troops might not be able to restrain the protesters. "If [Williams] finds he can not control the mob," Butler replied sternly, "open upon them with artillery."

The city officials sprang to their feet, condemning such violence. Butler remained implacable, replying, "Why this emotion, gentlemen? The cannon are not going to shoot our way and I have stood this noise and confusion as long as I choose to do." Monroe offered to go outside to ask the crowd to disperse. Butler consented, reiterating his demand that order be maintained in the public streets. The mayor, accompanied by Soulé and the city council, stepped onto the balcony and temporarily quieted the mob, warning that Butler had threatened to bring up the artillery. The general, still standing near the window, watched as some of the hooters wandered off, but most of the crowd remained "vast, fierce, and sullen" outside the hotel.[15]

Across the street Butler noticed a man wearing a scrap of cloth

14. *Butler's Book*, 374–75; Parton, *General Butler*, 286–88. Parton refers to Somers as Judge Summers.

15. *Butler's Book*, 375–76.

from the Stars and Stripes in his buttonhole. Asking one of Monroe's associates to identify the person, he learned from him that the man in question was William Mumford. Turning to an aide, Butler said, "Take a look at that man so that [you] would know him if [you] saw him again."[16]

The general attempted to resume the meeting, but catcalls from outside penetrated the walls of the ladies' parlor. "Where's old Butler?" came the chant. "Let him show himself; let him come out if he dare."

Butler timed his appearance well. With cap in hand he stepped out on the balcony, asking, "Who calls me? I am here." All eyes turned to the general and a hush fell over the crowd. Another noise, coming from St. Charles Street, diverted their attention as the 6th Maine Battery, comprising six Napoleons, came rattling over the blocks of the street. Captain Thompson, riding at the head of the battery, galloped furiously toward the hotel, driving every horse at full speed. The "terrible noise and clamor . . . and the wheels of the guns bounding up inches as they thunder[ed] over the uneven stones" terrified the crowd, and as Thompson sped by, the whole street cleared. By the time the Maine artillery formed in position on the sidewalk in front of the hotel, the street had become almost "as quiet as a children's playground." The guns remained in position, and "from that hour to the time I left New Orleans," Butler recalled, "I never saw occasion to move man or horse because of a mob in the streets of the city."[17]

His afternoon conference with Monroe had been so often interrupted that Butler postponed it until evening. The purpose of the meeting was to prepare the mayor and his advisers for the issuance of the general's proclamation, a document he had prepared on board the transport *Mississippi* and given that morning to the proprietor of the New Orleans *True Delta* for printing. Butler expected to have copies available in time for the evening conference, so in the late afternoon he returned to the vessel to pick up Mrs. Butler, her maid, and their baggage and bring them to the elegant and comfortable rooms at the hotel. At dusk, with trunks locked and strapped to the carriage, the hack driver refused to leave the levee until prodded by a bayonet.

16. *Ibid.*, 376.

17. *Ibid.*, 376–77; *Butler Correspondence*, I, 439. According to Mrs. Butler, there were four Napoleons instead of the six claimed by the general.

Then, with Mrs. Butler and her maid in one carriage and the general and his aide in another, the twin hacks rattled through the streets to the hotel without a single incident. For some unknown reason, nightfall always brought calm to the city.[18]

In the meantime, Butler learned that the publisher of the *True Delta* had refused to print his proclamation. He sent two officers and a squad of infantry back to the paper with orders to close it "until further orders." One of Butler's volunteer aides, Captain John Clark, former editor of the Boston *Courier*, set up the press, printed the proclamation, and departed, leaving the office locked and closed by order of the general. A day later the publisher appeared at headquarters with many apologies, and Butler struck an agreement with the owner and reopened the paper.[19]

In another part of town Federal officers searched for maps of the Mississippi Valley. They entered a bookstore on Canal Street, but the owner, Thomas T. White, refused to sell his inventory of maps. A short time later the officers returned with reinforcements, only to discover that during their absence, White had burned the documents.[20]

The meeting on the evening of May 2 in the vast dining room of the St. Charles Hotel did not go well for the mayor and his friends. With a scant meal set before them by a single waiter, Mrs. Butler and three members of the staff sat with the general at one end of the table, and the mayor, his council, and Soulé, the spokesman for the group, sat at the other end. During dinner Butler read extracts from a number of anonymous messages he had received that day, typical among them being, "We'll get the better of you yet, old cock-eye." Another warned him to "look out for poison in [your] food." Butler chuckled over most of the notes, but he considered the rebellious attitude of the town a serious problem. With reference to the populace, he spoke of conducting his administration with restraint, but he needed to discuss to what extent the municipal authorities would cooperate with him. As the meal ended, he sent a cue to the band waiting on the balcony and compelled his visitors to sit through a rendition of "The Star-Spangled

18. *Butler Correspondence*, I, 439; Parton, *General Butler*, 289.

19. General Orders No. 17, May 2, 1862, in *Butler's Book*, 377, 895; *Butler Correspondence*, I, 440; Parton, *General Butler*, 282–83.

20. "Reminiscent of War-Times," *Southern Historical Society Papers*, XXIII, 187–88.

Banner." Then he invited his guests to the ladies' parlor for the business meeting.[21]

Butler laid his proclamation on the table, and for three hours Monroe and Soulé argued vehemently against the general's demands. The mayor had stonewalled Farragut for several days and was determined to do the same to Butler, submitting to nothing less than what the conqueror was able to extort from the conquered. Soulé, a polished politician and long a favorite of the Creole population, also had the trust of the citizens-at-large, having been an influential member of the New Orleans Committee of Public Safety. Biographer Parton described him as similar in stature, complexion, and appearance to Napoleon, "only with an eye of marvelous brilliancy, and hair worn very long, black as night." Butler had met the Creole on several occasions in the past, and their relations had always been amiable. Unlike Butler, who often chose his words carefully, Soulé spoke fluently and manifested all the grace and courteous comportment that the general found difficult to match.[22]

All this did Soulé little good because the general's controversial proclamation sustained martial law—a condition already established by Lovell—forbade public assemblies, prohibited the flying of any banner other than the Stars and Stripes, restricted newspapers from publishing the movements of the army, issued licenses to places of business, and required all enemies of the United States to turn in their arms. For those who took the oath of allegiance to the Union, the document promised to protect their property "from the army of the United States," but the clause offered no protection to the property of those who remained loyal to the Confederacy. The proclamation also permitted the city government to continue its normal functions. Considering Butler's chilly reception and numerous death threats, the document was reasonable, but New Orleanians were accustomed to their independence. One clause in the proclamation disturbed many readers—a reference to New Orleans having been rescued by the Union "from the hands of a foreign government"—the government of the Confederacy.[23]

---

21. Parton, *General Butler*, 290.

22. *Ibid.*, 290–91; Monroe to Farragut, April 26, 1862, ORN, XXVII, 231–32; Bland, *Life of Butler*, 82; Johnson, "New Orleans Under General Butler," 469.

23. *Butler Correspondence*, I, 433; Butler's Proclamation, May 1, 1862, ORA, VI, 717–20; Johnson, "New Orleans Under General Butler," 447, 469–70.

Soulé eloquently argued for magnanimity, appealing at length to Butler's generosity. He suggested that Union troops be withdrawn from the city, arguing, "I know the feelings of the people so well that I am sure your soldiers can have no peace while they remain in our midst." The people would never submit, Soulé warned. "They were not conquered, and could not be expected to behave as conquered people. Withdraw your troops, general, and leave the city government to manage its own affairs. If the troops remain, there will certainly be trouble." The general doubted it and ignored the suggestion. He had his own methods for dealing with troublemakers. The troops would remain, and his only concession was to temporarily suspend his orders forbidding the use of Confederate currency, without which, Soulé and Monroe explained, the populace could buy nothing.[24]

To Soulé and the local magistrates Butler summarized his position simply and clearly:

> I wish to leave the municipal authority in the full exercise of its accustomed functions. I do not desire to interfere with the collection of taxes, the government of the police, the lighting and cleaning of streets, the sanitary laws, or the administration of justice. I desire only to govern the military forces of the department, and to take cognizance only of offenses committed by or against them. Representing here the United States, it is my wish to confine myself solely to the business of sustaining the government of the United States against its enemies.

Then to Soulé's warning he replied:

> I did not expect to hear from Mr. Soulé a threat in *this* occasion. I have been long accustomed to hear threats from southern gentlemen in political conventions; but let me assure gentlemen present, that the time for tactics of that nature has passed never to return. New Orleans *is* a conquered city. If not, why are we here? How did we get here? Have you opened your arms and bid us welcome? Are we here by your consent? Would you or would you not, expel us if you could? New Orleans has been conquered by the forces of the United States, and by the laws of all nations, lies subject to the will of the conquerors. Nevertheless, I

24. *Butler Correspondence*, I, 433; Parton, *General Butler*, 295; *Butler's Book*, 505–506; New Orleans *Daily Picayune*, May 3, 1862.

have proposed to leave the municipal government to the free exercise of all its powers, and I am answered by a threat.[25]

Soulé recanted his statement, declaring he meant it as a suggestion and not as a threat. Butler knew a threat when he heard one, and mindful of the stack of anonymous letters he had read at the supper table, he replied: "Gladly will I take every man of the army out of New Orleans the very day, the very hour it is demonstrated to me that the city government can protect me from insult or danger, if I choose to ride alone from one end of the city to the other, or accompanied by one of my staff. Your inability to govern the insulting, irreligious, unwashed mob in your midst has been clearly proved by the insults of your rowdies toward my officers and men this very afternoon." Butler gave his audience a moment to digest his statement before invoking a little anger. "I have means of knowing more about your city than you think, and I am aware that at this hour there is an organization here established for the purpose of assassinating my men by detail; but I warn you that if a shot is fired from any house, that house will never again cover a mortal's head; and if I can discover the perpetrator of the deed, the place that now knows him shall know him no more forever." Soulé protested, stating that New Orleans contained a smaller proportion of the mob element than any other city of equal size, but the general remained unimpressed.

Butler agreed to help the city bring in provisions and to give attention to the feeding of the poor, but it was not enough to satisfy Mayor Monroe. Dismayed over Soulé's inability to win concessions, Monroe announced that he would suspend the functions of civil government and Butler could do with the town as he wished. A council member disagreed, and Monroe consented to giving the matter further consideration in the morning, after which he would advise the general of his decision.[26]

Monroe's obstinacy, beginning the day he refused to lower the flag at city hall, had baffled even his own advisors. His antecedents were obscure, having come to New Orleans as a young man without a

---

25. Parton, *General Butler*, 295–96.

26. *Ibid.*, 296–97. Butler implies that an agreement was reached that night in *Butler's Book*, 378–79.

penny. He worked on the riverfront as a laborer and became the partner of his stevedore boss. Labor interests elected him to the city council in 1858, and two years later, at the age of forty, he became mayor,
beating two well-known competitors, although every other man on
his ticket lost. Monroe did not like Butler and made no effort to
appease him, and the general did not like hardheaded men.[27]

Without a great deal of ceremony, Monroe departed with his advisers. Flanked by a large crowd that had congregated outside the hotel,
they dispersed into the night. Minutes later, an unusual quiet per-
vaded the streets, and for the first time since daylight, the city was at
peace.

There was no doubt in the minds of many that night that the devil
had come down to Dixie. The rule of Ben Butler had begun.

27. Dabney, "The Butler Regime in Louisiana," 498.

6

Emergence of the Beast

BUTLER WENT TO BED on the night of May 2 satisfied that if the citizens of New Orleans demonstrated a willingness to improve their behavior, he would make an effort to win them over. He would not, however, allow the local magistrates to impose their demands on him, although he privately hoped the mayor would agree to maintain the city's elected government. He decided not to keep large numbers of soldiers in the city, and as other units arrived he planned to send most of them to outposts around the town to safeguard it from attack. Pierre Soulé had made several good suggestions, and although the general was not inclined to make concessions, he was willing to listen to the argument and test its validity. In the matter of the troops, however, he really had little choice. He sent General Phelps with several units to establish a permanent camp at Carrollton, General Williams went upriver with Farragut to capture Baton Rouge, a regiment remained across the river at Algiers, and smaller units occupied the two main forts at the entrance to Lake Pontchartrain.[1]

On the morning of May 3 the general published his proclamation, knowing that it would provoke a negative reaction. It did, but among the first to complain were the foreign consuls, accompanied by Brigadier General Paul Juge, who commanded the city's European Brigade. During the latter days of April, Juge had used his militia to quell disorder and prevent mobs from looting and sacking the city. Learning that his brigade had been disbanded, Juge offered to reorganize them to help maintain order. Butler remained skeptical and declined the offer, but he promised to reconsider it if looting continued. He then assured

1. Parton, *General Butler*, 298–99.

the consuls of his cooperation and promised to confine his activities to military matters, leaving domestic and foreign affairs to the city fathers. This appeased the consuls, and they departed with a favorable impression of the invading general. This was not to be Butler's last round with the consuls. They enjoyed a position of much importance among the businessmen of the city, supplying arms and munitions to the Confederacy, and as diplomats they mistakenly considered themselves beyond the grasp of Butler.[2]

The general's mood continued to improve when delegates from the mayor's office stopped at the hotel and agreed that "the city government should go on as usual." They asked that the troops posted at city hall be withdrawn to remove any impression that the government was acting according to the dictates of the military. Butler agreed and recalled the guard, and with everything going so smoothly, he reopened postal facilities.[3]

Three days after Butler reopened the *True Delta*, the repentant proprietor published an editorial far more favorable to Butler's proclamation than the general might have expected. "For seven years past," the article read, "the world knows that this city, in all its departments— judicial, legislative, and executive—has been at the absolute disposal of the most godless, brutal, ignorant and ruthless ruffians the world has ever heard of since the days of the great Roman conspirator. . . . The electoral system is a farce and a fraud; the knife, the slung-shot, the brass knuckles determining, while the sham is being enacted, who shall occupy and administer the offices of the municipality and the commonwealth. Can our condition then surprise any man?" The *True Delta* was clearly tired of the city's criminal element, even to the extent of condemning the mayor, and added, "We accept the reproach in the Proclamation, as every Louisianian alive to the fair fame of his state and chief city must accept it, with bowed heads and brows abashed." A local diarist read the proclamation and caustically noted, "It is written in the regular Butler style of nonsensical bombast."[4]

2. *Ibid.*, 298, 354; Winters, *Civil War in Louisiana*, 99.

3. Parton, *General Butler*, 298.

4. *Butler Correspondence*, I, 440; New Orleans *True Delta*, May 6, 1862, in Parton, *General Butler*, 299–300; "Reminiscent of War-Times," *Southern Historical Society Papers*, XXIII, 188.

On the afternoon of May 3 Butler turned his attention to the impoverished condition of the city. He attributed much of the turbulence in the streets to the starving condition of more than fifty thousand people, many of them women and children. With business dead the markets were empty. When Lovell abandoned the city he claimed there was food enough to last eighteen days. If so, Butler could not find it. A barrel of flour could not be bought for sixty dollars, Texas drovers had stopped bringing in cattle, steamboats from the Red River had ceased operations, and only the rich could buy food. The Free Market, an organization that for so long had fed the poor, collapsed, having become a free-for-all and stripped of every crumb. The crisis demanded immediate attention.[5]

Learning that in late April a steamer had been designated to pick up supplies at Mobile, Butler issued orders authorizing the trip and granted passes to the "owners and keepers of the flour." He also reopened the Opelousas Railroad, sending freight cars into the rich farmlands of western Louisiana with instructions to backhaul sugar, livestock, and cotton, all to be purchased at fair market value and paid for in specie. In both orders Butler allowed no passengers to be carried, but with food being so scarce, it was interesting that his instructions allowed for the purchase of cotton. Butler, a major stockholder in Middlesex Mills, could not ignore his investments.[6]

May 3 had been a comparatively good day for Ben Butler. He had gotten his way with the city fathers and with the consuls, but he astutely expected the situation to be temporary. More important, he had taken action to feed the public, but it was only the beginning. He must still earn the confidence of the public, revive business, restructure the banks, strengthen the currency, deal with the looming issue of finding work for the blacks, and at the same time attend to military matters in the field. On this day he had dipped into his pocket and contributed a thousand dollars to the immediate relief of the poor, half in cash and half in provisions. Someday he would get it back and write

5. Lovell's Testimony, April 10, 1863, ORA, VI, 565–66; Dabney, "The Butler Regime in Louisiana," 517–18.

6. General Orders No. 19, No. 20, May 3, 1862, ORA, VI, 720–721; "Reminiscent of War-Times," 183. See also A. Sellew Roberts, "The Federal Government and Confederate Cotton," *American Historical Review*, XXXII (1927), 264.

his own dividends, but the day had gone well and stirred his generosity.[7]

On May 4 Butler learned that a large shipment of provisions desig-nated for New Orleans had been detained at the mouth of the Red River. He issued passes for two steamers to go upstream, collect the supplies, and bring them back to the city, allowing six days for the voyage. Though the issuance of passes to bring in supplies was ab-solutely essential at this time, the practice rapidly expanded beyond the limits of pure necessity. In four weeks' time the price of a barrel of flour dropped from sixty to twenty-four dollars, but nineteen hundred families continued to be fed at public expense, and thousands more barely managed to subsist.[8]

Butler then discovered that "rebellious, lying, and desperate men" were ranging through the countryside encouraging planters to destroy their crops of sugar and cotton by telling them that the United States government was sending agents to confiscate them. The general reacted by circulating an order assuring all planters that if they shipped staples on authorized boats, they would be paid in specie and the provisions would be delivered "for the benefit of the poor of this city." For cotton and sugar sent to northern ports, he promised quick shipment and payment in cash.[9]

As supplies began to accumulate at the storehouses, Butler discov-ered that an element in the city was secretly siphoning off provisions as they came to the docks and transporting them to Lovell's encamp-ment at Camp Moore. He also became suspicious that some riverboat captains had been diverting goods to the Confederate army while operating under the protection of his permits. The general's nose for criminal activity had been sharpened through years of personal experi-ence, so on May 6 he established a military commission of five officers "for the trial of all high crimes and misdemeanors which . . . are pun-ishable with death or imprisonment for a long term of ten years."[10]

During the first two weeks of Butler's administration, even some of the most ardent secessionists admitted that the general's initial mea-

---

7. Parton, *General Butler*, 301, 303.

8. General Orders No. 20, May 4, 1862, *ORA*, VI, 721; Parton, *General Butler*, 304.

9. General Orders No. 22, May 4, 1862, *ORA*, VI, 722; New Orleans *Daily Picayune*, May 6, 1862.

10. General Orders No. 23, May 6, 1862, *ORA*, VI, 722; Parton, *General Butler*, 304.

sures had been marked by restraint. Economic conditions gradually improved, and the constant turmoil in the streets began to subside. On May 13 Lincoln raised the blockade and reopened the port of New Orleans to trade, effective the first day of June—a move certain to re-stimulate commerce. One of Butler's critics, Surgeon Charles S. Foltz of the USS *Hartford,* remained unimpressed. "General Butler's course is very pacific," he wrote, "a man of words, not deeds; a tricky politi-cian." When it came to "trickiness" in New Orleans, however, the general quickly became aware of his local competitors and his concilia-tory disposition began to change, not because of the rabble in the streets but because of the aristocracy, who had neither demonstrated the will to cooperate nor lifted a finger to help the poor. Butler loved a fight, and the ruling class of the Crescent City was about to awaken a slumbering lion.[11]

The general tried to insulate himself from the constant demands of the public but found it impossible. Somebody always wanted a pass to search for a missing slave, and to the applicant Butler would grant a one-minute audience and ask, "Have you lost your horse?"

"No, Sir."

"Have you lost your mule?"

"No, Sir."

"Well, Sir, if you had lost your horse or your mule, would you come and ask me to neglect my duty to the Government for the purpose of assisting you to catch them?"

"Of course not," the applicant replied sheepishly.

"Then why should you expect me to employ myself in hunting after any other article of your property?"

After fifteen seconds, most complainants departed by escort through the nearest exit to the street.[12]

During his first week in New Orleans, the general moved with his

---

11. Salmon P. Chase, *Diary and Correspondence of Salmon P. Chase in Annual Report of the American Historical Association for the Year 1902* (Washington, D.C., 1903), 297; Dabney, "The Butler Regime in Louisiana," 507; Rowland and Croxwell, eds., *Journal of Julia Le Grand,* 44; Foltz, *Surgeon of the Seas,* 237; New Orleans *Daily Picayune,* June 1, 1862.

12. Alfred F. Puffer, "Our General," *Atlantic Monthly,* XII (July, 1863), 114.

wife and her servants into a house owned by General David E. Twiggs, who had commanded the district before being relieved by General Lovell. Rising each morning at 6:00, he worked on his correspondence at the breakfast table and at 9:00 A.M. rode in a splendid carriage with a cavalry escort to his headquarters office at the customhouse. During the first hour or two he met with an array of military and civic officials on matters of sanitation, health, crime, labor, and public relief. By the time these meetings ended, a throng of callers lined the waiting room, many wanting passes to leave the city. To Captain Alfred F. Puffer, the aide in charge of issuing passes, Butler left instructions to flatly deny them. For Puffer, it was a thankless job. On several occasions he appealed to the general, declaring, "You must see some of these people. . . . If you would only hear their stories, you would give them passes." "That," Butler replied, "is precisely the reason why I want you to see them for me." [13]

An Englishman hauled unceremoniously before the general left an unflattering account, likening him to a "cunning trickster . . . a sort of compromise between the proud, semi-sanctified autocrat and the depraved sot. He had two eyes vastly different in expression. From one seemed to look out benignly [sic], and from the other, malignity." [14]

During the afternoon Butler scanned his correspondence, responding to some personally and leaving notations on those to be answered by his staff. Late in the day he visited the outposts on horseback, returning home for supper and another stack of letters and messages brought to the house by Puffer. At midnight the general went to bed. For more than seven months he seldom varied his daily regimen—working seven days a week. George S. Denison of the Treasury Department praised Butler's administrative output, writing Chase that the general "does more work than any other man in Louisiana. Every thought seems to be given to the interest of the Government, and his power[s] of endurance are remarkable. No other man could fill his place here. His popularity among Union men is great and increasing." The compli-

13. Nash, *Stormy Petrel*, 150–51; Puffer, "Our General," 108. Butler did issue passes; one in particular went by a messenger to Major General Pierre G. T. Beauregard to advise him of the serious illness of his wife.

14. Watson, *Life in the Confederate Army*, 410.

ment was easy to understand—it was the aristocracy of New Orleans who mainly challenged Butler's administration, not the city's poor or the handful of Unionists.[15]

Since his days at Waterville College, Butler had looked into the epidemiology of yellow fever, the tropical disease that had killed his father. Aware that the pestilence visited the city about once every three years, he knew it would be overdue during the summer of 1862. His men knew it too, and some became panic-stricken, constantly hounding him for permission to go home. The only known prevention was a rigid quarantine of incoming vessels. Butler researched the disease and became convinced that filth, more than anything else, had propagated the city's worst epidemics. On his trips about the town he located stinking ponds on which animal carcasses floated and ditches with foul, stagnant water that served the city as open sewers. Throughout the town huge piles of garbage lay rotting, and the general could not understand why the superintendent of streets did not find the enormous stink offensive. Hoping to stave off an attack of typhoid, typhus, and yellow fever, he ordered a quarantine station established at Plaquemine Bend, the town's garbage removed, and the sewage ditches flushed daily. These measures helped, but as the heat and humidity of summer intensified, soldiers, "especially the fleshy ones," developed prickly heat and boils, and it gave them a scare.[16]

After a week of progress, relations with city hall began to deteriorate and on May 9 Butler reminded the mayor that the streets were still filthy. Since the work was clearly a function of city government, Butler demanded that it be done promptly with "active, energetic measures" and without "resolutions and inaction." As the summer progressed, concerns for the public health increased daily. Thousands remained unemployed, and Butler admonished Monroe to put them to work with shovels and brooms. "It will not do to shift your responsibility from yourselves to the street commissioners," Butler warned. "Three days since I called the attention of Mr. Mayor to this subject, and nothing has been done."[17]

15. Chase, *Diary and Correspondence*, 316; Nash, *Stormy Petrel*, 151.

16. *Butler's Book*, 395–404; *Butler Correspondence*, II, 271–72.

17. *Butler Correspondence*, I, 456–57; Butler to Mayor *et al.*, May 9, 1862, ORA, VI, 723–24.

The messenger who carried the letter to city hall returned with a curt reply from Monroe, stating that on May 7 an additional three hundred workmen had been added as street cleaners. Butler dispatched members of his staff to verify the mayor's statement, but not a worker could be found.[18]

On May 9, rather than call the mayor a liar, the general issued an edict—General Orders No. 25—one certain to infuriate the council and strain the frail working relationship he had established with the aristocracy. He derided the city government for failing to provide relief for the poor and openly chastised the "wealthy and influential, the leaders of the rebellion, who have gotten up this war, and are now endeavoring to prosecute it without regard to the starving poor, the workingman, his wife and child." He blamed them for destroying the sugar and cotton that could have been used to purchase supplies for the poor, and accused them of trucking off what food they did not need for their own consumption and giving it to Lovell.

Butler's earlier proclamation had annoyed the elite, but this order made them livid. He enjoyed bearing down on the ruling class, who, he declared, "have betrayed their country, they have been false to every trust, they have shown themselves incapable of defending the State . . . although they have forced every poor man's child into their service as soldiers for that purpose, while they made their sons and nephews officers . . . they have plundered, stolen, and destroyed the means of those who had property, leaving children penniless and old age hopeless." For the poor, Butler had good news. His outposts had captured supplies on the way to the Confederate army, and he promised to distribute a quantity of beef and a thousand barrels of provisions to the "deserving poor of this city," even though "some of the food will go to supply the craving wants of the wives and children of those" now bearing arms against the United States.

Butler reminded the public that his men had come to New Orleans "ready only for war, we had not prepared ourselves to feed the hungry and relieve the distressed with provisions. But to the extent possible, within the power of the commanding general, it shall be done." And when a shipment of stores arrived from New York and delivered the

18. *Butler Correspondence,* I, 457.

army from its self-imposed scarcity, Butler authorized Captain John Clark, acting commissary, to "sell to families for consumption, in small quantities, until further orders, flour and salt meats . . . at seven and a half cents per pound for flour and ten cents for meats," accepting banknotes, specie, or treasury notes in payment. Butler made no mention of who would keep track of the money, and as during his days at Fort Monroe, kickbacks flowed through the quartermaster.[19]

On May 10 Butler followed up his orders by appointing Colonel George F. Shepley of the 12th Maine military commandant of New Orleans. Butler could no longer run the district alone, and his choice had little to do with the new commandant's military aptitude. The colonel was not known for his intellect, though he had been educated at Harvard and Dartmouth. As a prominent lawyer he had worked with Butler in politics. Besides being roughly the same age—Butler was forty-one, Shepley forty-two—the general and the colonel were alike in their motivations, as both were shrewd businessmen who had accumulated wealth by capitalizing on opportunities. The May 9 edict, followed by Shepley's advancement, marked a turning point in Butler's administration, and through the latter's efforts, Shepley, on July 18, 1862, became a brigadier general.[20]

No policy existed to define Shepley's administrative duties aside from what Butler told him to do. Washington viewed New Orleans as a military objective, and months passed before Lincoln gave much thought to its future status. With no instructions from the White House, and often no answers to important questions, administrative decisions—good and bad—remained mainly in the hands of Butler.[21]

One of Shepley's first acts as military commandant involved the bakeries, where owners had been gouging the public. Shepley set the prices: five cents for a seven-ounce loaf of bread; seven and a half

19. General Orders No. 25, May 9, 1862, ORA, VI, 724–25; *Butler Correspondence,* I, 457–59; Parton, *General Butler,* 306.

20. General Orders No. 24, May 10, 1862, ORA, VI, 724; Mark M. Boatner, *The Civil War Dictionary* (New York, 1959), 746; *Dictionary of American Biography,* IX, 78–79.

21. Thomas W. Helis, "Of General and Jurists: The Judicial System of New Orleans Under Union Occupation, May 1862–April 1865," *Journal of Louisiana History,* XXIX (Spring, 1988), 145.

cents for a pound of flour; eight cents for a pound of rice; ten cents a pound for beef, pork, and ham—and to make all food affordable, the Union commissary offered to sell provisions in small quantities at half the former prices.[22]

James Parton, Butler's first biographer and biggest fan, admitted that the general's "attitude toward the ruling class was warlike, and he strove in all ways to isolate that class, and bring the majority of the people to see who it was that had brought all this needless ruin upon their state." Parton's analysis, although correct as it related to Butler's war on the aristocracy, was an oversimplification of the general's motives. Accustomed as he was to stumping for votes, Butler did want approval for his actions from the lower classes, which represented up to 90 percent of the population. The aristocracy, however, held about the same percentage of the wealth and all of the influence. For Butler to have his way, the power of the elite had to be neutralized, and for the general this became both a personal challenge and a public necessity.[23]

On the heels of Butler's general orders, Governor Moore, who remained far enough away to not worry about repercussions from what he said, responded with heated denunciations. In an address "To the Loyal People and True of the City of New Orleans," Moore, seemingly content to see his people starve, forbade the interchange of goods, writing:

> General Butler's attempt to excite the poor against the more wealthy is characteristic of the man, and is as mean as it is contemptible. He springs from a race that has ever been purse-proud when fortune favored them, and idolatrous worshippers of the almighty dollar. He comes from a section of the country that has done more than any other to degrade and cheapen labor and reduce the laboring man to the condition of the slave. . . . Professions of regard for the people come with a bad grace from such a source.
>
> He appeals to your selfishness, and attempts to arouse the baser passions of your nature as though he was addressing Yankees, whose sole aspirations are the acquisition of money and the triumph of fanati-

22. Parton, *General Butler*, 306; New Orleans *Daily Picayune*, May 28, June 12, 1862.

23. Parton, *General Butler*, 323.

cism. . . . He seems wholly to forget that Southerners are a high-toned, chivalrous people, who entertain a holy abhorrence and hatred for traitors, cowards and petty tyrants. . . . He wishes to prejudice you against those in authority by falsehood and slanderous misrepresentations, as though you lacked the intelligence to think and act for yourselves.[24]

Because leaflets of Moore's address circulated liberally through the streets of the city, Butler blamed the press and clamped down on four of the town's newspapers. He closed *Le Propagateur Catholique* because of its secessionistic agitation and placed Father Napoleon Joseph Perché under house arrest. On May 13 he suppressed the *Bee* for printing an article endorsing the burning of cotton but allowed it to resume publication seventeen days later. He also closed the *Crescent,* and because the owner, J. O. Nixon, "was a rebel now in arms against the Government of the United States," he ordered the paper sold. He then took possession of the New Orleans *Daily Delta* and turned the press over to his own army printers. He permitted the *True Delta* and *Picayune* to operate with a minimum of censorship after the proprietors took the oath of allegiance. Later, he suspended publication of the *Estafette du Sud* for violating the terms of the proclamation and the *Daily Advocate* for speculating on the prospects of peace if Democrats gained in the fall elections, but he allowed both presses to reopen a few days later. Considering the outspoken nature of most editors, Butler practiced surprisingly lenient censorship.[25]

Butler later learned that a day of humiliation, fasting, and prayer had been scheduled for Friday, May 16, "in obedience to some supposed proclamation of one Jefferson Davis, in the several churches of this city." He canceled it, referring to his proclamation allowing churches to be kept open "as in time of profound peace," but not "upon the supposed authority" of Jeff Davis.[26]

Businessmen conscious of the importance of keeping their doors open to the public straddled Butler's edicts as best they could, but the

24. *Butler Correspondence,* I, 459–61.
25. *Ibid.,* I, 465, 476–77, II, 130, 475–76, 480; Special Orders Nos. 37 and 39, May 13, No. 42, May 24, and No. 513, November 14, 1862, *ORA,* XV, 421–22, 439, 595–96; Roger Baudier, *The Catholic Church in Louisiana* (New Orleans, 1939), 426.
26. General Orders No. 27, May 13, 1862, *ORA,* XV, 426.

same restraints were not observed by their wives and children. Dignified ladies strolled the streets ostentatiously, and if they crossed paths with a Union officer or soldier, they would contemptuously gather up their skirts, glare at the invader, and skitter away lest they be contaminated. If a soldier stepped onto a streetcar, all the fashionable women would get off, making as surly a scene as the limits of good manners allowed. Some ignored propriety and spat on the hated invaders. One woman made her point the hard way. When two officers approached, she flung herself off the sidewalk "so impetuously that she [landed] in the gutter." The officers rushed to her aid, but she growled that "she would rather lie there in the gutter than be helped up by a Yankee." General Williams, a frequent target himself, lamented, "Such venom one must see to believe. . . . I look at them and think of fallen angels."[27]

At least one officer deserved the scorn of the ladies. An intoxicated lieutenant of the 12th Connecticut boarded a streetcar, and immediately one of the ladies grimaced, gathered up her skirts, and shuffled toward the door. "Sit still, old girl," the lieutenant bellowed. "You needn't rise on my account." Incidents such as this worked against efforts of amelioration.[28]

Butler tolerated the insults for about two weeks, having on several occasions been the recipient of unladylike scorn. He found wealthy women especially annoying. They had become galvanizing influences, using the inviolability of their gender to agitate resistance. Riding on May 10 with an aide, Butler passed under a balcony where five or six women hovered above who, "with something between a shriek and a sneer," attracted the general's attention. Butler looked up just as the ladies whirled, throwing out their skirts and revealing their bottoms. Turning to his aide, he said loudly, "Those women evidently know which end of them looks the best." The demonstrators rushed inside, and Butler, having said his piece, enjoyed a good laugh.[29]

Balconies became lookout posts for mischievous ladies. One evening

27. *Butler's Book*, 415; George N. Carpenter, *History of the Eighth Regiment, Vermont Volunteers, 1861–1865* (Boston, 1886), 38; T. Williams, "Letters," 310–14.

28. De Forest, *A Volunteer's Adventures*, 45.

29. *Butler's Book*, 416.

Farragut was strolling through town with Colonel Henry Deming when a sudden shower of "not very clean water," originating from a chamber pot, descended and soaked them both. The tinkle-tosser claimed the act had been an accident, but the trajectory of the contents suggested otherwise. Dumping slops from upper windows on passers below had been an old city custom, but when Butler heard what had happened to Farragut, he did not find it amusing. To a friend in Boston he wrote dolefully, "Every opprobrious epithet, every insulting question was made by these bejeweled, becrinolined, and laced creatures calling themselves ladies, toward my officers and soldiers, from the windows of houses and in the street. . . . I had arrested the men who hurrahed for Beauregard,—could I arrest the women?" Butler did not know and asked himself—"What was to be done?"[30]

Support came from an unexpected source. The New Orleans *Picayune* expressed shock at the behavior of certain women and demanded their arrest "whether arrayed in fine clothes or in rags." Afterwards, no mention was made of whether the paper lost subscribers, but the editorial freshened the general's thoughts on searching for a solution. Mindful of a city ordinance prescribing a night in jail and a five-dollar fine for misdemeanors, Butler hoped the ladies of the city would take notice and improve their behavior.[31]

The practice, however, did not stop. The following day one of Butler's colonels dressed in his finest uniform to attend church. On the way he encountered two respectable-looking women approaching on the sidewalk, and as a gentleman should, he stepped to the outside to let them pass. As he did, one of the ladies stepped in front of the other and spit in his face. Butler learned of the incident the following day when he overheard the splattered colonel discussing it with Captain R. S. Davis.

"Why didn't you do something?" Davis asked.

"What could I do . . . to two women?" the colonel asked.

"Well," Davis replied, "you ought to have taken your revolver and shot the first *he* rebel you met."[32]

30. *Ibid.*, 417; *Butler Correspondence*, II, 35; New Orleans *Daily Picayune*, August 24, 1855.

31. New Orleans *Daily Picayune*, May 9, 1862; Dabney, "The Butler Regime in Louisiana," 503.

32. *Butler's Book*, 417–18.

For more than a week spitting became the preferred method of annoying the invaders, and Butler could not allow it to continue. He expected a measure of resistance from people who had poured so much blood and treasure into a government that had abandoned them, but the constant insults from the fairer sex demanded drastic steps. Arresting the assailants would only fill the jails with women and create martyrs, so he searched to find another way. He wanted to adopt an order that "would execute itself," something that would not "stir up more strife in its execution by the police than it would quell." Thinking he had found a solution, he drafted General Orders No. 28—the infamous Woman Order. The edict was a little out of character for Butler, whose reverence for women was well established and untarnished by any hint of personal scandal. The general, however, had a short temper, and this trait, combined with his penchant for stimulating controversy, often dominated his actions.[33]

A leading staff member read the draft, cautioning the general that "the troops may misunderstand the order." Worried that some of the ladies might be molested, he added, "It would be a great scandal if only *one* man should act upon it in the wrong way."

"Let us, then, have one case of aggression on our side," Butler replied. "I shall know how to deal with that case so that it will never be repeated."[34] So without changing a word, Butler issued the order on May 15:

> As the officers and soldiers of the United States have been subject to repeated insults from the women (calling themselves ladies) of New Orleans, in return for the most scrupulous non-interference and courtesy on our part, it is ordered that hereafter when any female shall, by word, gesture, or movement, insult or show contempt for any officer or soldier of the United States, she shall be regarded and held liable to be treated as a woman of the town plying her avocation.[35]

Word of the order hit the streets of New Orleans like a giant keg of gunpowder. The explosion thundered across the South, where noth-

33. *Butler Correspondence*, II, 35; *Butler's Book*, 418; Puffer, "Our General," 105–106.

34. Parton, *General Butler*, 327.

35. General Orders No. 28, May 15, 1862, ORA, XV, 426. See also *Butler Correspondence*, I, 490.

ing was more sacred than the honor of a woman. Then it resonated into the North and skimmed across the waves of the ocean to Great Britain, where the king's subjects interpreted the order as an invitation for soldiers in the army to engage in rape, a common practice among some dueling nations. Sixteen-year-old Clara Solomon, who referred to Butler as simply "the Wretch," asked a question of her diary, "Can a woman, a Southern woman, come in contact with one of them and allow her countenance to retain its wanted composure? Will not the scornful feelings in our hearts there find utterance?"[36]

The edict was as astounding as it was effective, and the anger it stimulated in the South elevated Butler's image to new levels of hatred. From Corinth, Mississippi, General Beauregard wrote: "MEN OF THE SOUTH: Shall our mothers, our wives, our daughters, and our sisters be thus outraged by the ruffianly soldiers of the North, to whom is given the right to treat at their pleasure the ladies of the South as common harlots? Arouse, friends, and drive back from our soil those infamous invaders of our homes and disturbers of our family ties." Beauregard's sister did not agree with his antipathy, remarking calmly that she had "no interest in or objection to" the Woman Order because "it does not apply to me."[37]

Governor Moore, operating from the new seat of state government at Opelousas, condemned the order, and like Beauregard, he encouraged New Orleanians to rise against such tyranny and hurl the invaders out of the South. The appeal was more patriotic than practical. If the forces of the Confederacy could not save the city, how could a disarmed populace accomplish it? Nobody had been more forcible than Governor Moore in orchestrating Louisiana's secession, but he never accepted any responsibility for the misfortunes of its people. Instead, he kept up the fight from a safe distance, encouraged guerrilla warfare within the city, and on May 24 issued a proclamation:

36. Kendall, *History of New Orleans*, I, 278; Clara E. Solomon Diary, May 17, 1862, in Louisiana and Lower Mississippi Valley Collections, Louisiana State University Libraries, Louisiana State University, Baton Rouge; Ashkenazi, ed., *Diary of Clara Solomon*, 367, 370.

37. General Orders No. 44, May 19, 1862, *ORA*, Vol. X, Pt. 2, p. 531; Puffer, "Our General," 106.

The annals of warfare between civilized nations afford no similar instance of infamy than this order. It is thus proclaimed to the world that the exhibition of any disgust or repulsiveness by the women of New Orleans to the hated invaders of their home and the slayers of their fathers, brothers, and husbands shall constitute a justification to a brutal soldiery for the indulgence of their lust.

Louisianians! will you suffer such foul conduct of your oppressors to pass unpunished? Will you permit such indignities to remain un-avenged? A mind so debased as to be capable of conceiving the alterna-tive presented in this [Woman Order] must be fruitful of inventions wherewith to pollute humanity. . . . Strike home to the heart of your foe the blow that rids your country of his presence. If need be let his blood moisten your own grave. It will rise up before your children as a perpetual memento of a race whom it will teach to hate now and evermore.[38]

The New York *Tribune* reported that on the heels of the Woman Order, the Jackson *Mississippian* had offered ten thousand dollars for the head of Ben Butler. "A gentle, soft-hearted little Southern lady," wrote the general, "published that she wanted to subscribe her mite to make the reward sixty thousand dollars, so that my head would be sure to be taken." In Baton Rouge young Sarah Morgan tried to understand the order and decided that the ladies of New Orleans turned up their noses and gathered up their skirts "owing to the odor" of the Union soldiers, "which is said to be unbearable even at this early season of the year."[39]

In the British House of Commons, Lord Palmerston, convinced that the South was about to win the war, received cheers when he declared that "no man could have read the proclamation . . . without a feeling of the deepest indignation. . . . An Englishman must blush to think that such an act has been committed by one belonging to the Anglo-Saxon race . . . [and] by one who had raised himself to the rank of general, is a subject undoubtedly of not less astonishment than pain." After venting his vituperatives on the House of Commons, Palmerston chided Charles Francis Adams, American minister to Great Britain: "I

38. Moore's Proclamation, May 24, 1862, ORA, XV, 743–44.
39. New York *Tribune*, June 4, 1862; *Butler's Book*, 421; Charles East, ed., *Sarah Morgan: The Civil War Diary of a Southern Woman* (Athens, Ga., 1991), 76, 151.

will venture to say that no example can be found in the history of civilized nations, till the publication of this order, of a general guilty in cold blood of so infamous an act as deliberately to hand over the female inhabitants of a conquered city to the unbridled license of an unrestrained soldiery." The Briton's outburst amused Adams, who noted laconically, "Palmerston wants a quarrel!" Butler could see no difference between his Woman Order and the king's recently established "Order of the Garter"—given as an emblem of good conduct.[40]

For several weeks the diplomatic kettle boiled hot between Palmerston and Adams, the former suggesting that Lincoln remove Butler and the latter referring the matter to Seward, warning of the London *Times*'s demand that Great Britain intervene on the side of the Confederacy. "General Butler," Adams cautioned, "is furnishing [the British with] a good deal of material." Seward apologized, calling the British uproar a misunderstanding of "phraseology which could be mistaken or perverted." Butler, however, remained defiant and neither Seward nor Lincoln showed any inclination to revoke the order.[41]

When France announced its loathing of the order, Charles Sumner mirthfully wrote Butler from the Senate chamber: "I understand that the French government has forbidden the papers to mention your name. The name of Marlboro was once used in France to frighten children,—more than a century ago. You have taken his place."[42]

Neither echoes from abroad, proclamations from the governor, nor rewards for the general's head acquired the same longevity as the locally adopted sobriquet "Beast" Butler. Marion Southwood praised it as perfect, and on May 21 diarist Mary Boykin Chesnut, learning of the Woman Order, wrote, "There is said to be an order from Butler, turning over the women of New Orleans to his soldiers. Then is the measure of his iniquities filled. We thought the generals always

---

40. *Butler's Book*, 420; Charles Francis Adams, Jr., *Charles Francis Adams* (Boston, 1900), 248–49; Henry Adams, *The Education of Henry Adams* (Boston, 1918), 136; Parton, *General Butler*, 341; Coulter, *Confederate States of America*, 189.

41. Holzman, *Stormy Ben Butler*, 87–88; Herbert Asbury, *The French Quarter: An Informal History of the New Orleans Underworld* (New York, 1989), 227; Clifford Dowdey, *Experiment in Rebellion* (Garden City, N.Y., 1946), 170.

42. *Butler Correspondence*, II, 520.

restrained by shot or sword, if need be, the brutal soldiery. This hideous cross-eyed beast orders his men to treat ladies of New Orleans as women of the town. To punish them, he says, for their insolence."[43]

President Davis commented dourly that northerners were "the only people on earth who do not blush to think [Butler] wears the human form," and New Orleanians could not refrain from muttering "Beast" on every occasion calling for invectives. One poet sprinkled southern papers with a popular acrostic:

> Brutal and vulgar, a coward and Knave;
> Famed for no action, noble or brave;
> Beastly by instinct, a drunkard and sot;
> Ugly and venomous, on mankind a blot;
> Thief, liar, and scoundrel in highest degree;
> Let Yankeedom boast of such hero[e]s as thee;
> Every woman and child shall ages to come,
> Remember thee, monster, thou vilest of scum.[44]

The Confederacy now had a scapegoat, "Beast" Butler, the meanest and vilest Yankee in the South, and no newspaper operating in Dixie would permit readers to forget their hatred of the general. The Woman Order, however, produced results in New Orleans. "A marked change has been the result," a naval officer noted. Insults to Union soldiers stopped, life on the streets reverted to a modicum of its former civility, and the only disorderly ladies who got themselves into trouble with the law spent a night in the local jail—wards of the local police and not as victims carried away to sate some soldier's sexual appetite. Although the South continued to condemn the order as long as anybody would listen, Butler never regretted it. The North supported it as the best way to subdue unrepentant Rebels, and Captain De Forest reported that "the citizens have dropped their surly air, and show a willingness to talk civilly if not cordially." The captain may have been

43. Southwood, *"Beauty and Booty,"* 109; C. Vann Woodward, ed., *Mary Chesnut's Civil War* (New Haven, 1981), 343.

44. James D. Richardson, *A Compilation of the Messages and Papers of the Confederacy, Including the Diplomatic Correspondence, 1861–1865* (2 vols.; Nashville, 1906), I, 269–74; Coulter, *Confederate States of America,* 370.

too generous when he added, "For the present General Butler is rather popular with them than otherwise."[45]

To a friend in Boston, Butler defended the Woman Order, writing grimly: "We were two thousand five hundred men in a city seven miles long by two to four wide, of a hundred and fifty thousand inhabitants, all hostile, bitter, defiant, explosive, standing literally on a magazine, a spark only needed for destruction. The devil had entered into the hearts of the women of this town to stir up strife in every way possible. . . . How long do you suppose our flesh and blood could have stood this?"[46]

Many women still demonstrated "the ingenuity of the sex" by averting their eyes and holding their skirts aside when an officer approached, and those with pianos made an extra effort to play only Rebel tunes when bluecoats passed below their balconies. If an officer entered a streetcar, female occupants would spread out, leaving no room for a man to sit down. Another trick was to feign nausea if offered a hand, which led the *Daily Delta* to remark "that the ladies should remember that but for the presence of Union forces *some* of the squeamish stomachs would have nothing in them." If prizes had been awarded for originality, however, the prostitutes of the French Quarter would have taken the honors. When General Butler's portraits first appeared on the street, the ladies of the bordellos took them to their rooms and pasted them to the bottom of their tinkle-pots. A detachment of soldiers raided the red-light district, confiscated all the potties, and destroyed them. Some said the general wielded a hammer and smashed a few himself.[47]

Butler cared little about what his enemies said beyond the borders of the lower Mississippi, asserting he could not "carry on war with rose-water." If the British did not like his methods, so much the better, for Europeans were distinctly friendly to the South. Secretary of State Seward agreed with the general, accusing the British of overlooking their own double standards, reminding them that their national arms

---

45. Roe's Diary, ORN, XVIII, 773; *Butler's Book*, 419; De Forest, *A Volunteer's Adventures*, 22; Carpenter, *History of the Eighth Vermont*, 39.

46. *Butler Correspondence*, II, 35.

47. Parton, *General Butler*, 328; Asbury, *The French Quarter*, 227–28.

displayed the motto "Evil to him who evil thinks." Assistant Secretary of the Navy Fox applauded Butler, writing, "The most delicate, but the most important duty is entrusted to your hands viz: drawing back into the ark the wanderers and the deluded. This requires more brains than it does fight." Lincoln, who received both diplomatic and internal pressure to repudiate the order, never did.[48]

During the early days of the occupation, Sarah Butler confided to her sister: "I think Mr. Butler would rejoice at some demonstration from a mob that he might sweep the streets, and make these people feel that there is a power here to sustain or crush them according as they merit protection from the government or deserve punishment for their traitorous deeds. . . . He fears them not." She added, "This *city will be governed*, and made to wear the *outward* forms of *decency*, however much they struggle against it."[49]

The general did not "sweep the streets," but within the borders of the Department of the Gulf, and especially in New Orleans, he did much as he pleased. For those who questioned his authority, the general acted swiftly and decisively. Mayor Monroe and the city council would have to learn the hard way.

Sixteen-year-old Clara Solomon expressed it differently. "A gloom has settled o'er my spirit," she wrote, "a gloom envelopes our dearly beloved city." A schoolgirl, not the mayor, found the words to articulate the feelings of the city.[50]

---

48. *Butler's Book*, 420–21; New York *Tribune*, June 19, 1862; *Fox Correspondence*, II, 301; John G. Nicolay and John Hay, *Abraham Lincoln: A History* (10 vols.; New York, 1914), V, 284. The British motto is written in French—"Honi soit qui mal y pense."

49. *Butler Correspondence*, I, 487.

50. Clara Solomon Diary, May 4, 1862, quoted in Lang, "Gloom Envelops New Orleans," 281.

Sarah Butler, the general's wife and companion. From *Autobiography and Personal Reminiscences of Major General Benjamin F. Butler.*

Abraham Lincoln, who placated Butler because he needed the general's political support. Courtesy U.S. Army Military History Institute.

Secretary of War Simon Cameron, who championed Butler's desire for a large
command. From *Battles and Leaders of the Civil War*.

Major General George B. McClellan, who supported the idea of burying Butler in the Gulf. Courtesy U.S. Army Military History Institute.

Admiral David Glasgow Farragut, one of the few naval officers who was able
to get along with Butler. Courtesy Naval Imaging Center.

Major General Benjamin F. Butler waiting on Ship Island for Farragut to get his warships into the river. From *Battles and Leaders of the Civil War.*

Commander David Dixon Porter, who developed a deep distrust of General Butler. Courtesy Naval Imaging Center.

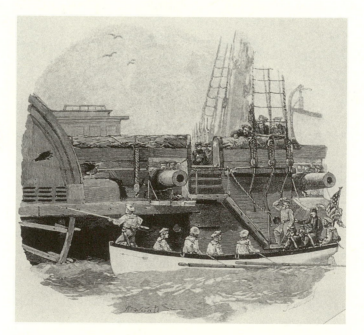

Commander Porter receiving the surrender of Forts Jackson and St. Philip—Butler's missed opportunity. From *Battles and Leaders of the Civil War*.

The Union fleet arriving off New Orleans. From *Battles and Leaders of the Civil War.*

Captain Bailey and Lieutenant Perkins on their way to city hall to demand the surrender of New Orleans. From *Battles and Leaders of the Civil War*.

Major General Mansfield Lovell, who turned the city over to the mayor and departed with his troops. From *Battles and Leaders of the Civil War*.

Federal officer lowering the state flag at city hall. From *Battles and Leaders of the Civil War*.

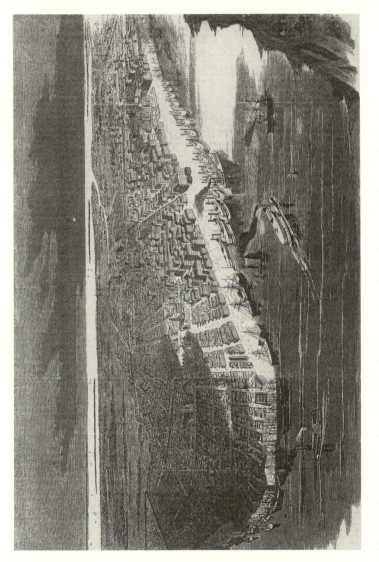

New Orleans' waterfront before the war. From *Harper's Pictorial History of the Great Rebellion*.

The U.S. customhouse, headquarters of the Union occupation force. From *Autobiography and Personal Reminiscences of Major General Benjamin F. Butler*.

The St. Charles Hotel, Butler's first headquarters. From *Autobiography and Personal Reminiscences of Major General Benjamin F. Butler*.

Ben Butler and his New Orleans staff. Engraved from a photograph. From *Autobiography and Personal Reminiscences of Major General Benjamin F. Butler.*

The U.S. mint at New Orleans, where William Mumford was executed. From *Autobiography and Personal Reminiscences of Major General Benjamin F. Butler.*

Women of New Orleans insulting Federal officers. From *Autobiography and Personal Reminiscences of Major General Benjamin F. Butler.*

Governor Thomas O. Moore. Had New Orleanians adhered to his numerous proclamations, most of the populace would have starved. Courtesy Walter L. Fleming Collection, Louisiana and Lower Mississippi Valley Collections, LSU Libraries, Louisiana State University.

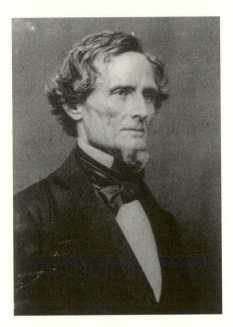

Confederate president Jefferson Davis, who ordered Butler captured and executed. Courtesy U.S. Army Military History Institute.

Pierre Soulé, whose differences with Butler led to his arrest. From *Battles and Leaders of the Civil War*.

Brigadier General George F. Shepley, whom Butler elevated to military commandant of New Orleans. Courtesy U.S. Army Military History Institute.

Colonel Joseph H. French, Butler's provost marshal. Courtesy U.S. Army Military History Institute.

Secretary of War Edwin M. Stanton, who supported Butler against detractors in Lincoln's cabinet. Courtesy U.S. Army Military History Institute.

Secretary of State William H. Seward, who lobbied with Lincoln for Butler's recall. Courtesy U.S. Army Military History Institute.

Arrest of Anne Larue for misbehavior in the streets. From *Autobiography and Personal Reminiscences of Major General Benjamin F. Butler.*

Feeding the poor of New Orleans. From *Harper's Pictorial History of the Great Rebellion.*

"Colonel" Andrew Jackson Butler, the general's troublesome brother. From *Autobiography and Personal Reminiscences of Major General Benjamin F. Butler.*

Secretary of the Treasury Salmon P. Chase, who trusted Butler despite rumors of corruption. Courtesy U.S. Army Military History Institute.

Brigadier General John W. Phelps, the abolitionist who initiated the practice of recruiting fugitive slaves. Courtesy U.S. Army Military History Institute.

Major General Godfrey Weitzel, whom Butler promoted from lieutenant to brigadier general. Courtesy U.S. Army Military History Institute.

7

A Bad Day at City Hall

MAYOR MONROE PROBABLY THOUGHT he was taking the proper action when he challenged Butler's Woman Order, but it only stirred up the general. If Butler wanted to abolish city hall, he had the authority to do it, and since he had elevated Colonel Shepley to the post of military commandant, the publicly elected officials were rapidly becoming obsolete. He continued to tolerate them despite a constant undercurrent of opposition. They had agreed to remove the filth from the streets but did not. They hired three hundred "hangers-on of City Hall" as street cleaners who would not lift a shovel. When Butler decided to reinstate the city's European Brigade, Monroe disbanded it. Confederate bank notes, which had fallen in value to thirty cents, were redeemed by the city government at par, thereby taxing the city one hundred cents to "give thirty to the favorites of the mayor and his council"—at least it appeared that way to the general.[1]

On May 16, one day after Butler issued the Woman Order, he received a stinging protest from Monroe that contained all the rhetoric of a challenge:

> I cannot, holding the office of chief magistrate of this City, chargeable with its peace and dignity, suffer it [Woman Order] to be promulgated in our presence without protesting against the threat it contains, which has already aroused the passions of our people and must exasperate them to a degree beyond control. . . . I did not, however, anticipate a war upon women and children, who . . . have only manifested their displeasure at the occupation of their City by those whom they believe to be their enemies, and will never undertake to be responsible for the

1. General Orders No. 24, May 10, 1862, ORA, VI, 724; Parton, *General Butler*, 329.

peace of New Orleans while such an edict, which infuriates our citizens, remains in force.

Butler told the mayor that if he could not control the populace he would be forced to lock him in jail for his own protection. The general explained that he considered the order essential because it enabled the female element to classify themselves as ladies or common women.[2]

The general expected Monroe's reaction to the Woman Order, but he was surprised to read in the New Orleans *Bee* that on May 10 the mayor had invited the heavily armed French fleet to visit New Orleans. As a preamble to the resolution inviting the French to New Orleans, Monroe had written: "This council, bearing in grateful remembrance the many ties of amity and good feeling which unite the people of this City with France, to whose paternal protection New Orleans owes its foundation and early propriety, and to whom it is especially grateful for the jealousy with which they guard all rights of property, personal and religious freedom of its citizens, *Be it resolved*."

Butler grasped the situation quickly. Monroe's letter to the French read like an invitation to come and recapture the city. Farragut had taken his squadron upriver, and with the exception of Porter's small flotilla—which the French fleet could walk right over—there was little in the Gulf but sailing vessels to stop an attack. Louis Napoleon III had imperialistic designs on Mexico, and his only hesitation in declaring war on the United States was wanting Great Britain to do it first. If Napoleon decided to go it alone, where better to start than with a surprise attack on Butler's weak force? With the French navy in the river, Farragut could not obtain supplies unless he made a juncture with Flag Officer Charles H. Davis' Mississippi flotilla above Memphis. Whether his vessels could get that far up the well-defended falling river was questionable, and if he did so, the heavy sloops of war could become stranded and the entire Gulf left in possession of the enemy. Butler notified the mayor that meddling in foreign affairs "is simply an invitation to the Calaboose or the Hospital," and "The action of the City Council . . . must be reversed."[3]

With two problems, both authored by the city fathers, Butler dis-

2. *Butler Correspondence*, I, 490, 497–98, 500–501.
3. *Ibid.*, I, 496–97; New Orleans *Bee*, May 10, 1862.

patched Provost Marshal French to bring the mayor to headquarters. Monroe must have realized that he had finally stretched the limits of the general's patience. In crisp terms, Butler told him that the language of his letter "would not be tolerated," and if he could no longer control the "aroused" passions of the public, he would be relieved of all responsibility and sent to Fort Jackson—Butler's prison on the river. After a "paroxysm of anger," Monroe declared that he only wanted "to vindicate the honor of the virtuous women of the City." Butler replied that vindication was not necessary because the order "did not contemplate any virtuous women." He believed that virtuous women would not insult "by word, gesture, or movement" any soldier. Boxed in by Butler's logic and conscious of the consequences, Monroe agreed to repudiate his letter, calling it a "mistake of fact, and being improper in language." Butler accepted the apology, and the mayor returned to city hall with his nerves shattered.[4]

When Monroe informed the council of his meeting with the general, they unanimously objected to the withdrawal of the city's letter. On May 17 the mayor, now bending to a force composed of his associates, sent a note to Butler rescinding his apology and demanding that the general place a notice in the newspapers assuring all decent ladies that the Woman Order did not apply to them. Monroe, counting upon universal sentiment to condemn the edict as "inhuman," told Butler that he would be at his office prepared to suffer arrest.

Butler waited two days before taking action, as six men on parole had been arrested and were being interrogated. On May 19 he once again sent Captain French to city hall, and the provost guard herded the mayor and his council over to headquarters. Butler remarked that he was tired of being played with like a "weathercock" and opened the meeting by advising the city fathers that six parolees, calling themselves the "Monroe Guard," had just confessed their plans to attack and overpower Union pickets and escape to the Confederate army. After implicating Monroe and some prominent citizens for supplying the men with money and weapons, the sextet had been sentenced to death. Butler, thinking this news might startle the mayor, then asked why he wished to withdraw his apology. Monroe refused to speak for himself and deferred the question to his attorney, Judge Kennedy.

4. *Butler Correspondence*, I, 498–95; Puffer, "Our General," 105–106.

After a brief interview with the judge, the chief of police, and D. G. Duncan, the mayor's secretary who helped write the letter, Butler looked squarely at Monroe and said, "Mr. Mayor, you have played with me long enough. The boat leaves for Fort Jackson this afternoon, and you must be ready to take passage on her at four o'clock." Monroe wanted to know if his apology would be withdrawn, and the general assured him it would.[5]

Butler no longer needed the mayor to run city hall. With General Shepley functioning as military commandant and French as provost marshal, he added Major Joseph M. Bell as provost judge, mainly because all the local judges had quit. The major had been law partner and son-in-law to the great Rufus Choate, who had befriended Butler at a time when the general was a struggling young lawyer. Bell, another of Butler's Massachusetts chums, had served for several months without pay as the general's volunteer aide and military secretary. As provost judge, his role was twofold: to court-martial enlisted personnel for breaches of military discipline, and to try civilians for petty violations of martial law. For the next four months Union army officers became the sole source of justice in the city, and Bell's workload soon grew to a hundred cases a day. On occasion Butler acted as criminal judge, especially if the case involved a defendant he particularly disliked. Shepley took quick steps to reorganize city government. French became the city's military mayor, Bell made a few judicial appointments, and within a few days the municipal revolution was accomplished with little disturbance—at least insofar as Butler was concerned.[6]

When all but eleven of the existing police force refused to take the oath of allegiance, French reorganized the department and advertised for five hundred replacements. By June 1 the department was functioning around the clock and maintaining civil order. As an extra precaution, French issued an order forbidding the assembly of more than three persons on the streets or in the public squares.[7]

5. *Butler Correspondence*, I, 499–501; Record of the Military Commission, May 15, Monroe to Butler, May 16, 17, 1862, in Butler Papers, LC; General Orders No. 36, May 31, 1862, ORA, XV, 467; Puffer, "Our General," 106.

6. Butler to Stanton, August 16, 1862, ORA, XV, 552; Parton, *General Butler*, 336–37; *Butler's Book*, 521; Helis, "Of Generals and Jurists," 147–49, 151. Butler gradually began to restore civil courts in the fall of 1862, *ibid.*, 151–52.

7. Dabney, "The Butler Regime in Louisiana," 513–14.

For a while the city council attempted to function under military rule, but they were eventually dismissed for refusing to take the oath of allegiance. Butler now held absolute reign over the city, and he was patient and shrewd enough to build a justifiable case for doing it. Even Commander Porter, who seldom had anything good to say about the general, later stopped on his way to Vicksburg and wrote, "General Butler was not popular at New Orleans, although the city was never so clean, healthy, and orderly as under his *régime*."[8]

During the turmoil leading to the arrest of Mayor Monroe, Captain French captured William Mumford, who seemed not to have enough sense to remove the shorn Stars and Stripes from his buttonhole. Besides desecrating the flag, Mumford always managed to be present during civil disorder, and French concocted additional charges such as "aiding and abetting" the rebellion and acting with "treasonable and wicked" purposes. Mumford blamed his arrest on the New Orleans *Crescent* for exposing him as the instigator of the flag-shredding episode, which, he claimed, was done by somebody he did not know. Mumford, who at forty-two was a rather "fine-looking man, tall, black-bearded . . . bold, reckless, and defiant," acted as overlord to the city's gamblers but was well educated, owned property, and exerted considerable influence among the lower class. Thomas A. Dryden, a police officer, testified that he knew the prisoner, heard him admit being "the first man who put a hand on the flag," and declared that Mumford was accustomed to hard drinking and had a reputation for lying. That was enough for Butler, and he ordered Mumford executed on the morning of June 7.[9]

New Orleanians expressed shock at the order, never believing the general would carry out the sentence. Butler waited for the appeals to come, but "no good man petitioned for his release, but the bad men, the blacklegs and blackguards, assembled in large numbers and voted that he should not be executed." If Mumford died, the protesters vowed to murder Butler "by any and every possible means." They discussed forming a committee to take the threat directly to the general, but when they found no one brave enough to serve on the committee,

8. *Ibid.*, 512; Porter, *Incidents and Anecdotes*, 73.
9. Record of the Military Commission, May 14, 1861, in Butler Papers, LC; *Butler Correspondence*, I, 482–83; *Butler's Book*, 439, Parton, *General Butler*, 346.

they decided to write letters. The following day Butler received fifty anonymous notes containing violent language and depictions of pistols, coffins, and skulls with crossbones.

"Their performances frightened one man besides myself," Butler recalled. "He was my secret service man, who had attended the meeting and made a speech on behalf of my being shot." The infiltrator was so shaken by the meeting that he warned Butler not to execute Mumford. The general ignored the advice. "I thought I should be in the utmost danger if I did not have him executed, for the question was now to be determined whether I commanded the city or whether the mob commanded it." The spy, however, had seen enough and asked to be detached and sent back north. Butler wrote out the order and went to bed—but, he wrote, "I did not sleep."[10]

Mumford, however, sat in jail showing neither fear nor contrition, expecting at any moment to have his sentence commuted. An almost universal belief prevailed that Mumford would be brought to the gallows and there reprieved, in keeping with the blank-cartridge practice of weak governments. The six captured parolees also waited in jail for their executions, scheduled "immediately after reveille" on June 4.[11]

Butler felt pressure from all sides. In the matter of the six soldiers his officers pleaded with him, and Union men of the city implored him to save their lives. Some argued that the prisoners were only "poor, simple, ignorant souls," and at the arraignment before the commission one had declared that he understood nothing about paroling or what it meant. "Paroling is for officers and gentlemen," he said, and "we are not gentlemen." This simple remark probably saved their lives. Those words meant something to a southerner where a gentleman must keep his word, but "we poor people may get away if we can."[12]

Two local Unionists, J. A. Rosier and Julian Durant, delivered an appeal to Butler to spare the lives of the six men on the general's death row. By now, even Butler had begun to question the need to execute the men, but in Rosier and Durant's appeal he saw an opportunity to perform a personal favor that in politics required something

10. *Butler's Book*, 440.

11. General Orders No. 36, May 31, 1862, ORA, XV, 467.

12. *Butler Correspondence*, I, 573–74; Puffer, "Our General," 106–107; Parton, *General Butler*, 347–49.

in return later. "You ask for these men's lives," Butler replied. "You shall have them. You say that the clemency of the government is best for the cause we all have at heart. Be it so." On June 4 Butler commuted the sentence of the parolees and ordered them transported to Ship Island to perform hard labor.[13]

Only the issue of Mumford, scheduled to hang on June 7, remained. Mrs. Mary Mumford hoped a personal appeal to the general might yet save her husband, and on June 5 she sent a note asking if she and her children could speak with him. He rode to her home, uncomfortably aware that carpenters in front of the mint had already begun work on the gallows. The moment the general entered the convicted man's parlor, he knew the visit would be a tear-wrenching experience. "Mrs. Mumford wept bitterly," Butler recalled, "as did the children, who fell about my knees, adding all those moving acts which perhaps they had been instructed to say or do, or which perhaps naturally came to them." Butler, however, would not bend to the wails of the family. Instead, he urged Mrs. Mumford to come to the jail and encourage her husband to make preparations for his death. "Mumford believes he will not be executed," Butler declared, and "I wish you to convince him that he is mistaken. Whether I live or die he will die. . . . Let him in the few hours he has to live look to God for his pardon." He then apologized for "the great affliction that was to come to her and her children," but in departing he promised to come to the aid of the family should she or her children ever require his help in making ends meet.[14]

The general returned to his office and found Dr. William N. Mercer, an octogenarian and one of the most respected gentlemen in the city, waiting to see him.

"Give me this man's life," begged the doctor. "I must soon go to meet my Maker; let me take with me that I have saved a fellow-creature's life."

Butler remained obdurate. "The question now to be settled is whether law and order or a mob shall govern."

13. *Butler Correspondence*, I, 571–72, 573–74; Butler to Stanton, June 10, Rozier and Durant to Butler, Butler to Rozier and Durant, Butler to French, June 3, 1862, *ORA*, XV, 465, 467–68, 468–69.

14. *Butler's Book*, 441; Special Orders No. 70, June 5, 1862, *ORA*, XV, 469.

"A scratch of your pen will save him," Mercer pleaded, moisture welling in his aged eyes.

"True, Doctor, and a scratch of that same pen would put you in his place. . . . Having this great power I must use it judiciously. I cannot [save Mumford]."

Mercer rose and departed, and his sorrow filled the room.[15]

Butler claimed the act of carrying out the execution would solidify his authority in Louisiana and preserve order in the city. He had also promised Farragut he would do it, although the flag officer never actually endorsed the idea. The entire populace waited, many expecting the general to remit the sentence, but on June 5 he issued the final order for Mumford's execution—two days hence. Butler's determination to kill Mumford may have been influenced by Major General John A. Dix, who at the war's start declared, "If any one attempts to tear down a United States flag, shoot him on the spot!"[16]

On the morning of June 7 Mumford spoke his final words, claiming that his so-called offense was committed under excitement, and the misdemeanor did not justify a penalty of death. In an appeal to those who came to hear his words, Mumford implored them to act justly in their relations with each other—peculiar words coming from a gambler. He told them "to rear their children properly; and when they met death they would meet it firmly." And if Butler was listening, Mumford added that he was prepared to die, "and as he had never wronged any one, he hoped to receive mercy."[17]

This was exactly the type of rhetoric that created martyrs, and when Mumford began his fatal trip to the mint, a huge crowd assembled to witness the execution—or as some hoped, the anticipated commutation. Butler noticed that one of his staff officers failed to attend the execution—a quiet if not sullen protest. All eyes followed the tall, handsome gambler to the scaffold, but they were silent, shocked by what they were watching. Following an old Spanish custom, Butler had ordered the gallows built at the scene of the crime, a good substitute for "shooting him on the spot." At the appointed time the trap

15. *Butler's Book*, 442–43.

16. *Butler Correspondence*, I, 574; Morgan Dix, ed., *Memoirs of John Adams Dix* (2 vols.; New York, 1883), I, 374.

17. Parton, *General Butler*, 351–52.

sprang, Mumford dropped halfway through the scaffold, his neck snapped, and for several minutes spasms rippled through his body— and then he became still. A murmur swept through the crowd, but they turned away and quietly dispersed—confused, dumbfounded, and silently angry. But the confusion would not last, and anger found other ways to express itself.[18]

Like much of the town, sixteen-year-old Clara Solomon reacted privately, noting in her diary, "Everyone is fired with indignation at the atrocious wonder of yesterday, the hanging of Mumford for tearing down the U.S. flag from the mint. . . . God help us to revenge it." To others Butler remained simply a beast, a bloated tyrant no better than the barbaric Hun who raided and looted Rome. Deprecated from every corner of the South, Butler provided the perfect image of a cruel despot everybody could hate, and after word of Mumford's execution worked its way across the Confederacy, the event gained in fanciful embellishments what it lost in accuracy. By the time the news reached Richmond, the press reported that as Mumford ascended the scaffold, he turned to the onlookers and bravely declared that the manner of his death "will be no disgrace to my wife and children." Stories like this convinced southerners of Butler's injustice and Mumford's innocence.[19]

After clearing the scaffold of Mumford's body, Butler ordered the Stars and Stripes raised over city hall. Thirty-four guns blasted a salute, followed by a series of patriotic speeches in Lafayette Square. Fifteen thousand spectators "mad with excitement" participated in the ceremony.[20]

The roar echoed east, stirring passions in Charleston, the seat of secession, where anger raged unabated. The editor of the *Courier* offered a reward of $10,000 "for the capture or delivery of the said Benjamin F. Butler, dead or alive, to any proper Confederate authority." This, together with the $10,000 offered by the Jackson *Mississippian* in

18. Butler to Stanton, June 10, 1862, ORA, XV, 465–66; *Butler's Book*, 443; Parton, *General Butler*, 352; Clarence Edward Macartney, *Lincoln and His Generals* (Philadelphia, 1925), 56.

19. Ashkenazi, ed., *Diary of Clara Solomon*, 399; Southwood, *"Beauty and Booty,"* 107–108; Coulter, *Confederate States of America*, 72–73; Edward Pollard, *The Lost Cause* (New York, 1866), 260.

20. New Orleans *Daily Delta*, June 7, 8, 1862.

the aftermath of the Woman Order, raised the price on Butler's head to $20,000. The Charleston *Mercury* offered no money but recommended that Butler be poisoned or stabbed if he could not be caught and hanged. "If they do it," Butler remarked, "it will only place General Phelps in command, and if they are satisfied with that arrangement I have nothing to say."[21]

To incite public reaction against the execution of Mumford, Governor Moore published a proclamation "To the People of Louisiana." In a lengthy appeal for the public to keep the fires of rebellion burning hot, he placed the "noble heroism of the patriot Mumford . . . high on the list of martyred sons." After condemning Butler for the monstrous miscarriage of justice, Moore explained how the provost guards brought Mumford in full view of the scaffold, where his "murderers hoped to appall his heroic soul by the exhibition of the implements of ignominious death." According to the governor's version of the event, Butler offered to spare Mumford's life if the gambler took the oath of allegiance, but, Moore stated, "He spurned the offer. Scorning to stain his soul with such foul dishonor, he met his fate courageously and transmitted to his countrymen a fresh example of what men will do and dare when under the influence of fervid patriotism. I shall not forget the outrage of his murder," Moore added, "nor shall it pass unatoned."[22]

In Virginia, General Robert E. Lee received a letter from Secretary of War George W. Randolph explaining the recent "murder" in New Orleans and declaring that Mumford's desecration of the Stars and Stripes occurred before the city surrendered. Lee had just driven General McClellan's Army of the Potomac back down the peninsula and had it holed up at Harrison's Landing. "Under these circumstances," said Lee to General McClellan, "the execution of Mr. Mumford is considered as a murder of one of our citizens." Lee demanded an answer, warning that "outrages of such a character" would not be tolerated without retaliation. McClellan, once again confronted with a bothersome issue involving Butler, shed the matter quickly and forwarded Lee's demand to Washington. A month later Jefferson Davis still waited for an answer.[23]

21. Nash, *Stormy Petrel*, 155; New York *Tribune*, June 4, 14, 1862.

22. Moore's Proclamation, n.d., *ORA*, XV, 509.

23. Lee to McClellan, July 6, Randolph to Lee, June 29, Davis to Lee, August 1, 1862, *ORA*, Ser. 2, IV, 134–35, 793, 835. Lee's July 6 correspondence includes the coverage of Mumford's execution as reported by the New Orleans *Daily Delta*.

Mumford's execution continued to fester in the Confederate capital, and on December 24 Davis issued a lengthy proclamation condemning the United States for "failure to make an early reply" to Lee's letter. Davis, however, wanted retribution, and if Lincoln would not deal with Butler's act of unjustified murder, then Davis, whom Butler had once tried fifty times to nominate for president, would do so himself. He proclaimed the general a "felon, deserving of capital punishment."

> I do order that he [Butler] be no longer considered or treated simply as a public enemy of the Confederate States of America, but as an outlaw and common enemy of mankind, and that in the event of his capture the officer in command of the capturing force do cause him to be immediately executed by hanging; and I do further order that no commissioned officer of the United States taken captive shall be released on parole before exchange until the said Butler shall have met with due punishment for his crimes.[24]

At the time of the proclamation, Butler had been recalled from New Orleans for numerous questionable and unexplained activities. Hans Louis Trefousse, one of the general's more recent biographers, wrote, "Had Jefferson Davis deliberately tried to make his former friend more popular in the North, he could not have succeeded more readily than he did by these actions." Davis, however, may have saved Butler's military career. If so, the South would collect its dividends during the campaigns of 1864.[25]

In the days following the execution, Mumford's family became the sacred trust of the people, and his children the ward of the Confederacy. Considerable sums were raised, and during the years of the war the Mumfords lived in comfort. When Butler returned north in late 1862, he never expected to hear from the Mumfords again, but in 1869 he received a letter from a lady in Malden, Massachusetts, who informed him that "Mrs. Mumford was . . . in the greatest distress." Butler remembered his promise to give aid to the widow should ever she ask and invited her to come to Washington.

Much to his surprise, she came, appearing much older than he re-

---

24. Davis' Proclamation, December 24, 1862, *ORA*, XV, 906.
25. Trefousse, *Ben Butler*, 115.

membered her. Mary Mumford explained how after her husband's death she had received a great deal of money, much of it in Confederate currency, and that she entrusted the care of it to a clergyman, who promised to take the money to Wytheville, Virginia, and build a home for her and the children. The trustee ran off, leaving a mechanic's lien on the house, and the property was to be sold to satisfy the lien. Butler paid it in Mrs. Mumford's name, and because there was no school at Wytheville, he suggested she rent the property and come to Washington. Then, quietly using his influence, he secured a position for her as clerk with the Department of Internal Revenue. Later, when the office was reorganized along political lines, Mrs. Mumford lost her job, and Butler searched until he found an opening with the postal service. "I saw the boys from time to time," he recalled. "They called to see me with their mother and they seemed very gentlemanly and bright." Butler was a man of many facets. He vowed to hang William Mumford, and he did. He also promised to help the family and did so.[26]

Butler's justice extended beyond Mumford and into the ranks of his own command. Nobody complained when nine days later the general hanged four men—three northerners and one southerner—for forcibly entering eight homes of peaceful New Orleans citizens in an attempt to steal money and jewelry under the pretense of searching for arms and contraband. A fifth burglar, a New Orleans lad of eighteen, escaped the gallows on an appeal from his mother, but spent time at hard labor on Ship Island. A sixth member of the gang turned state's evidence and escaped the gallows, having his sentence commuted to five years at hard labor. Yankees and Rebels fought through four years of war, but when it came to stealing, they learned how to get along with each other.[27]

Nobody praised Butler for cleansing the city of another crime ring, nor did he expect it. A man hated has few friends. A man loved has few enemies. Butler could be both at the same time, and he seemed to live his life attentive to neither.

26. *Butler's Book*, 443–46. There are many letters between Mary Mumford and the general in the Butler Papers, LC, dating from August 19, 1866, to April 16, 1881.

27. Special Orders Nos. 98 and 103, June 13, 14, 1862, *ORA*, XV, 476–77, 478; New Orleans *Daily Picayune*, June 15, 17, 1862.

8

Butler's War
with the Consuls

WITH A PRICE ON HIS head, Butler took surprisingly few precautions against being assassinated. He spent much of his time at the office, and when working he kept a loaded revolver on his desk. After an aide pointed out that the weapon was accessible to anyone who might want to shoot him, Butler unloaded it and put it back on the desk, but kept a loaded one handy and out of sight. When traveling the streets he always carried a revolver and by accident one day earned the reputation for being a crack shot. Approaching a wall on horseback, he spied a limb full of oranges dangling above the sidewalk, pulled out his revolver, hit a branch, and brought down a bagful of fruit. The shot created the myth of Butler's skill as a marksman. Howard P. Nash, who told the story, wrote, "This was a useful reputation for a man who was probably threatened with assassination oftener than anybody except a Russian czar."[1]

Butler's daily trips through the city had little to do with demonstrating his marksmanship and much to do with restoring business. When shopkeepers refused to reopen their stores, Butler fined them one hundred dollars each for every day they stayed closed. New Orleans depended on its commerce, and contractors and mechanics who refused to work on the clutter of shipping tied to the levee were thrown into prison and put on bread and water until they changed their minds. The general reactivated the railroads as far as Union lines extended, and through cajoling and intimidation he restored the normal services of

1. Nash, *Stormy Petrel*, 155–56.

the city before the execution of Mumford. "It was half affectation, half terror," he recalled, "the men only needed such a show of compulsion as would serve them as an excuse to their comrades."[2]

After issuing his May 1 proclamation, Butler realized that the internal and external commerce of New Orleans would continue to be paralyzed in the absence of a defined currency. Confederate paper money, worth about thirty cents on the dollar, remained the only legal tender available. Coins had vanished from circulation, and streetcar tickets, drinking-house shinplasters, and odd pieces of scrip substituted for small change. At the request of Pierre Soulé, Butler agreed to allow the worthless monetary system to exist temporarily, but on May 16 he issued an order forbidding the circulation of Confederate money after May 27. He distrusted the banks, and to guarantee their compliance he offered a reward of one-quarter of the value of the transaction to any informant who, after May 27, discovered an exchange in Confederate notes or bills. The order would have been less troublesome for the banks had Butler not blamed them publicly for causing the collapse of the local currency.[3]

New Orleans banks had suspended specie payments the past September and initiated the practice of circulating Confederate banknotes as currency by substituting them for coins, notes, and drafts— thereby shifting the burden of worthlessness to the public at large. Even the *True Delta* recognized the practice as "patriotic swindling."[4]

While Farragut had been holding the city under his guns and waiting for Butler, Mayor Monroe yielded to the banks and added to the monetary turmoil by declaring shinplasters legal tender redeemable by the Committee of Public Safety. Bankers, intent upon safeguarding their own welfare, looked for ways to cut their losses and advised the public that money not withdrawn during the next ten days would be held on deposit at the risk of the depositors. When Butler discovered that the banks had transported their bullion out of the city and were now refusing to accept the very notes they had printed and were still distributing, he attempted to stop it. On May 19 he issued an order

2. Parton, *General Butler*, 407.
3. General Orders No. 29, May 16, 1862, ORA, XV, 426; *Butler's Book*, 505–507.
4. New Orleans *True Delta*, May 9, 1862.

compelling the banks to discontinue the practice of paying depositors in Confederate notes, demanding that all deposits be paid in "the bills of the bank, United States Treasury notes, gold, or silver." The general then authorized incorporated banks to issue new bills of one- to five-dollar denominations, substituting them for Confederate currency. He also compelled the banks to redeem shinplasters and all forms of scrip; if a bank refused, he threatened to confiscate it and sell off its assets and the property of its directors to compensate the depositors. To make it possible for the banks to comply with the order, Butler promised to provide a military guard for the safe conduct of bullion back from its hiding places to the vaults. This angered Confederate authorities in Richmond who wanted the specie to finance the war.[5]

Bank presidents descended on Butler's headquarters questioning whether the bullion would be free from confiscation. The general assured them that gold and silver were private property and would be held "inviolate like any other property" under his proclamation. But, the general added, it "must be in the hands of its owners and held in the usual course of business. If it is concealed, hid away so that it cannot be in public or private use, I shall hold that [it] is not within my proclamation. Therefore, you gentlemen who have got your gold concealed behind the altars, in the tombs, or elsewhere, better get it back into your own vaults. . . . If I find it elsewhere I shall not recognize it as your property. But I now give you the opportunity to get it, and when you do get it, certify to me that you have it, and the amount of it."

A cashier from one of the banks approached Butler for permission to go up the river on one of the boats buying provisions on the Red River. Butler suspected the purpose of the trip and gave him a pass. A few days later the cashier returned with $350,000 in gold, all packed in barrels of beef. The banks, however, had already recovered much of the bullion they had hidden, except for thousands still at large behind enemy lines.[6]

5. General Orders No. 30, May 19, 1862, ORA, XV, 437–38; *Butler Correspondence*, I, 480; *Butler's Book*, 507–509; Dabney, "The Butler Regime in Louisiana," 509.
6. *Butler's Book*, 506.

In guaranteeing the banks protection of their capital, Butler also warned that he would not hesitate to "retake, repossess, and occupy" all the property of the United States confiscated by the banks—including, if necessary, recovery from the directors. At the time, Butler did not know that this sum involved about $3 million—$500,000 from the mint, $150,000 from customs, and more than $2 million in unpaid commercial transactions. After repudiating the debts, New Orleans bankers proceeded to place the obligations beyond their power to ever pay them. They did not have to read between the lines of the order to see that Butler intended to exclude from protection those deposits held for the Confederacy.[7]

No matter how much the financial community complained, Butler upheld May 27 as the last day in the life of Confederate bills. This placed the Citizens' Bank of Louisiana in an awkward position because it held Confederate deposits of $219,090.94 and an equal amount in Confederate treasury notes that it wanted to set off against the deposits. Butler ruled that the deposits now belonged to the United States and demanded they be paid in money or property—not in worthless Confederate treasuries. Other rebellion-related deposits brought the bank's obligations to the United States to $434,911.83, a sum they could not meet.[8]

Strange events followed in the wake of Butler's edict. A black man informed Lieutenant Kinsman that an immense number of kegs had been recently removed from Citizens' Bank and taken to the office of a liquor dealer named Amedée Couturié, a Frenchman, and placed in a large vault. Butler made inquiries of depositors looking after their own interests and detailed Captain Samuel D. Shipley and a squad of soldiers to ask the liquor dealer if he was holding any specie for a local bank. The Dutch consular flag flew from the Frenchman's office, so Couturié believed that by saying no, his visitors would leave. When Shipley persisted with more questions, Couturié declared that his building "contained nothing but the property belonging or appertaining to the consulate, or to himself" and demanded that the soldiers

---

7. *Butler Correspondence,* I, 480; Bragg, *Louisiana in the Confederacy,* 39–40; Winter, *Civil War in Louisiana,* 14.

8. *Butler Correspondence,* I, 589–91. See also ORA, XV, 475–76.

leave. Shipley doubted it and asked permission to search the vault. The Frenchmen became quite angry and demanded that a note be carried to Count Méjan, the French consul.[9]

Shipley let Butler read the note before sending it to the count. The general suspected that Méjan was as involved in the cover-up as the Dutch consul, so he kept the note and sent Shipley back to arrest Couturié and search the premises. Joined now by Lieutenant Kinsman, Shipley found the Frenchman in a surly mood and unwilling to surrender the key to his vault. Couturié invoked diplomatic immunity, but Kinsman ordered him to shut his mouth and detailed a pair of soldiers to strip the consul down to his stockings and find the key. They found it in his pants, opened the door to the vault, and discovered $800,000 in Mexican silver coins packed in kegs and bearing the mark of the Citizens' Bank of Louisiana. After rummaging through the vault they also uncovered bonds, dies, bankplates, engraving tools of the bank, and a stock of paper with plates to print Confederate treasury notes. Shipley held the consul under arrest, placed a guard over the money, and returned to headquarters for further orders. In the morning, Shipley removed all the silver, dies, and plates and moved them to the United States mint.

As the transfer was being made, Edmund J. Forstall, acting as power of attorney for Hope & Company of Amsterdam, claimed the money for his client. Butler doubted the claim because steel dies and plates bearing the mark of the Citizens' Bank lay among the coins. Forstall, however, demanded that the money—all 160 kegs—be returned to him for shipment to Europe. He accused Butler of illegally meddling in the affairs of the Netherlands by raiding its consul's office.[10]

On the heels of breaking into Couturié's vault, Butler received a protest signed by eighteen consuls living in New Orleans who demanded to know whether the general intended to unilaterally revoke all the treaties existing between their governments and the United States. The general promptly ruled that the flag of the Netherlands "was made

9. Butler to Stanton, May 16, 1862, *ORA*, Ser. 3, II, 116; Parton, *General Butler*, 364–65.

10. Forstall to Butler, May 11, Couturié's Statement, May 10, 13, Butler to Stanton, May 16, 1862, *ORA*, Ser. 3, II, 116–19, 119–21, 123–24; *Butler Correspondence*, I, 490.

to cover and conceal property" of Citizens' Bank for the purpose of shielding it "from the operation of the laws of the United States." Butler professed great respect for the flags of all nations, but he assured the consuls of having sufficient proof to discredit all the claims of Hope & Company.[11]

With backing from the consuls, Couturié protested, adding to his complaint "rough handling" by Butler's soldiers. He demanded the return of the money and an apology from the government. Since the incident took place during the time of the proposed visit of the French fleet, Couturié advised Butler that he had placed the matter in the hands of the French consul. Butler remained unimpressed, writing Couturié, "So far as I can judge . . . you have merited . . . the treatment you have received, even if a little rough, having prostituted your flag to a base purpose, you could not hope to have it respected."[12]

The general naturally suspected Forstall and the consul of collaborating with the bank and practicing a conspiracy to keep the coins out of the public's hands. He attempted to explain his position in a letter to Stanton:

The claims of these consular gentlemen are most extravagant. Men who have lived here all their lives now claim perfect immunity from the ordinary laws of war for themselves and all property they can cover, although they have been in arms against the United States. Many of these pretensions are too absurd to be for a moment entertained. . . . Almost all property, therefore, useful to the United States which has not been burned or carried off will be found to be held here by persons who have lived in Louisiana all their lives, but now claim to be foreigners. Every schooner and fishing smack that cannot venture out of the river raises a foreign flag. May I ask direction of the Department on this subject?[13]

Couturié, finding Forstall's efforts unproductive, submitted the case to Roest Van Limburg, the Dutch foreign minister in Washington, who in turn laid the matter before the secretary of state. At first Seward could not understand the issue because the only information he had

11. Consuls to Butler and Butler to consuls, May 12, 1862, ORA, Ser. 3, II, 121, 122.
12. Couturié to Butler, May 16, Butler to Couturié, May 14, 1862, *ibid.*, 122–23, 124.
13. Butler to Stanton, May 16, 1862, *ibid.*, 116.

was contained in Couturié's correspondence. Stanton, however, produced Butler's report, giving Seward a basis to argue that the general's action was justified because Couturié chose to stand on diplomatic immunities and failed to clarify the contents of his vault. Had he done this, Seward explained, "and then referred Major-General Butler to yourself, or to this Government, the President now thinks that it would have been the duty of the general to have awaited special instructions from the Secretary of War. . . . Nevertheless," Seward admitted, "this error of the consul was altogether insufficient to justify what afterward occurred." Seward officially apologized for Kinsman's "unnecessary and rude" strip search, and for that he blamed Butler. He did not, however, release the money or bonds but only promised to return them to the consul after further investigation.[14]

This did not end the matter. Van Limburg excused himself from the investigation, knowing that no consular seals had been placed upon the kegs of silver. The absence of consular seals led him to believe that Hope & Company's ownership would be validated and the innocence of the consul verified. He expected Couturié to have his commission and exequatur returned and Butler removed from New Orleans. Because Seward had suddenly become hounded by complaints from other disgruntled consuls, he was already discussing with the president what to do with Butler.[15]

The general's battle over the bank's silver was only the beginning of his trouble with foreigners. Some forty thousand of them lived in the city at the beginning of the occupation. They sympathized with the South and supported it but claimed they were neither Rebels nor loyalists and thus entitled to neutral treatment. So whenever they had a problem with Butler, they sought remedies through their local consul, who in turn engaged his country's foreign minister in Washington, thereby involving Seward in every issue, large or small.[16]

While difficulties with the Netherlands continued to fester, Butler learned that a British Guard had been formed in New Orleans to protect the town against Union attack. The small company contained about sixty Englishmen, most of them longtime residents of New Or-

14. Seward to Van Limburg, June 5, 1862, *ibid.*, 132–33.
15. Van Limburg to Seward, June 6, 7, 1862 *ibid.*, 133–37.
16. Johnson, "New Orleans Under General Butler," 507 n. 347.

leans, large property owners, and successful businessmen. They decided to disband when the city fell and voted to ship their arms, accoutrements, and uniforms to General Beauregard. A few days after occupying the city, Butler learned of the incident and sent for Captain J. J. Burrowes, the unit's commander, and directed him to bring his company to headquarters dressed in their uniforms and with their arms— anyone failing to do so would have to leave the city within forty-eight hours or be sent to Fort Jackson. Burrowes, of course, claimed immunity. Butler reminded the captain that the act of raising arms against the United States represented a breach of neutrality, to which the British government had pledged itself. Baffled by his predicament, Burrowes asked if some arrangement could be made for those members of the company who had disbanded but not sent their arms to the Rebel army. Butler assented and ordered them to bring their arms and uniforms to headquarters—the others to obey his order to leave the city or suffer arrest.[17]

The following day George Coppell, the acting British consul, appealed to Butler on behalf of the British Guard, calling the incident an excusable violation of international law. Referring to the Guard as British subjects, Coppell suggested that the men "were ignorant of the importance that might be attached to [delivering their arms to the Confederacy] and did it with no idea of wrong or harm." The consul, using Butler's own argument, declared that if it was not proper for the British Guard to serve as Louisiana militia, then it would be improper for them to report to the general to serve the United States. Butler, however, was simply trying to determine who among the Guard retained their arms and equipment and who did not. Coppell, of course, knew this, but his role was to protect British subjects from arrest or banishment.[18]

Since childhood, Butler's disdain for the British had remained among his greatest prejudices, and he vented some of this contempt on Coppell. "These people," he argued, "thought of it as no consequence that Beauregard should have sixty more uniforms and rifles. I think it of the same consequence that he should have sixty more of these faithless men. . . . I intend this order to be strictly enforced. I am

17. Butler to Coppell, May 11, 1862, ORA, Ser. 3, II, 126–27.
18. Coppell to Butler, May 8, 1862, *ibid.*, 124–25.

content for the present to suffer open enemies to remain in the city of their nativity; but law-defying and treacherous alien enemies shall not." Butler accused Coppell of not having the required credentials to act as consul. Coppell produced letters addressed to him and signed by Earl Russell and Lord Lyons, but he could not produce the required exequatur because the official consul had departed. He continued to act for Great Britain, however, and claimed that after another conversation with Captain Burrowes he now doubted whether any arms or uniforms had actually been forwarded to Beauregard. A few days later every man but Captain Burrowes and one other fled from the city. Butler sent the pair to Fort Jackson along with a third Englishman, Samuel Nelson, who "refused to be investigated." Coppell protested, and Butler ignored it.[19]

Coppell laid his case before Lord Lyons, the British foreign minister in Washington, who called upon the secretary of state. Butler's relationship with Seward had long been guardedly antagonistic, so it was no surprise to the general when the secretary attempted to placate Lord Lyons by upholding the illegality of the British Guard but recommending the release of Butler's English prisoners. By then the situation in New Orleans had drastically changed, and the general was fully engaged in a war with the consuls. Captain Puffer, Butler's aide, blamed Coppell for declaring "an offensive and defensive war of the guerrilla stamp" against every effort of the general for the sole purpose of exposing the weakness "of our Government."[20]

Seward had been cautiously tiptoeing through an international minefield, trying his best to keep France and Great Britain out of the war. The Dutch had also been sympathetic to the South, and Butler's antagonistic attitude toward the strongest nations in Europe did not bode well for Seward's efforts. Conferring with Lincoln on possible solutions, they dismissed the idea of recalling Butler and decided to elevate Colonel Shepley from military commandant of New Orleans to military governor of Louisiana. The order looked good on paper, and Seward hoped that the bothersome ministers would accept the change

19. Butler to Coppell, May 11, 16, *ibid.*, 127, 129; Coppell to Butler, May 13, 16, 1862, *ibid.*, 127–29; Puffer, "Our General," 104.

20. State Department Memorandums, May 30, 31, 1862, ORA, Ser. 3, II, 130–32; Puffer, "Our General," 104; Parton, *General Butler*, 358–59.

as a censure of Butler. To placate Van Limburg, Seward also announced that Reverdy Johnson would go to New Orleans to investigate the complaints of the consuls. Not wishing to express any dissatisfaction toward Butler, Stanton toned down the appointments, assuring the general that the changes were made to support him. Butler saw through the transparency and continued to operate with the same autocracy as he had in the past. He felt bitter, speculating that Johnson had been sent by Seward to decide in favor of the consuls "if it could be done without concessions too palpably humiliating."[21]

The general knew that Shepley was *his* man, and the only threat would come from the presence of sixty-six-year-old Reverdy Johnson, a powerful Maryland legislator with whom he had quarreled during the Democratic Convention of 1860 and again in 1861 when he occupied Baltimore and arrested Ross Winans. The appointment contained the ingredients of a bad mix because the pair were perceived as enemies. Postmaster General Blair wrote Butler of his concerns, saying that he opposed the appointment and had reminded Seward that Johnson had once lied to Butler. "Yes," Seward replied, "but he was paid to do that. Now he is paid to lie the other way." Stanton, also aware of the potential conflict, wrote Butler, "Mr. Seward is quite sure that Mr. Johnson has the kindest feelings toward yourself, and will perform his duties in a manner entirely satisfactory to yourself." Johnson and Butler had two things in common—they were both lawyers, and in 1860–61 they had both fought to keep the South in the Union. Apart from that, they did not like each other.[22]

Shepley, in his first act as military governor, appointed Lieutenant Weitzel mayor of New Orleans. Next he invited Couturié, with Butler's blessing, to resume his consular functions, and on June 9 Seward promised Van Limburg that "no time shall be lost" investigating the matter of the silver removed from the consul's office, though it remained at the mint with Butler. Reverdy Johnson, however, did not

21. State Department Memorandum, May 31, Stanton to Seward, June 3, Stanton to Shepley, June 10, 1862, ORA, Ser. 3, II, 131, 141, 142; Stanton to Butler, June 10, 1862, ORA, XV, 471; *Butler's Book*, 522; Parton, *General Butler*, 356.

22. *Butler Correspondence*, I, 581; Stanton to Butler, June 10, 1862, ORA, Ser. 3, II, 140; Holzman, *Stormy Ben Butler*, 23, 34; Bernard Christian Steiner, *Life of Reverdy Johnson* (Baltimore, 1914), 58; Faust, ed., *Historical Times Illustrated*, 398.

establish an office in New Orleans until July 10, and by then the general had become deeply embroiled in conflicts with all the consuls.[23]

Having upset the Dutch and the British, Butler now engaged the Greeks. When the port of New Orleans reopened on June 1, products hoarded by foreign shippers came out from their hiding places. Stamatz Covas, co-owner of the shipping company of Covas & Negroponte, conjointly with Ralli, Benachi & Company, had purchased 3,205 hogsheads of sugar worth $200,000. On June 10 Butler detained the shipment and sent his staff to investigate. The owners admitted the sugar had been purchased between January and March but claimed the transaction was strictly mercantile and the shipment of sugar must not be delayed. Butler, sniffing through Covas' records, concluded that the Greek shipper was purposefully buying Confederate notes and giving them for sterling exchange, thereby transferring abroad the credit of the South by enabling these bills to be converted into bullion for purchasing arms and munitions in Britain and France.[24]

By detaining the sugar, Butler expected a protest from Covas, but he was curious to see who else might complain. The following day Coppell, the British consul, Méjan, the French consul, and N. M. Benachi, the Greek consul and co-owner of the sugar, sent a joint message to Butler claiming the transaction was "strictly mercantile" and the property of British, French, and Greek subjects. They reminded the general of his May 1 proclamation protecting the property of foreigners and begged that "the sugars be at the disposal of the purchasers to do with them as they see fit."[25]

Having convinced himself that proceeds from the sugar would only result in more arms shipments to the South, Butler replied that his proclamation "was not an amnesty to murderers, thieves, and criminals . . . nor a mantle to cover the property of those aiders of the rebellion." After a lengthy written harangue to the joint consuls, he added: "In order to prevent all misconception, and that for the future you gentlemen may know exactly the position upon which I act in regard

23. Seward to Van Limburg, June 9, Johnson to Butler, July 10, 1862, *ORA*, Ser. 3, II, 139, 213; New Orleans *Bee*, June 3, 1862.

24. *Butler Correspondence*, I, 604, 605–607; Coppell, Méjan, and Benachi to Butler, June 11, 1862, *ORA*, Ser. 3, II, 159–60.

25. Coppell, Méjan, and Benachi to Butler, June 11, 1862, *ORA*, Ser. 3, II, 160.

to foreigners resident here, permit me to explain to you that I think a foreign resident here has not one right more than an American citizen, but at least one right less; *i.e.*, that of meddling or interfering, by discussion, vote, or otherwise, with the affairs of government."[26]

Since Seward's emissary was en route to New Orleans, Butler detained the shipment to await the arrival of Reverdy Johnson. Coppell and Méjan, having never received any satisfaction from Butler—and expecting none on the sugar issue—also decided to wait for a more pliable mind to resolve the problem. Before Johnson had time to organize his office for work, Butler had stirred up another controversy, this time with an American company.

The general's scouts had developed a new sport called steamboat hunting. When Farragut came up the river, many shipowners took their vessels into impenetrable bayous and swamps where no respectable Yankee would look. During one of these hunts, a small steamer named *Fox* fell into Union hands, a mailbag was discovered, and its contents were forwarded to headquarters. In sifting through the mail Butler discovered that Kennedy & Company had bought cotton at Vicksburg, hid it in a bayou along the coast, and loaded it on a blockade runner for Havana. From there it was reshipped to another office of the Kennedys in England—all this in defiance of President Lincoln's proclamation. Butler believed he had a strong case and fined Kennedy & Company $8,948.50, their portion of the value of the shipment. Knowing the assessment would be contested, he held the money and waited for a ruling from Johnson.[27]

By the time Johnson settled into his office on July 10, he had a dozen cases pending, all of them involving Butler's disputes with the consuls. His first chore was to investigate the claim of the Dutch foreign minister that a Union force had illegally entered the office of their consul and departed with $800,000 in silver specie owned by Hope & Company. In the meantime, William M. Evarts had studied the case in New York and felt that the silver had been "directly or indirectly" involved in financing the Confederate war effort, but he

26. *Butler Correspondence*, I, 605–607. See also Butler to Coppell, Méjan, and Benachi, June 12, Butler to Stanton, June 17, 1862, *ORA*, Ser. 3, II, 153, 160–62.

27. *Butler Correspondence*, II, 55, 56; Johnson to Butler, Butler to Johnson, July 22, 1862, *ORA*, Ser. 3, II, 242–43, 243–45.

also believed it should be retained in New Orleans at the Citizens' Bank, with Hope & Company being compensated by the bank through bills of exchange on its London branch. Lincoln, though he agreed with Butler's protection of national interests, was also anxious to restore trade on the Mississippi and would, if necessary, make a few concessions to do it. Seward, speaking for the president, urged Johnson to settle claims because the normalization of trade would "deprive foreign powers of all excuse for sympathy with the insurgents."[28]

In the meantime, Butler discovered another transaction involving Citizens' Bank in which Edouard Dupasseur & Company had withdrawn $716,196 in silver coin at daybreak, April 20, and deposited it with the French consul, Count Méjan. Dupasseur claimed to have purchased the coin on speculation, intending to make a profit of $30,000 after the blockade was raised, and he admitted moving it to the French consulate at an unusual hour on the Sabbath to prevent it from being stolen. Since this was the last of the silver held by Citizens' Bank, Butler naturally suspected that collaboration existed between the bank and the British, French, and Dutch consuls. He asked Johnson to examine both cases in this light, paying careful attention to Dupasseur. "I need not remind you," Butler wrote, "of the improbability of such a transaction . . . in such dangerous times, with such hope of profit, and the entire uncertainty of even being able to ship the specie . . . with our cannon at that moment thundering on the forts, and the city in fear daily of bombardment."[29]

Word quickly circulated among foreigners that Johnson had arrived. Joseph Deynoodt, the Belgian consul, visited Seward's envoy Johnson at the customhouse with a new claim, alleging that Butler's men had also entered his consulate and removed an unspecified amount of silver coin. Butler denied it. "It is the first time I have heard of such claims," he replied. "Several gentlemen called for their tin trinkets and I ordered them to be given up." He promised to investigate the charge but suspected it was both bogus and larcenous. Eventually he discovered that part of the coin removed by Dupasseur had been

28. *Butler Correspondence*, II, 56; Evarts to Seward, June 10, Seward to Johnson, June 27, Johnson to Butler, July 10, 1862, ORA, Ser. 3, II, 139–40, 179, 213.

29. *Butler Correspondence*, II, 80; Johnson to Butler, July 15, Butler to Johnson, July 16, 1862, ORA, Ser. 3, II, 229–30.

transferred to the Belgium consulate because of insufficient room in the French vault.[30]

On July 21 Johnson asked Butler to return $18,000 in bonds, not to Couturié but to Forstall. Butler agreed, and Johnson sent Puffer to get the key to the box from Couturié so the bonds could be removed. The Dutch consul refused, so Puffer sprung the box, removed the bonds, and advised Couturié he could pick up the smashed box and the rest of its contents at his convenience. Couturié again refused and the box remained in the customhouse. For Johnson, the episode demonstrated the recalcitrance of the consuls. What Couturié wanted was the coin, which remained under guard. Dupasseur retained possession of his coin, but Butler would not permit him to move it or ship it.[31]

In late July, Johnson returned to Washington, leaving most of the issues between Butler and the consuls unresolved. Debate over the disposition of Hope & Company's $800,000 and Dupasseur & Company's $716,196 went on for months, mostly because Butler did not believe either firm was entitled to the coin. Johnson concurred that the silver had been owned by the bank but that the transactions were proper in order to assure interest payments on loans abroad. "The United States can have no interest in the coin," Johnson concluded, "except upon the ground of forfeiture, and for that there was not at the time, nor is there now, the slightest pretense." Johnson did not believe the funds were ever intended to be used to purchase arms for the Confederacy, but he admitted there was no proof one way or the other.[32]

Meanwhile, Butler neither released the coins nor agreed with Johnson, and on August 20 Seward asked Van Limburg whether he wanted the silver delivered to Couturié, Forstall, or the Citizens' Bank of New Orleans. The Dutch minister designated Couturié, and Seward promised to make the transfer as quickly as possible. On September 30 Butler still held the silver, but Shepley promised that he was ready to deliver it to Couturié.[33]

30. Butler to Johnson, July 16, 1862, ORA, Ser. 3, II, 229–30.

31. Johnson to Butler, July 21, Puffer to Johnson, July 26, 1862, *ibid.*, 240, 263–64.

32. U.S. Congress, *Papers Relating to Foreign Affairs, 1862*, 37th Cong., 3rd Sess., Executive Document No. 16; *Butler Correspondence*, II, 148.

33. Johnson to Butler, July 26, 1862, in Butler Papers, LC; Seward to Van Lim-

Exactly when Couturié took possession of the silver or when Dupasseur received clearance to ship his coins to France is unclear, but Butler enjoyed the irony that followed. He obtained a copy of a letter written on September 26 by Henry S. Sanford, United States minister to Belgium, to Seward. In Belgium Sanford learned that shipments of military supplies to the Confederacy had been detained for payment but that the funds were expected shortly from the French consul in New Orleans. "It would be well," Sanford suggested, to make inquiries into "who the depositors of the money sequestered by Butler were, and for whom it was intended."[34]

After this accidental discovery, Butler sent his secret police into the offices of several French shippers and in November confirmed that at least $405,000 in silver coin had been designated to cover Confederate purchases of military supplies, and that another $800,000 in contracts had been processed through Count Méjan, all involving the silver sequestered by Butler. "I leave the consul [Count Méjan] to the Government at Washington," the general declared. "I will take care sufficiently to punish the other alien and domestic traitors concerned in this business. . . . I am glad my action here has thus been vindicated and that the Government of the United States will be able to demand of the French Government a recall of its treacherous and hostile [consul]." Butler's warlike attitude toward consuls continued to fret Seward and caused Lincoln considerable anxiety.[35]

The silver, however, was gone, carried to Europe on a Spanish warship and delivered to the French. The first shipment of supplies entered the Confederacy through Brownsville, Texas, and Butler suspected that a second shipment was already on its way.[36]

After leaving New Orleans, Reverdy Johnson dispensed with Butler's other cases. He reversed Butler on Kennedy & Company and told the general to return the $8,948.50 fine imposed on the cotton mer-

---

burg, August 20, September 4, Van Limburg to Seward, August 30, Watson to Seward, September 5, Watson to Seward, September 30, 1862, *ORA*, Ser. 3, II, 488, 503, 511, 515, 622–23; Parton, *General Butler*, 376–77.

34. Sanford to Seward, September 26, Watson to Butler, October 22, 1862, *ORA*, Ser. 3, II, 677, 678.

35. Butler to Stanton, November 13, 1862, *ibid.*, 766–69.

36. *Ibid.*, 768.

chant. Of the seizure of 3,205 hogsheads of sugar owned by Covas & Negroponte, Johnson ruled it a normal mercantile transaction and released it. He returned to Washington to write his report, and when Butler read it he lamented to Seward that the elder lawyer from Baltimore had done everything in his power to support the interests of the Confederacy.[37] Johnson, however, waited for four months before airing his opinion publicly, declaring that the state of fraud and corruption in New Orleans was "without parallel in the past history of the country."[38]

These reversals did not make Butler charitably inclined toward foreign emissaries, and after Johnson departed he resumed his campaign against the consuls. On July 31 he arrested Charles Heidsieck, producer and dealer of Heidsieck champagne, who was found operating under a false name and serving as a bartender on a vessel protected by a Butler permit. After arresting Heidsieck for carrying secret dispatches for the French, Swiss, Spanish, Prussian, and Belgian consuls, the general sent him to Fort Jackson. Viscount Jules Treilhard, the French minister, intervened with Seward, and Count Méjan protested to Butler, eventually leading to the release of the French spy. "If Heidsieck had not been taken out of my hands by the action of my government," Butler wrote, "I should have ordered him before a court for trial, and I believe he would have suffered for his crimes against the country."[39]

Having no regard for any European power, Butler also created friction with Spain. Prior to the occupation, Captain Thomas T. Craven captured the Confederate steamer *Magnolia* as it attempted to break through the blockade. The prize crew recovered a mailbag containing a letter revealing that Juan Callejon, the Spanish consul in New Orleans, was to collect a 5 percent share from the profits of a proposed sale

37. *Papers Relating to Foreign Affairs*, 1862, 37th Cong., 3rd Sess., Executive Document No. 16; Johnson to Butler, July 22, Butler to Seward, September 19, 1862, *ORA*, Ser. 3, II, 242–43, 571–72.

38. Quoted from the New York *World*, December 4, 1862, by Trefousse, *Ben Butler*, 124.

39. Butler to Halleck, September 10, Halleck to Butler, October 20, 1862, *ORA*, Ser. 3, II, 534–35, 674; *Butler Correspondence*, II, 213, 276, 372–73; Parton, *General Butler*, 363.

of eighty thousand muskets to the Confederate government. Months passed, and Callejon one day protested that his mail was being searched. Butler recalled the *Magnolia* incident and replied caustically that mail should be sent through the postal service and not on blockade runners.[40]

When Union scouts captured the runner *Fox* in May, Butler's staff began to sift through stacks of papers found on board the steamer. Documents, invoices, and bills of exchange between the Avendano Brothers of New Orleans and agents in Havana provided proof that the firm had been running arms, powder, lead, quicksilver, and medical supplies into the Confederacy for many months. When Butler paid the brothers a visit, they admitted their blockade-running ventures. He fined them the value of the cargo, and the Avendanos promised to desist from further illegal ventures. After Johnson appeared in New Orleans and began overruling Butler, the Avendanos sent a lawyer to the general to recover their money. Although the Avendanos had been residents of New Orleans since birth, this erupted in an international dispute between Seward and Gabriel Garcia y Tassara, the Spanish minister. Spain finally dropped its case and moved on to other problems with the general.[41]

In late June, Union quarantine officers detained the Spanish steamer *Cardenas*, laden with a cargo of fresh fruit, at Fort St. Philip for the mandatory health inspection. *Roanoke*, an American vessel also having loaded at Havana, passed through the checkpoint without being subjected to the mandatory quarantine. After *Roanoke* deposited its cargo at New Orleans, Callejon would not grant clearance for the vessel to sail back to Havana and demanded it be delayed the same number of days that *Cardenas*, whose fruit had spoiled, had been detained at Fort St. Philip. Butler's reply implied that Callejon should make plans to depart from New Orleans whenever *Cardenas* sailed. Incensed,

40. Craven to Welles, February 19, Dewhurst to Welles, March 5, 1862, *ORN*, XVII, 137–38; Clifford L. Egan, "Friction in New Orleans: General Butler Versus the Spanish Consul," *Journal of Louisiana History*, IX (Winter, 1987), 45.

41. Watson to Seward, Watson to Butler, September 10, Seward to Tassara, September 9, 10, 11, Butler to Seward, September 10, Seward to Stanton, September 11, Butler to Stanton, October 27, 1862, *ORA*, Ser. 3, II, 533, 534–37, 687–90; *Butler Correspondence*, II, 387–89.

Callejon complained to Tassara, who involved Seward and submitted a bill for $16,347 to cover the cost of the spoiled fruit. Before Seward could untangle the matter, Butler's officers quarantined *Blasco de Garay*, another Spaniard. When the vessel finally cleared, it came up to New Orleans and attempted to depart with several Confederate passengers and an escaped murderer on board. Two other Spanish vessels also drew Butler's ire when numerous Rebels were found on *Pinta* and *Maria Galanti*. Several of these cases remained unsettled until July, 1863, and it was not until well into Butler's administration that the general met with Callejon and discovered that a large part of the trouble stemmed from an "insuperable language barrier." Eventually, Seward sided with Butler, who was no longer there to enjoy a rare moment of support.[42]

The general's disputes with the consuls received much notice in New Orleans, the *Daily Delta* observing: "If Gen. Butler rides up the street, the consuls are sure to come in body, and protest that he did not ride down. If he smokes a pipe in the morning, a deputation calls upon him in the evening to know why he did not smoke a cigar. If he drinks coffee, they will send some crude messenger with a note asking in the name of some tottering dynasty why he did not drink tea." Since the army controlled the *Delta*, its sympathetic views may not have been shared by the public.[43]

Independent of Seward's knowledge, Butler attempted to make a statement to all foreigners by showing them that the power of the United States was a tangible reality they must learn to respect. Left to his own devices, the general had intended to subdue the consuls. His strategy collapsed after Johnson's arrival, and on September 19 Butler wrote Seward:

> Indeed, sir, I beg leave to add that another such commissioner as Mr. Johnson sent to New Orleans would render the city untenable. The town got itself into such a state while Mr. Johnson was here that he

42. Tassara to Seward, June 28, August 21, 26, September 3, 11, 1862, ORA, Ser. 3, II, 426–27, 529–30, 537, 551–55, 558; Puffer, "Our General," 104–105; Egan, "Friction in New Orleans," 45–49. The *Cardenas* affair involved the Puig brothers; this account is in *Butler Correspondence*, II, 205, 368–69, 370–71.

43. Bland, *Life of Butler*, 126.

confessed to me he could hardly sleep from nervousness from fear of [an uprising], and hurried away, hardly completing his work. . . . The result of his mission here has caused it to be understood that I am not supported by the Government; that I am soon to be relieved; that all my acts are to be overruled, and that a rebel may do anything he pleases in the city, as the worst will be a few days imprisonment, [and] when my successor will come he will be released.

To such an extent has this thing gone that the inmates of the parish prison, sent there for grand larceny, robbery, and forgery, in humble imitation of the foreign consuls, have agreed together to send an agent to Washington to ask for a commission to investigate charges made by these thieves against the provost-marshal, by whose vigilance they were detected.[44]

Thieves came in all shapes and sizes—some wore rags and some wore blue uniforms—and General Butler's activities were not confined to the consuls. He knew exactly where he stood with the powers in Washington, and he doubted whether Lincoln would risk recalling him before the November elections—if then. In the interim, he had his own agenda. "Mr. Seward," Butler wrote, "was in distress whenever I did anything that caused a little whipper-snapper emissary from some government in Europe to complain of my just treatment of a man who claimed to be a consul, and this caused perpetual interference and annoyance. Otherwise I was supreme. Having supreme power, I used it."[45]

And so he did.

44. Butler to Seward, September 19, 1862, *ORA*, Ser. 3, II, 571–72.
45. *Butler's Book*, 426.

9

Bearing Down on New Orleans

THE CONSULS WERE NOT alone in their antipathy toward Butler—the banks distrusted him also, as did virtually every professional practitioner or businessman with assets to protect. The general seemed to be especially keen on locating funds belonging to the United States, and his first step, beginning with the Bank of Louisiana, was to make it known that deposits of the Confederacy would not be recognized. The financial community naturally protested, but Butler, anxious to recover specie, had his way.[1]

In looking into the records of the Bank of Louisiana, Butler came to the conclusion that the directors, who owned one-tenth of the bank's capital, took the other nine-tenths—about $3 million—without consulting the owners, and "sent it flying over the country in company with fugitive property-burners among the masses of a disorganized, retreating, and starving army, whence it is more than likely never to return again." When A. Durand, a depositor in the bank, sued the president and cashier to recover his deposits in cash, the defendants appealed, using as a defense their inability to pay in specie. Butler intervened and compelled the bank to give Durand bills instead of money, thereby making Durand the creditor of the bank. Once this ruling hit the streets, all bilked depositors became instant creditors of the banks.[2]

Aside from the kegs of coin shifted to foreign consuls, Butler suspected the banks would not bring back their hidden specie and

1. *Butler Correspondence*, I, 480, 504–505.
2. Butler to Mercer, May 22, Butler's decision on Bank of Louisiana, June [?], 1862, ORA, XV, 438–39, 472–73; *Butler Correspondence*, I, 481, II, 27–30.

detailed his secret police to locate the loot. Slaves knew their masters' hiding places, and Butler, who bragged that "he had a spy in every household," encouraged them to spy on their owners. If a bank returned specie to its vaults, Butler asked no questions, but if his police located a hoard under suspicious circumstances, he condemned it as Confederate property and compelled the holder to provide incontrovertible evidence of ownership. Such were the circumstances when in late May Butler discovered fifty thousand dollars in gold hidden in two kegs found in the banking house of Samuel Smith & Company.[3]

To the general, the gold looked exactly like the type of specie taken from the mint. When questioned, Smith did not seem to be aware of the value in the kegs, and since it appeared to have been cloistered under Smith's care by the Canal Bank of New Orleans, Butler assumed it was the property of neither Smith nor the bank but gold pilfered from the United States. To test his theory, Butler formed a commission led by General Shepley to hear testimony. Smith appeared before the tribunal, was flustered through the examination, and looked guilty. So certain was Butler of the gold being government property that he did not wait for a ruling from his own committee. Having insufficient funds to meet his division's payroll—some men had not been paid since entering the service—he used Smith's gold to pay his soldiers, or so he said. A few days later he had second thoughts, writing Chase, "I should have sent the specie to you, but . . . I would not let my soldiers go longer unpaid. It was injuring the credit of the Government with our foes and breeding sickness and discontent among my men."[4]

Butler, however, did not do as he claimed. He borrowed money from the bank to pay the soldiers and held both kegs of gold. Smith wanted his gold returned and hired a good lawyer to sue Butler. The general then attempted to have the government accept responsibility for holding the gold, but the Treasury Department wanted nothing to do with the transaction. Smith's attorney prevailed, forcing Butler to hand over the gold and pay all legal costs, which had grown to a hefty

3. Southwood, *"Beauty and Booty,"* 82; *Butler Correspondence*, I, 565–67; Kendall, *History of New Orleans*, I, 284.

4. Butler to Chase, July 2, 1862, *ORA*, XV, 513; *Butler Correspondence*, I, 566, 567, II, 14, 31–32. See also testimony in Smith case, May–June, 1862, in Butler Papers, LC.

sum. The case, filed in January, 1863, lasted two years, taking its final form in 1865 before the House of Representatives when James Brooks, a New York Democrat, called Butler a "bold robber." The general, who at the time had just been relieved of command of the Army of the James, demanded an apology, and Brooks, on January 23, replied that he had erred and meant to say "gold robber." Butler's supporters rushed to his aid, and Brooks countered by reminding his assailants that the general had voted for Jefferson Davis fifty times at the 1860 convention. Butler deserved embarrassment over the gold incident, but this, like all the setbacks in his life, never slowed him down.[5]

In late June, Butler's spies, who seemed to be everywhere, discovered an underground market in Rebel notes, which rose and fell in value depending upon Confederate successes or failures in the field. With the press censored, Butler did not know how the brokers obtained their information, so he put his informants to work. He learned that the brokers "were principally Jews, and as Benjamin, the Confederate Secretary of State, was a Jew, and his brother-in-law was a broker," Butler concluded that some of the Jewish brokers could get intelligence from Richmond. The spies continued to study the transactions, and when the brokers discovered they were being investigated, they suspended trading temporarily. The operation seemed to be harmless, so the general lost interest in it.[6]

By early July Butler believed he had brought most of the New Orleans banks to a state of liquidity, and this enabled him to press the city a little harder. On July 8 he issued General Orders No. 48, compelling every bank, company, or individual to pay to any claimant of the United States whatever was due them "since the fraudulent ordinance of secession." This created another wave of dissension against Butler's monetary policies, but the general quashed it.[7]

5. Butler to Army of the James, January 8, 1865, ORA, Vol. XLVI, Pt. 2, p. 70; *Butler Correspondence*, III, 7, 476–77, 560–63, 595–96, IV, 385, V, 280, 352, 340–41, 411, 420, 524, 689–91; Edwards Pierrepont, *A Review by Judge Pierrepont of Gen. Butler's Defense Before the House of Representatives, in Relation to the New Orleans Gold* (New York, 1865); Samuel Smith versus Benjamin F. Butler, in Edwards Pierrepont Papers, Special Collections, Hill Library, Louisiana State University Libraries, Louisiana State University, Baton Rouge.

6. *Butler's Book*, 510.

7. *Butler Correspondence*, II, 52–53.

New Orleanians found it especially offensive to be constrained to take the oath of allegiance or suffer consequences analogous to outright robbery. Butler had started the ball rolling on June 6, issuing General Orders No. 40:

> Any person who has in his possession, or subject to his control, any property of any kind or description whatever of the so-called Confederate States, or who has secreted or concealed, or aided in the concealment of such property, who shall not, within three days from the publication of this order, give full information of the same . . . to the Assistant Military Commandant, Godfrey Weitzel,—shall be liable to imprisonment and to have his property confiscated.[8]

After allowing four days to elapse, the general issued a second edict— General Orders No. 41:

> The Constitution and laws of the United States require that all military, civil, judicial, and legislative officers of the United States, and of the several States, shall take an oath to support the Constitution and Laws. If a person desires to serve the United States, or to receive special profit from the protection of the United States, he should take upon himself the corresponding obligations. This oath . . . "I do solemnly swear (or affirm) that I will bear true faith and allegiance to the United States of America, and will support the Constitution thereof" . . . will not be, as it has never been, forced upon any.
>
> Be it further ordered, that all persons ever heretofore citizens of the United States, asking or receiving any favor, protection, privilege, passport, or to have money paid to them, property, or other valuable thing whatever delivered to them, or any benefit of the power of the United States extended to them . . . must take and subscribe the oath . . . before their request can be heard, or any act done in their favor by any officer of the United States within this Department.[9]

He aimed a special clause at foreigners, declaring that if they had lived in the United States for five or more years, but had not claimed or received the protection of their government more than sixty days

8. *Ibid.*, I, 563.
9. *Ibid.*, 574–75.

prior to the order, they would be deemed natural citizens and required to take the regular oath as opposed to a special oath designed for foreigners, which read:

"I, _____ , do solemnly swear (or affirm) that so long as my Government remains at peace with the United States I will do no act, or consent that any be done, or conceal any that has been done, that shall aid or comfort any of the enemies or opposers of the United States whatever." [10]

The two orders infuriated every southern sympathizer in Louisiana and drew special vituperatives from foreign consuls, but Butler, after being compelled to modify the special oath, tried to make it stick. In simple terms, he told the foreigners and their consuls that if they did not like the order, to go home, and some of them did. He then sent copies of his correspondence to Stanton with the recommendation that certain foreigners be deported from New Orleans for their "unneutral conduct." [11]

Seward, pestered by European ministers over Butler's policy of demanding oaths of allegiance from foreigners, questioned the policy and asked Stanton to order Butler to discontinue the practice and "cancel any such obligations which may thus have been compulsorily contracted." Seward was more concerned about his own problems than Butler's and advised Stanton, "It is preferable for the maintenance of harmonious relations with foreign powers that misconduct on the part of their citizens or subjects within our jurisdiction should not be anticipated, but that its actual development should be awaited." While Seward worked long hours in an effort to keep Great Britain and France out of the war, Butler continued to engage their hostile consuls on another front. On June 29 Stanton ordered Butler

10. *Ibid.*, 576.

11. Butler to Stanton, June 17, Coppell to Butler, June 14, Callejon *et al.* to Butler, June [?], 1862, ORA, Ser. 3, II, 153, 154, 154–56; *Butler Correspondence*, I, 597–600, 600–604; Felix Grima to Victor Grima, November 12, 1862, in Felix Grima Family Papers, Mss 99, Folder 58, Historic New Orleans Collection, Wallace Research Center, New Orleans; Auvignac Dorville to Anatole de Ste. Gême, October 26, 1862, in Auvignac Dorville Papers, Mss 100, Folder 396, Historic New Orleans Collection.

to desist, but the consuls had no trouble finding other reasons to complain.[12]

Americans, however, had the choice of going out of business or taking the oath. Solomon Benjamin, brother of Judah P. Benjamin, the Confederacy's secretary of state, took the oath in preference to closing his business. On the day Solomon Benjamin endorsed his oath, the general acted as witness and stood by "preaching Unionism," causing brother Judah to develop "an enormous grudge at me for doing so."[13]

New Orleans offered a dismal future to citizens who refused to take the oath, making it impossible for anyone to transact business unless he was in compliance with the general's edict. Fines and imprisonment awaited those violating the order, and in the matter of transfers, even the clerk recording the transaction faced jail. Butler saw right through efforts by persons attempting to shield their property from confiscation by transferring it to minors or to foreigners, and by August 7 the provost marshal reported that 11,723 citizens had taken the oath, 2,499 foreigners had taken the neutral's oath, and 4,933 privates and 211 officers of the Confederate army had given the required parole. For Butler this was not enough, and on September 24 he ordered all persons, male and female, eighteen years of age and above who had ever been citizens of the United States but still held allegiance to the Confederacy to report to the nearest provost marshal by October 1 to give their occupation and address and register all their property. If they took the oath they would be restored with full rights as citizens of the United States. If they declined, a certificate would be issued proclaiming them enemies of the United States. By the end of October the rigors of Butler's administration induced 69,920 Louisianans to take the oath, and only 4,000 refused to do so. Eventually Confederate holdouts did not judge the oath-takers too severely, for they believed that an act of expediency did not change the fundamental attitudes of people required to earn a living.[14]

12. Seward to Stanton, June 24, Stanton to Butler, June 29, 1862, *Butler Correspondence*, II, 9–11; General Orders No. 82, July 21, 1862, ORA, Ser. 3, II, 234–35.

13. Butler to Stanton, June 28, 1862, ORA, XV, 502; *Butler Correspondence*, I, 595–96, 619; *Butler's Book*, 546.

14. General Orders No. 73, September 18, 1862, *Butler Correspondence*, II, 305–306; General Orders No. 71, September 13, General Orders No. 76, September

At first nothing stirred the emotions of the obstinate more than learning the names of those who had taken the oath. The local newspapers added to the storm by publishing the names of the oath-takers, bringing down the wrath of the holdouts. Ladies spurned gentlemen known to have taken it, and a few tenants were ejected from their boardinghouses. Unreconstructable secessionists kept books on defectors, vowing vengeance in the days ahead. Men accused of taking the oath denied it; others admitted they took it only to secure temporary advantages, stating "their readiness to take as many oaths as Picayune Butler thought it necessary to impose; as no faith was to be kept with Yankees." The holdouts suffered. Soldiers searched homes for contraband, and the sight of furniture, silver, jewelry, and clothing being auctioned in public only embittered the people toward the general. Emma Walton, whose husband was a colonel in the Confederate army, wrote that "prudence forbids her writing a letter." Only Butler's recall in December saved many civilians from absolute ruin.[15]

Among those who disdained the edicts of the general were Mayor Monroe and archsecessionists like Pierre Soulé. Their situations were different but connected. Butler sent Monroe to Fort Jackson for opposing the Woman Order, but he sent Soulé to Fort Lafayette in New York under the pretext of treason to rid himself of a highly regarded and influential dissident fully capable of inciting hostility. Butler then moved Monroe to Fort Pickens after the deposed mayor refused to take the oath of allegiance. When the general received word that Monroe's son lay dying, he sent the mayor's wife to visit her imprisoned husband and to encourage him to take the oath. At the pleading of his wife, Monroe decided to sign it, but he read an announcement

24, 1862, ORA, XV, 571, 575–76; Parton, *General Butler*, 462, 474; Caskey, *Secession and Restoration*, 60–61; Bland, *Life of Butler*, 128; Coulter, *Confederate States of America*, 95. The adjutant general's office could only account for about six thousand, leaving some doubt concerning the accurate number. See Johnson, "New Orleans Under General Butler," 500.

15. New Orleans *Daily Delta*, July 17, 1862; New Orleans *Daily Picayune*, August 12, 1862; Parton, *General Butler*, 462–63, 584; Johnson, "New Orleans Under General Butler," 501; Emma Walton to Colonel J. B. Walton, July 27, August 6, 1862, Emma Walton Papers, Mss 135, Folders 16, 17, Historic New Orleans Collection, Wallace Research Center, New Orleans.

in a newspaper stating that France had recognized the Confederacy, made the mistake of believing it, and refused to take the oath. Butler eventually released Soulé, whose health was failing, on a provisional parole that he not return to New Orleans or commit any act hostile to the United States.[16]

Too many stubborn secessionists failed to comprehend Butler's determination to rule New Orleans and restore it to the Union. If they wanted more evidence, they had no further to look than Jackson Square, where the equestrian statue of Andrew Jackson had stood for many years without an inscription on its base. Choosing the deceased president's own words, Butler had it inscribed "The Union Must and Shall Be Preserved."[17]

The general showed little patience with any person practicing the slightest disregard for his orders. On June 30 he sent Fidel Keller to serve two years at hard labor on Ship Island for exhibiting a human skeleton labeled "Chickahominy" in the window of his bookstore. Passersby stared with contempt at the bones of a supposed dead Yankee killed on the outskirts of Richmond, and that was enough for Butler to close down Keller's operation.[18]

The general's war on skeletal remains extended to John W. Andrews, an elderly member of the deposed city council who made the mistake of fashioning a cross from the bones of a "Yankee soldier" and displaying it in the Louisiana Club. The general ruled the act a "desecration of the dead" and an impiety toward the "blessed Saviour," so Andrews joined Keller on the boatload of convicts headed for Ship Island's penal colony. Andrews swore that he had destroyed the cross before the city surrendered, but the general harbored a special contempt for council members and dismissed the testimony. Friends who saw Andrews off doubted if he would return alive.[19]

John H. Larue and his wife, Anne, found themselves in separate

16. Thomas to Thompkins, June 15, 21, Thomas to Burke, June 19, Butler to Stanton, November 14, Townsend to Burke, November 27, 1862, *ORA*, Ser. 2, IV, 23, 41–42, 49, 707, 760; *Butler Correspondence*, I, 431–32; Parton, *General Butler*, 335, 338; Dabney, "The Butler Regime in Louisiana," 498.

17. Asbury, *The French Quarter*, 52 n.

18. Special Orders No. 151, June 30, 1862, *ORA*, XV, 511; Parton, *General Butler*, 441.

19. Special Orders No. 152, June 30, 1862, *ORA*, XV, 511–12; Walker to Davis, September 13, 1862, *ibid.*, Ser. 2, IV, 881–82.

prisons, John for being a vagrant gambler and Anne for wearing a Confederate flag in public, inciting a riot by distributing handbills falsely announcing the capture of General McClellan, and endangering the life of a Union soldier. Butler sent her to Ship Island on July 10 but remitted her sentence three weeks later. He allowed her to return to New Orleans providing she did not object to being restored to her worthless husband, whom he also released.[20]

The city at large voiced disgust when Provost Marshal French arrested Mrs. Eugenia Levy Phillips for enjoying a children's party on her balcony and laughing as a funeral procession transporting the remains of Lieutenant George De Kay, who had been shot on board a gunboat by guerrillas, passed unnoticed on the street below. Looking into Mrs. Phillips' antecedents, Butler discovered that aside from being the wife of a former congressman from Alabama, she had been apprehended in Washington for espionage, where her staunch loyalty to the Confederacy was well known. He then discovered that her husband was an influential Jewish lawyer in New Orleans and a personal friend of Judah Benjamin. To blacken her soul further, he remembered her as one of the ladies in James Buchanan's "boudoir cabinet" of traitors. He asked why she was laughing during a funeral, and she coolly replied, "I was in good spirits that day." Butler suggested she apologize for her insensitivity, but she refused, claiming no offense had been intended. The general, she recalled, then flew into a rage and accused her of training her nine children to spit upon Union officers. She also remembered a sign over the general's desk that read, "THERE IS NO DIF-FERENCE BETWEEN A HE AND A SHE ADDER IN THEIR VENOM." For a little merriment and a spatter of benign expectorate, Mrs. Phillips paid a harsh penalty. Butler reduced her social status to "a common . . . bad, and dangerous woman," and for "stirring up strife and inciting to riot" he sent her with the others to Ship Island "until further orders." Mrs. Phillips was allowed to take one servant and permitted to speak only with Fidel Keller or the general.[21]

For reasons unknown, the bookseller asked to be spared Mrs. Phillips' company, and Butler granted his wish. The episode shocked southern-

20. *Butler Correspondence*, II, 57.

21. Special Orders No. 150, 151, June 30, 1862, ORA, XV, 510–11; Walker to Davis, September 13, 1862, ORA, Ser. 2, IV, 881; *Butler Correspondence*, II, 24,

ers. They believed that Keller's refusal to socialize with Mrs. Phillips stemmed from Butler's demotion of her social status to prostitute. Near the close of her diary, sixteen-year-old Clara Solomon lamented Butler's action, as it humiliated the mother of one of her closest friends. She quoted the *Daily Delta* as saying, "It will cause a hullabaloo in certain circles," but what she missed in the equation was Butler's aversion to Jews.[22]

A "hullabaloo" erupted in New Orleans over the incident—partly because no foundation existed for so harsh a penalty and partly because Mrs. Phillips had nine children—but a plot to rescue her died with the unlikelihood of the mission ever succeeding. Efforts continued through diplomatic channels, and on September 14 Butler released Mrs. Phillips on her parole "to give no aid, comfort, or information to the enemy." Nobody praised the general for magnanimously remitting an unfair sentence. Hate festered unabated. Once so gay and active, Julia Le Grand grumbled to her friends, "There is no hope left in me. I do not talk much, but the suppressed life of pain which I lead is enough to kill a stronger person."[23] One of Butler's aides believed that "if the Rebel newspapers had not taunted the General so much," Mrs. Phillips would have been home much sooner.[24]

Fidel Keller, the banished bookseller who refused to socialize with Mrs. Phillips, remained on Ship Island for a few more days. His wife, "a very modest, respectable little woman," made frequent visits to headquarters to appeal the plight of her famished family. Butler would not see her but Captain Puffer did, and his constant lobbying with the general led to her husband's release in early October.[25]

Writing from Ship Island on September 13, Alexander Walker,

36–37; Ashkenazi, ed., *Diary of Clara Solomon*, 429–30; Eugenia Levy Phillips, "A Southern Woman's Story of Her Imprisonment During the War of 1861 and 1862" (manuscript), in Philip Phillips Papers, LC; Philip Phillips, "A Summary of the Principal Events of My Life," in *ibid.*; Parton, *General Butler*, 438–39, 587–88.

22. Special Orders No. 151, June 30, 1862, ORA, XV, 511; Southwood, *"Beauty and Booty,"* 148–49; Ashkenazi, ed., *Diary of Clara Solomon*, 430.

23. Butler's order, September 14, 1862, ORA, Ser. 2, IV, 516; Eugenia Levy Phillips, "A Southern Woman's Story," in Phillips Papers; Rowland and Croxwell, eds., *Journal of Julia Le Grand*, 50.

24. Puffer, "Our General," 108.

25. *Ibid.*, 107–108.

plantation owner, former editor of the New Orleans *Daily Delta,* and one of sixty-some prisoners consigned by Butler to hard labor, expressed his anger in a letter smuggled to Jefferson Davis: "I have thought it my duty at every risk to communicate to you some . . . incidents of the administration of the brutal tyrant who has been sent by the United States Government to oppress, rob, assault and trample upon our people in every manner which the most fiendish ingenuity and most wanton cruelty could devise and in gross violation of all the laws and usages of the most remorseless wars between civilized and even savage nations and tribes." Walker had been arrested for using seditious language, and he attempted to entangle Reverdy Johnson in an investigation of Butler's penal system. Seward's emissary dodged the issue by stating that his mission only involved Butler and the foreign consuls.

Among the prisoners on Ship Island, Walker found an "elderly and weakly" man named Shepherd whose only crime was holding the correspondence of a Confederate naval officer. Dr. Moore, a druggist fastened to a ball and chain, worked at hard labor for smuggling "a few ounces of quinine" through Union lines. For the act of denouncing those who after taking the oath to the South abrogated and swore allegiance to the United States, James Beggs, a New Orleans alderman, worked daily on the island's fortifications. Aside from a few Rebel soldiers who had broken their paroles, many of the prisoners on the island came from the city's elite. George C. Laurason, former collector of customs, suffered arrest when he applied for a passport to go to Europe. Walker also reported that Dr. Charles H. Porter, a wealthy dentist and member of the city council, was "imprisoned for requiring the Citizens' Bank, the pet bank and place of deposit of Butler and his agent in his vast schemes of corruption and extortion, to pay checks in the currency which Butler alone allowed the banks to pay." What Walker meant by extortion pertained to Butler's assessments on certain citizens who had subscribed funds to finance the war. Walker's letter covered dozens of abuses and created great consternation in Richmond. Butler's taxes infuriated the wealthy but contributed to feeding the poor. Others considered the assessment "light," depending upon whether they were among those forced to pay it.[26]

26. Walker to Davis, September 13, 1862, ORA, Ser. 2, IV, 880–85; *Butler Correspondence,* II, 331–32; Alexander Walker, "A Prisoner's Own Story," 3–12, in Louisiana

Not every nonconformist served time. When a shopkeeper refused to sell shoes to a Union soldier, the provost marshal raised a red flag over the store and sold the entire inventory at auction.[27]

Walker's account of Butler's administration was a combination of prejudices and truths. There is no question that the general intended to suppress critics and members of society having sufficient political influence to make trouble. Walker, having been the outspoken editor of the *Daily Delta*, condemned Butler for confiscating the press and making it an organ for his administration. When he protested, Butler sent him to Ship Island, and when he wrote his scathing letter to Davis, he used his writing skills to present the worst possible impression of the general's conduct toward civilians. Johnson's report on Butler's mismanagement of the consuls added credibility to Walker's charges.

Inconsistencies exist between the claims of those imprisoned, who referred to Butler's regime as a reign of terror, and Butler's official records, which convey the impression of a man whose early efforts at conciliation were frustrated by a recalcitrant public led by the elite. Like most contentious issues, the extremes cloud the facts and the truth exists somewhere in the middle. Butler, however, had a personality built upon extremes, and as a self-appointed protector of the masses he could be quite brutal and inconsiderate toward the rich and powerful, whom he blamed for dissolving the Union, starting the war, and challenging his administration. For that, he would make them pay.[28]

Butler also had his differences with the clergy. He found some preachers to be as rabid on the issue of secession as his old friend Pierre Soulé. After denying a day of fasting and prayer at the bidding of Jefferson Davis, Butler tried to let the pulpits conduct services without interference, but secessionists sought the immunity of the sanctuary to preach resistance. When the clergy refused to take the oath of allegiance, Butler did not force it, but when some of them declined to

and Lower Mississippi Valley Collections, Louisiana State University Libraries, Louisiana State University, Baton Rouge; W. M. Geddy to George Moss, September 3, 1862, in George Moss Papers, Record Group 58, Louisiana State Museum, New Orleans.

27. Macartney, *Lincoln and His Generals*, 56.

28. Carpenter, *History of the Eighth Vermont*, 44; *Butler Correspondence*, I, 476; Dabney, "The Butler Regime in Louisiana," 500–504.

include the president of the United States in their weekly blessings, his staff made the rounds and gathered the names of the offenders.[29]

At Sunday service in the Episcopal church across from General Twiggs's home, Major Strong took a seat in the front pew. When the president's prayer was omitted, he stopped the proceedings and ordered the church closed. The general invited the noncomplying pastors to headquarters and learned that in place of the required prayer, attendees received a few minutes of silence to pray for whatever they wished, including the "triumph of treason."[30]

Three of the biggest offenders, the Reverends W. T. Leacock, William Fulton, and Charles Goodrich, confessed that their orders came from the Right Reverend Major General Leonidas Polk, their ecclesiastical superior, who claimed religious immunity from Butler's unholy enactments. Leacock lectured the general, accusing him of "eating up God's people, as it were bread. You have possessed them with such fear, that they are rushing, innocent and weak women . . . guiltless and timid men, most ingloriously . . . to their destruction, through fear of being deprived of their substance or of their personal liberty. . . . The law under which you act does not call for this universal wickedness," Leacock argued. He then protested against the oath of allegiance, declaring that it would force half of his congregation to perjure themselves.

Amused by the statement, Butler replied, "If that is the result of your nine years of preaching; if your people will commit perjury so freely, the sooner you leave your pulpit the better."

Stunned by the general's remark, Leacock replied scornfully, "You elevate your will above the law for people to bow down and obey; and in their obedience they deny God and rush into the arms of Satan— and whose is the sin?"

Butler ignored the implication that the sin was his, but he would not tolerate having his supremacy challenged.

At length Leacock asked, "Well, general, are you going to shut down the churches?"

29. General Orders No. 27, May 13, 1862, ORA, XV, 426.

30. Parton, *General Butler*, 482–83; James Earl Bradley Diary, October 1, 1862, in James Earl Bradley Papers, Special Collections, Hill Library, Louisiana State University Libraries, Louisiana State University, Baton Rouge.

"No," Butler replied, "I am more likely to shut up the ministers," and he did.

He denied General Polk's claim of precedence and shipped Leacock, Fulton, and Goodrich to Fort Lafayette, the military prison in New York, "so that they will at least be out of mischief during the remainder of the war." Marion Southwood called the Beast's skirmish with the clergy the "Battle of St. Paul's," but the trio had been flies in Butler's ointment for six months before the general lost patience and sent them north, filling their vacancies with army chaplains. Miss Southwood thought it strange when Reverend Hodges' church burned to the ground "accidentally" one windy night, and she could not shake the notion that Butler's firebrands had started it.[31]

There were exceptions. Father James Ignatius Mullen of St. Patrick's Church defied Butler with such spirit that the general permitted the fierce little Irishman to conduct his services as he wished. He declared the seventy-year-old priest the bravest man he had ever met. Butler liked the Irish. Back home they brought him votes.[32]

On October 31 Reverend F. E. R. Chubbock, Butler's post chaplain, entered Christ Church on Canal Street with orders from the general to obtain the keys to the buildings. Chubbock declared the pews "free" and asked permission of Charles L. Harrod, the senior warden, for use of the church plate on Communion Sunday. Harrod agreed, and for a year Chubbock returned the plate immediately following the service—and then it disappeared with Chubbock. The church blamed Butler, who left the department before the plate vanished. On July 15, 1865, Christ Church reverted to the parish, but the silver plate and a massive and elegantly carved oak pulpit were still missing. The general received the blame because by his order Christ Church had been seized. Harrod learned later that Chubbock never received an order to

31. Butler to Stanton, October 25, 1862, *ORA*, Ser. 2, IV, 650; W. T. Leacock to Butler September 26, 1862, Butler Papers, LC; Southwood, *"Beauty and Booty,"* 111, 114; Parton, *General Butler*, 481–85; *Butler Correspondence*, II, 407–408; Bland, *Life of Butler*, 130; Helen Gray, "The Three Clergymen of New Orleans and Gen. Benjamin F. Butler," in Suzanne Hiller Herrick Papers, Howard-Tilton Library, Tulane University, New Orleans.

32. Baudier, *Catholic Church in Louisiana*, 422.

remove any of the property and suspected that the chaplain had shipped it to Massachusetts for his own use.[33]

Typical of a seasoned politician, to those who cooperated or refrained from challenging his authority Butler demonstrated unusual acts of kindness. Catholics obeyed his edicts and functioned harmoniously under his administration. Nuns—Butler called them "delicately nurtured holy women"—often passed through camps "scattering blessings in their path" and ministering to the wounded and dying. He provisioned their orphanages, repaired damages to their churches, and extended whatever charitable assistance they required to sustain their schools, hospitals, and asylums. When public funds ran low, he dug into his own deep pockets and donated five hundred dollars to the orphans at St. Elizabeth. It was like reaching out to the farm girls who once worked at the mills and lived in his mother's boardinghouse.[34]

Butler also showed kindness to secessionists who supported the rebellion but conducted their affairs in a respectful manner. When Mrs. Cora Slocomb applied for a pass to take her daughter to their country home in North Carolina, Butler interviewed her and learned she had equipped from her private purse Louisiana's famous Washington Artillery, among the crack artillery units serving the South. One of the first acts of the Confederate congress had been to confiscate all debts due northern creditors and make them payable to the Confederate treasury. When Butler discovered that Mrs. Slocomb felt honor bound to pay the debts of her deceased husband to a northern ironmaker, he became interested in her plight. She had even attempted to send a shipment of cotton in payment of the debt, but Confederate authorities stopped the vessel and detained it at New Orleans.[35]

Butler agreed to give the ladies a pass if they would take the oath of allegiance. Mrs. Slocomb declined, explaining that her son and son-in-law were officers in the Washington Artillery and it would defy

33. Charles L. Harrod, "Christ Church and General Butler," *Louisiana Historical Quarterly*, XXIII (October, 1940), 1241–57; Charles L. Harrod Journal, October 31, 1862, and *passim*, in Howard-Tilton Library, Tulane University, New Orleans.

34. Santa Maria Clara to Butler, September 2, 1862, in Butler Papers, LC; Parton, *General Butler*, 320–21.

35. *Butler's Book*, 423; Boatner, *Civil War Dictionary*, 893.

them if she did so. Butler understood and as an alternative asked if she would give up her spacious townhouse for his use if he granted her a pass. She said she could not, that her house was "endeared to her by a thousand tender associations, and was now dearer to her than ever." There was something about Mrs. Slocomb that may have reminded Butler of his mother. She was frank without being brusque or impolite. He granted the pass, promising that her home would not be occupied unless the city fell to the ravages of yellow fever.[36] From Mrs. Slocomb, Butler received a rare note of appreciation:

> Permit me to return my sincere thanks for the special permit to leave, which you so kindly granted to myself and family, as also for the protection promised to my property.
>
> Knowing that we have no claim for any exception in our favor, this generous act calls loudly upon our grateful hearts; and hereafter, while praying earnestly for the cause we love so much, we shall never forget the liberality with which our request has been granted by one whose power here reminds us painfully that our enemies are more magnanimous than our citizens are brave.[37]

Butler considered the deplorable condition of the poor the most serious problem facing his administration. He blamed their destitution partly on the southern army, which carried away the available food supply, but he blamed the war entirely on the rich. More than eleven thousand bales of cotton had been burned along with millions of dollars in property, more than enough to feed all of Louisiana.[38]

He also discovered that a committee composed of city council members acted as trustees of the Touro fund, a large sum of money left by its donor for the support of orphans. Instead of allocating the money to the needs of children, they outraged their trust by diverting large sums for the purchase of munitions. Butler brought them under guard to headquarters, used choice words to articulate his contempt, and sent them all to Fort Pickens until such time as "every cent of the money they had so wantonly diverted" had been repaid.[39]

36. *Butler Correspondence*, II, 1; *Butler's Book*, 424–25.
37. *Butler Correspondence*, I, 631.
38. Sandburg, *Abraham Lincoln*, I, 475.
39. Puffer, "Our General," 113–14.

His idea of a special tax on the upper class translated into salvation for the poor, and it brought him immense support among the lower classes. The problem of feeding and clothing the poor had increased daily by the continuous flood of fugitive slaves crossing Union lines and straggling into the city—men, women, and children, all hungry and looking for work. At first Butler returned the runaways to their masters, but on they came, settling around camps or squeezing into the city—thousands more mouths to feed. To contend with the swelling crisis, Butler issued orders on July 2 calling for the appointment of a superintendent and an assistant to cope with the burgeoning problem. He repeatedly attempted to make work for the unemployed, and when this proved only partly successful, he conceived the idea of assessing funds from leading secessionists.[40]

Determining whom to tax led Butler directly to documents produced by the Committee of Public Safety and to a list of cotton brokers printed in an October edition of the New Orleans *Crescent.* Taking every name listed, Butler levied a special tax equaling 25 percent of their subscription to the Committee of Public Safety and a flat fee ranging from one hundred to five hundred dollars on cotton brokers for "advising planters not to send produce to New Orleans, in order to induce foreign intervention in behalf of the rebellion." Calling such acts "treasonable," he designated August 11 as the final day of collection and threatened to seize the property of the delinquents, sell it at auction, and imprison the taxpayers until the assessment was paid. Butler justified the scheme by appealing to the popular belief that firing on Fort Sumter had produced a rich man's war but a poor man's fight. The general raised $300,000, spent it, and on December 9, 1862, reinstated the order and initiated a second collection.[41]

Though dozens of foreigners had subscribed to the Committee of Public Safety's defense fund or acted as cotton brokers, they did not feel obliged to pay Butler's tax. They naturally protested through channels, but the general remained adamant. When the French and Prus-

40. *Butler Correspondence*, I, 514, 554–55, 564, II, 30–31; Winters, *Civil War in Louisiana*, 143; Johnson, "New Orleans Under General Butler," 472–74.

41. General Orders No. 55, August 4, 1862, ORA, XV, 538–41; *Butler Correspondence*, II, 152–53; *Butler's Book*, 436; New Orleans *Daily Picayune*, December 12, 1862; Southwood, *"Beauty and Booty,"* 95.

sian consuls complained, he reminded them that members of the firms assessed were officers in the Rebel army who had taken the oath of the Confederacy and could not claim immunity. He also produced a document showing that more than 80 percent of the ten thousand families receiving aid were foreigners, the others being either American or black. At one point, as many as 32,450 "souls" were fed daily, and Butler put many to work as fast as he could find jobs for them.[42]

In early June, the general ordered Shepley and his probational city council to make jobs for the poor, paying them fifty cents a day plus regular army rations for cleaning the streets and all public places. Later he increased the pay to a dollar a day. That did not satisfy members of the council, who now wished to reingratiate themselves with the public. They passed a resolution spurning Butler's dollar with the claim that when they ran city government, laborers received $1.50 a day. Butler accepted the mild rebuke and declared that "in administering the affairs of the city, to be paid for by its tax, I thought I ought to be economical; but as that was to be paid for by taxation of the city, and the city government wanted to pay fifty cents more, I would raise the price to one dollar and fifty cents, although plenty of good labor had been employed at a dollar a day." On June 18 the city surveyor, the controller, and the treasurer resigned and sent the keys for their offices to General Shepley. Tired of bickering with the council, Shepley dissolved it, supplanting it with a bureau of finance under Edward H. Durell and a bureau of streets and landings under Julian Neville. He then announced that self-government would be restored as soon as the city demonstrated a willingness to obey the laws of the United States. In the interim, the acts of municipal government would be subject to the inclinations of the commanding general.[43]

By midsummer New Orleans had never been cleaner, and the city

---

42. Treilhard to Seward, August 29, Butler to Stanton, October [?], 1862, ORA, Ser. 3, II, 567–68, 720–25, 731.

43. *Butler Correspondence*, I, 554–55; *Butler's Book*, 429; New Orleans *Daily Picayune*, June 6, 28, 1862; Johnson, "New Orleans Under General Butler," 499–500; Toxie L. Bush, "The Federal Occupation of New Orleans" (M.A. thesis, 1934), in the Louisiana and Lower Mississippi Valley Collections, Louisiana State University Libraries, Louisiana State University, Baton Rouge. This form of government continued until March, 1865. See also Kendall, *History of New Orleans*, I, 282–83.

reported only two cases of yellow fever—imported from Nassau by sailors who slipped by the quarantine station near the mouth of the river. A break in the levee had been repaired, and on a daily schedule the streets were swept and shoveled clean, the gutters flushed, and the drainage canals purged of sewage. Marion Southwood, who hated Butler with a passion, had to admit that he was the "best scavenger they ever had." All this favorable news did not relieve the diplomatic strain on Seward, although the Battle of Antietam had just been fought and the legions of General Robert E. Lee had been driven out of Maryland.[44]

Butler, however, could not keep himself out of mischief. Seeds of corruption took root and spread at a frenetic pace, and for a man with a larcenous mind, the opportunities to turn a profit seemed limitless.

44. *Butler's Book*, 408; Southwood, *"Beauty and Booty,"* 182.

10

The Brothers Butler

NOBODY EVER QUESTIONED Butler's ability to make money.
He had taken leave from his law practice but not his investments.
From Boston, Richard S. Fay, Jr., wrote: "The Middlesex [Mills] flour-
ishes wonderfully. I think we must pay 10% this 6 months in spite of
all I can do to keep down the profit and loss account." The general
undoubtedly welcomed the news, but the dividends represented a pittance compared with the mother lode at New Orleans.[1]

On July 17 President Lincoln signed a second act expanding the
rights of the military to confiscate the property of rebellious citizens.
When it passed, Butler was already several weeks ahead of the act in
terms of his own confiscations. He had taken the home of General
Twiggs for his personal use and the adjacent home of Colonel Daniel
Adams to house General Shepley. He ordered the property of John
Slidell, the Confederate commissioner to France, confiscated and
made it available to members of his staff. Rowena Florence, a young
lady occupying the Twiggs home, claimed ownership of the deceased
general's swords and a box of family silver. Butler dismissed the
woman's claim, sent the swords to President Lincoln, but retained the
silver. Creoles noted the action with disdain, clamoring that the general stole not only weapons but also spoons. His enemies embellished
the tale when he then confiscated the silver plate of a Frenchman
named A. Villeneuve, and the acts led to the legend of "Spoons Butler." The general eventually purchased Twiggs's silver and sent it to his
mother, but transactions of this sort went unnoticed by the public. As

1. *Butler Correspondence*, I, 465. Fay had functioned as one of Butler's aides earlier in the war.

far as they were concerned it was not necessary for a man of Butler's wealth to steal anybody's spoons.[2]

In April, while the general was still on Ship Island, he had privately acquired cotton and turpentine worth about five thousand dollars, loaded it on a transport as "ballast," and shipped it to Richard Fay, his agent in Boston, with instructions to sell it. Captain William W. McKim, assistant quartermaster at Boston, could not see how the cargo could be the property of Butler if it had been transported on a government vessel. Caught in a small swindle, the general maintained that his purchases helped to restore confidence among the planters and factors while saving the government the expense of ballasting the vessels. Before Fay could resolve the issue with the government, a shipment of cotton and sugar arrived on another transport. Quartermaster Meigs authorized Fay to auction the goods, pay Butler's expenses, and deposit the balance to the credit of the Treasury Department. He mildly censured Butler, and the War Department halted the practice, circumspectly writing, "General Butler's action . . . has evidently been wise and patriotic. He has incurred much responsibility, and ought to be protected. At the same time, as a public officer, he ought not to be involved in private trade and profits arising out of his official power and position." Treasury Secretary Chase warned, "Be on your guard . . . against the appearance of evil." Subsequent shipments arrived under clear title to the government, but the general's reputation had been tarnished, compelling him to find other ways to turn a profit.[3]

Two months elapsed before Stanton resolved the matter of the captured cotton, and by then the commanding general had mastered the fine art of conversion. Under the broad powers of the Confiscation Act, Butler could attach property under the guise of legality and through multiple transactions skim from the proceeds by using his staff

2. *Ibid.*, II, 393, III, 531–33; Parton, *General Butler*, 467–68, 615; Basler, ed., *Collected Works of Abraham Lincoln*, V, 552–53; Orcutt, "Ben Butler and the 'Stolen Spoons,'" 67–72; Bush, "The Federal Occupation of New Orleans," 112; After the war, the swords were returned to Twiggs's daughter, *Butler's Book*, 568n.

3. Chase to Butler, June 24, 1862, John Niven, ed., *The Salmon P. Chase Papers* (3 vols.; Kent, Ohio, 1993–96), III, 218; *Butler Correspondence*, I, 445–47, 465–66, 533–34, 579–80, 612–13, 628, 632, 634–35; *Butler's Book*, 483–84.

of co-conspirators. He also issued permits for trade within Confederate lines, and he was well positioned to use his authority corruptly. Persons applying for passes at times offered as much as three thousand dollars to get one, and though nobody ever admitted taking a bribe, the temptation must have been compelling.

Nowhere could profits be reaped faster than among the planters in enemy territory. Because of the Confederate government's cotton boycott, the commodity had become virtually worthless in the South but in high demand everywhere else. Sugar sold for three cents a pound in New Orleans but for six cents in New York. Turpentine brought thirty-eight dollars a barrel in the North but could be bought for three dollars on the Mississippi, while flour, which could be bought for six dollars a barrel in the Northeast, cost twice as much in New Orleans. In New York, dry goods could be purchased at prewar prices and sold for several times their cost in the Crescent City, and with a monetary exchange advantage as high as 15 percent. A speculator could not lose, and for a man of Butler's multiple talents, marvelous opportunities existed to make money at both ends. Governor Moore reacted by announcing that any person found with a Butler pass would be hanged instantly without trial. Since many of Butler's permits were for humanitarian purposes, Moore disregarded the woes of the starving populace when he issued his edict.[4]

Deceit and rapacity flourished at all levels, though most of the confiscations were cloaked with legitimacy. Whenever headquarters issued a pass it listed the articles to be carried through the lines, and the applicant pledged to transport nothing else and to apply the articles for only the use specified. Nobody, however, crossed Union lines without being searched. Inspectors examined every box, trunk, container, and boat. Permits were abused because secessionists did not consider it dishonorable to lie to a Union officer. A lady begging for a pass to take a barrel of flour across the lake to her "starving children" concealed a packet of quinine in the middle. Inspectors found trunks with false bottoms, percussion caps secreted in barrels of potatoes, and

4. *Butler's Book*, 385; Parton, *General Butler*, 411, 486; Dabney, "The Butler Regime in Louisiana," 491–92; Johnson, "New Orleans Under General Butler," 482–83.

letters containing military intelligence hidden in shoes and clothing, but these were mild transgressions compared with the organized efforts of the general's agents.[5]

One "agent," Andrew Jackson Butler, had followed his brother to Ship Island and then accompanied him to New Orleans. Everyone called him "Colonel," but he lost that distinction because the Senate denied his commission. When General Butler took command of New Orleans, he lost no time in employing Andrew—"jovial, fat, and shrewd "—who was under no military restraints other than those imposed by brother Ben. Andrew had a little of his own money for speculation, but he also had the wealth of his brother for operations well beyond the scope of the general's rather liberal prerogatives. Early in Butler's administration Andrew obtained passes through Union lines, entered Confederate Texas, and brought back a herd of cattle to ostensibly feed the poor. There is no record of what Andrew paid for the beef, but the method Butler used to recover from the government was to forward the invoice to Boston, have his agent apply a generous markup, and pass the bill to the quartermaster for payment.[6]

Brother Andrew did not have to travel far to make money, and what part collusion played is obscure, but it looked bad when the general issued orders forbidding the sale of liquor because General Phelps could not keep his men from getting drunk after payday. Andrew went from store to store buying up all the intoxicants at reduced prices, and when he had the market cornered, the general lifted the ban. The "Colonel," who could be a tough negotiator when it came to money, sold every drop back at a huge profit. Mrs. Butler may have had more insight into her brother-in-law's manipulations than her husband's when she wrote a friend, "I am a little afraid people will think the General is speculating from [Andrew's] being engaged in it. But he will go north as soon as he exchanges his freight for cotton, sugar, etc. I am glad of it." But Andrew did not go north—not for many months.[7]

5. Parton, *General Butler*, 486–88.

6. *Butler Correspondence*, I, 360; Parton, *General Butler*, 303; Henry Warren Howe, *Passages from the Life of Henry Warren Howe, Consisting of Diary and Letters Written During the Civil War, 1861–1865* (Lowell, Mass., 1899), 128–29.

7. Porter, "Journal of Occurrences," 371; *Butler Correspondence*, I, 489.

When the general learned the blockade would be lifted on June 1, he dispatched Andrew to purchase $60,000 in ground sugar packed in hogsheads. Butler admitted that he had "no right to buy this property with the money of the United States, even if I had any of it, which I have not. But I have bought it with my own money and upon my individual credit." The statement was partially true. Butler borrowed $100,000 from banker Jacob Barker, bought the sugar, and reserved $40,000 for other acquisitions. The general must have anticipated great returns, otherwise he would not have pledged all his assets—$150,000—against the loan. In his communication to Stanton, Butler excluded any reference to his brother, who acted as the general's front man on every purchase and pocketed an extra five dollars per hogs-head as a freight-handling charge. When Butler later learned that his purchases—made, he said, for purely patriotic reasons—were not winning the approbation of Washington, he discontinued the advisories but not the practice. Contrary to Butler's assertion that the sugar purchase had "gone very far to assure the planters and factors" of a fair price, Andrew had acquired it for a pittance, admitting that he had gotten back his investment after the first twelve days of grinding. In July the general complained to Reverdy Johnson that "these deluded people" still believed that their crops would be confiscated when they reached New Orleans. Had he been serious in seeking the source of this distrust, he would not have found reason to search beyond his brother.[8]

Goods began to flow into the Crescent City from northern ports, and how much money Andrew collected from the trade may never be known. Vessels once again began to tie to the wharves, and on June 8 the first cargoes of ice arrived. Compared with prewar years, when steamboats lined the levee five deep and the masts of high seas traders rose like a forest above the great river, the charred warehouses and the occasional arrival of a few steamers made the waterfront a picture of near desolation, but trade was improving.[9]

Andrew's multiple monopolistic business ventures probably did

8. *Butler Correspondence*, I, 490–95, 612–13, II, 94; Butler to Stanton, May 16, 1862, ORA, XV, 423; *Butler's Book*, 384; Parton, *General Butler*, 407–409.

9. Dabney, "The Butler Regime in Louisiana," 507.

more to retard the revival of the city's stores than brother Ben's proclamations. In mid-September, when prices stabilized and employment improved, a great number of stores and offices remained closed, their names blacked out as if they were "in mourning." In November, a reporter for the *Daily Picayune* wrote sadly, "Old times and old arrangements have passed away. . . . A few have been enriched, but tens of thousands have been ruined." Auvignac Dorville, a French merchant living in New Orleans, referred to "the lowly position" of the city's residents and grumbled about his inability to buy cotton and ship it to France.[10]

For the Butler brothers, Lincoln's signing of the second Confiscation Act created new opportunities for enrichment. Property belonging to Confederate civil or military officers could be confiscated upon detection and without restraint. Every Confederate soldier had sixty days to lay down his arms and swear allegiance to the United States. Dissident civilians received the same terms, and in September, when Butler induced all people to register their names, occupations, and property with the provost marshal, some four thousand persons refused to take the oath of allegiance and received certificates branding them as "registered enemies" of the United States. Once they were identified, Butler exiled them. He permitted them to cross through enemy lines with personal clothing and not more than fifty dollars, and he banned them from returning to the department. He then sequestered the property of soldiers fighting for the Confederacy and the remaining property of those whom he banished, selling it at auction at a fraction of its value.[11]

When William Newton Mercer of 144 Canal Street felt unobliged to take the oath, he wrote Butler claiming the right to retain some three thousand dollars in gold because he had "maintained strict neu-

10. New Orleans *Daily Picayune*, September 18, November 6, 1862, quoted in Johnson, "New Orleans Under General Butler," 483; Auvignac Dorville to Anatole de Ste. Gême, August 12, September 1, 1862, in Dorville Papers, Mss 100, Folders 394, 395.

11. General Orders No. 71, September 13, General Orders No. 76, September 24, 1862, ORA, XV, 571, 575–76; Parton, *General Butler*, 467–68; Wickham Hoffman to Hamilton Fish, September 30, 1862, in Hamilton Fish Papers, LC; Winters, *Civil War in Louisiana*, 140, 142; New Orleans *Daily Picayune*, August 16, 1862.

trality." Butler replied, "There is no such thing as neutrality by a citizen of the United States," demanding that Mercer choose between being a friend or an enemy. Butler forced Mercer, like so many others, to make a choice, and most of them, to protect their wealth, did so. Those who refused found their banking privileges denied.[12]

Andrew added his own interpretation to the Confiscation Act when he circulated among the sugar growers advising them that they could no longer take off their crop without his permission, and if they did, General Butler would seize it. To do the work, Andrew hired two New Orleans firms who employed only white laborers. After the Butlers departed from New Orleans, growers came forth with horror stories of how Andrew's agents, acting on behalf of the general, had entered plantation homes and stripped them clean. One angry grower, Frank Webb, claimed the marauders took his wife's wardrobe and jewels and drove off all the blacks. These actions were contrary to Butler's standing orders, but the promulgation of the July Confiscation Act expanded the prerogatives of the military to plunder private property.[13]

Having achieved great success from his local ventures, Andrew began importing northern flour soon after the blockade lifted, selling it at a huge profit. He soon acquired a monopoly on all imported groceries, medicines, and staples, and because he controlled flour, brother Ben made it possible for him to seize and operate the city bakery. As one lady observed, both Butlers colluded in wresting certain enterprises from the owners, but Andrew, who was not encumbered by official position, became the front man.

Persons seeking special favors from the general had a greater likelihood of success if they first spoke to Andrew, who charged a handsome "fee" for discouraging his brother from confiscating their property. If the general imprisoned a person of importance, Andrew could get him released if the money was right. When the general learned that the government disapproved of his method of ballasting government vessels with commodities purchased on his own account, he shifted the

12. Mercer to Butler, September 26, Butler to Mercer, September 27, and Butler Circular to the Bank of New Orleans, October 4, 1862, in William Newton Mercer Papers, Special Collections, Hill Library, Louisiana State University Libraries, Louisiana State University, Baton Rouge.

13. Mulford *et al.* to Benjamin, December 23, 26, 1862, ORA, Ser. 2, V, 792; *Butler Correspondence*, I, 634–35; *Butler's Book*, 383–85.

practice to his brother. Andrew's methods were much sharper. When sugar and cotton seized by Union troops found its way into New Orleans, the "Colonel" bought it at auction at a ridiculous price, shipped it to New York, and sold it for three or four times his cost. The general transferred Andrew's payment for the cotton to the government account, and the Butlers got the price paid at New York. An even more insidious occupation involved Andrew's share of the profits gleaned from smuggling medicines and supplies through Union lines and into the Confederacy, an act punishable by ten years at hard labor if committed by a secessionist.[14]

These surreptitious operations did not go unnoticed. Commander Porter, who in mid-June attempted to bring his mortar flotilla to Farragut's aid at Vicksburg, encountered difficulty in getting his vessels to New Orleans because Butler failed to provide the promised towboats. Part of the problem involved Andrew, who operated nine steamers intended for military use. Escorted by Union infantry and operating under the general's permits, the sole mission of these vessels was to collect medicine, salt, cotton, and sugar and transport it to New Orleans for auction. "This service," wrote George Denison from New Orleans, "[is] unpopular with officers and men, who enlisted for the benefit of the country and not of speculators." When title passed to Andrew, he loaded everything on steamers and sent them to New York or Boston. This contributed to the congestion in the river, and the captain at Fort Jackson in charge of managing the towboats took his orders from Butler. "I don't hesitate to say that there has been a deliberate attempt made to deceive and trifle with me," Porter reported as he waited for towboats below. He noted that many of the vessels were those captured by the navy and turned over to Butler. "We have traitors enough to fight against," complained Porter, "without finding them holding office under our Government at posts of honor which have for the moment become so lucrative that the holders thereof fear to miss the golden opportunity, and intend to make hay while the sun shines."[15]

In late June, Secretary of the Treasury Chase, one of Butler's close

---

14. Porter, "Journal of Occurrences," 372; Velazquez, *The Woman in Battle*, 242; Parton, *General Butler*, 411; Winters, *Civil War in Louisiana*, 138.

15. Porter to Farragut, June 16, 1862, ORN, XVIII, 559; Chase, *Diary and Correspondence*, 321–22.

friends, warned him that a "discordant note" had circulated within the department that "you were availing yourself of your military command to engage in mercantile speculation." Chase assured the general that he doubted the rumor but was sending two special agents— George Denison, another friend of Butler's, and M. F. Bonzano—to help with "your arduous duties." Denison, collector of customs, arrived in early July, found the city in starving condition, and soon discovered that everybody from government officers down to "rebels" recognized Andrew Butler as a "partner or agent" of the general. Referring to the fraudulent "Colonel," Denison wrote: "He does a heavy business and by various practices has made between one and two million dollars since the capture of the City. Gov. Shepley and especially Col. French (Provost Marshal) are supposed to be interested, but these officers, I believe to be entirely under the control of Gen'l Butler, who knows everything, controls everything, and should be held responsible for everything."[16]

Denison worried about appearances, especially in regard to his friend the general. On August 26 he warned Chase that "[Andrew Butler] is not a government employee. He is here for the sole purpose of making money. . . . I regret his being here at all, for it is not proper that a brother of the commanding general, should devote himself to such an object. It leads to the belief that the General himself is interested with him, and such is the belief of our enemies and some of our friends."[17]

By coincidence, as Denison was writing the Treasury Department, the general was writing his wife in praise of his brother. "Andrew is shipping Fisher some thousand hogsheads of sugar. It will be of prime quality and will pay, he thinks." The very next day he wrote her again: "Andrew is shipping much larger amounts of sugar to Fisher than I supposed." From the letters it appeared that the Butlers may have also entered the shipping business, as Fisher's vessel had "not yet arrived here."[18]

---

16. *Butler Correspondence*, I, 632–34; Chase to Butler, June 24, 1862, ORA, Ser. 3, II, 173–74; Chase, *Diary and Correspondence*, 321; Denison to his mother, July 6, 1862, in George S. Denison Papers, II, LC. See also Niven, ed., *Chase Papers*, III, 218–19.

17. Chase, *Diary and Correspondence*, 312.

18. *Butler Correspondence*, II, 234, 236.

Word of Butler's infamy spread to Richmond, where John B. Jones, a clerk in the war office, noted, "[Governor Pettus of Mississippi] says he don't know that he has received the consent of 'Butler, the Beast' (but he knows the trade is impossible without it)." On November 10 he added, "Is it not certain that 'Butler, the Beast,' is a party to the speculation?" The South already knew what the North did not want to admit. "Butler is preparing to do a great business," Jones wrote, "and no objection to the illicit traffic is filed by the [Union] Secretaries of State or Treasury."[19]

Denison's infatuation with Butler soon began to waver. On Lake Pontchartrain he discovered a smuggling operation and directed a customs inspector to seize an offending schooner laden with 1,000 sacks of salt. Denison then advised Butler, who acted indignant that someone would be carrying salt to the Rebels. Later in the day the Treasury agent learned from the provost marshal that Butler had released the vessel, calling the detention a mistake because the captain and the shipper carried a permit from the general. Denison protested because Butler did not have the authority to release customs seizures, but by then it was too late. He later learned that 600 sacks, costing $2 each, had been carried across the lake—400 were sold to the Confederate army at $25 a sack and 200 were sold to civilians for $36 a sack. The owners cleared $6,000, but Denison did not discover their names until later. By October some 10,000 sacks of salt had made the trip across the lake. Quite by accident, the 9th Connecticut's surgeon, George W. Avery, remained behind enemy lines to care for some wounded men and noticed a pile of sacks waiting by the railroad. He asked a Confederate officer what they were. "We bought that salt from Col. Butler," the officer replied. "We paid $5. per sack for the privilege of shipment from New Orleans. To-day that salt goes to Richmond for the army. To-morrow or the next day another cargo will arrive. . . . The Yankees 'will do anything for money.'"

Denison discovered that Shepley issued the passes on General Butler's demand, but he began to suspect that every transaction originated through the bogus "Colonel." Soon after Captain Charles H. Cornwell

---

19. John Beauchamp Jones, *A Rebel War Clerk's Diary* (2 vols.; Philadelphia, 1866), I, 185, 187, 189.

of the 13th Connecticut took his company to New Canal for three weeks of picket duty, he detained a number of schooners crossing the lake laden with medicines and other contraband. He sent Lieutenant John C. Kinney of the 3rd Connecticut to headquarters for instructions. "Go to Governor Shepley," Butler said, "and ask him if he does not *know* that these articles will go right into the hands of the enemy." Kinney located Shepley, who replied, "Return to Gen. Butler and say I consulted *him* before giving this permit." The lieutenant repeated the conversation to Butler, who simply shrugged and said, "Well, let it go, since Governor S[hepley] has granted a permit." A few days later Cornwell discovered more violations and sent another messenger to headquarters. The courier returned with Butler's endorsement scratched on the back—"Gov. Shepley's passes *must* be respected." Denison reported the matter to Chase, commenting glumly, "Captain Cornwell now wants to go home."[20]

On the heels of Denison's reports, Commander Porter returned to Washington after a brief stop at New Orleans and warned Assistant Secretary of the Navy Fox:

> The people of New Orleans are eminently disgusted with Butler rule (and I think they have reason) and will kick out the traces the first chance they get. There is not a Union man from the mouth of the Mississippi to Vicksburg. . . . New Orleans will either be in the hands of the rebels in 40 days, or it will be burnt. Rest assured of that unless another man is sent in Butler's place. [The people] are great fools for not wishing to keep him there, as he is supplying the Rebels with all they want by way of the Pearl River (Salt, Shoes, Blankets, Flour, etc.) for which he charges license, which goes, God knows where![21]

The continuous flow of trade across Lake Pontchartrain annoyed Denison, but he had no authority to stop it. Don D. Goicouria, a speculator from New York, arrived at New Orleans in June and secured a permit from Shepley. In four months he turned a profit of $200,000 by acting as an intermediary between General Butler and Judah Benjamin to exchange ten sacks of salt with the enemy for one bale of cotton. Denison noted that two hundred bales of cotton had been recently

20. Chase, *Diary and Correspondence*, 322–25.
21. *Fox Correspondence*, II, 125.

collected for shipment north. He also learned from Goicouria that "Colonel" Butler had bragged of sending eight thousand hogsheads of sugar to New York, pocketing between $800,000 and $900,000.[22]

By September Denison felt manipulated. On several occasions he questioned the practice of trading with the enemy, only to be told by Butler that "it *was the policy of the Gov't* to get cotton shipped from this port." Denison assumed the instructions came from Washington, but Chase gave him no confirmation. Butler's only authority seemed to have come from Reverdy Johnson, who on one occasion—and only one—suggested that it would be proper to exchange salt with an English cotton dealer in Mobile providing the cotton went to England to the account of the United States. Johnson's advice was incredibly bad, but Butler used it to his advantage. The general's flow of special orders and his liberal policy of issuing permits all benefited brother Andrew, enabling brother Ben to continue his trading by proxy. But Denison, in spite of his suspicions, admitted that he could not "discover any good proof that Gen. Butler has improperly done, or permitted, anything for his own personal advantage. He is such a *smart* man, that it would in any case, be difficult to discover what he wished to conceal."[23]

Denison tried again to convince Butler that trading with the enemy was degrading the character of the government, demoralizing the army, and disgusting loyal citizens. Butler listened to the argument, agreed halfheartedly that it "ought to be stopped," and said he "didn't see why Shepley granted such permits." Butler departed for a visit to Ship Island and promised to discuss the matter when he returned. A week passed before Denison met with Butler and Shepley. Both officers promised to stop the trade providing Denison allowed two more vessels to cross the lake. The Treasury agent agreed, and with his faith in the commanding general restored, he wrote Chase, "Gen. B[utler] has more brains and energy than any other three men in New Orleans. He does an immense amount of work, and does it well"— which demonstrates the ease with which Butler could hoodwink his friends.[24]

22. Chase, *Diary and Correspondence*, 324.
23. *Ibid.*, 313, 322, 325; *Butler Correspondence*, II, 120–21.
24. Chase, *Diary and Correspondence*, 325, 327.

With Denison looking over his shoulder, the general turned to other equally profitable pursuits, again covering his schemes by using his brother and other cooperative speculators. For the Butlers, the Confiscation Act created a marvelous opportunity for broadening their operations, and on September 24, as provided by Congress, the general began confiscations in earnest, sequestering the property of Confederate officers and the four thousand "registered enemies" residing in the department. When that well went dry, Federal troops under General Weitzel entered Bayou Lafourche and captured the rich plantation lands west of the Mississippi. Butler quickly established the District of Lafourche and assigned Weitzel to the area, with Captain Truman K. Fuller, provost marshal, Major Joseph M. Bell, provost judge, and Lieutenant Colonel Kinsman, Butler's personal aide, who well understood the general's objectives. Weitzel's mission was to identify the "disloyal" citizens and separate them from their property. He delegated the work to Kinsman, and in six weeks more than a million dollars in property passed over the auction block at New Orleans. Denison noted that the proceeds were deposited to the credit of the United States, but he made no mention of what or how much was bought by Andrew Butler.[25]

The "Colonel" then infiltrated the Lafourche with a few speculators and operated with customary autonomy. The general used various methods to cover his brother's dealings, and in the Lafourche, Colonel James W. McMillan of the 21st Indiana worked for Andrew and acted as military attaché. McMillan was also a key player in the salt traffic, fronting for Andrew, and whenever he encountered resistance the "Colonel" would usually find a way for his brother to remove the obstruction. As one observer noted, the auctions in New Orleans were often rigged, enabling Andrew to purchase sugar and cotton at absurdly low prices.[26]

25. Butler's Report, October 24, Weitzel's Report, October 25, 29, General Orders No. 76, September 24, General Orders No. 91, November 9, 1862, *ORA*, XV, 158–60, 166–70, 575–76, 595–94; Chase, *Diary and Correspondence*, 329–30; *Butler's Book*, 521–22; George Denison to James Denison, November 14, 1862, in Denison Papers; Parton, *General Butler*, 581, 583–84.

26. Porter, "Journal of Occurrences," 372; W. C. Corsan, *Two Months in the Confederate States*, ed. Benjamin H. Trask (1863; rpr. Baton Rouge, 1996), 18. In *General*

By mid-November the general had beguiled Denison into believing that Andrew, although he had made a little money, acted only as a staunch patriot with a wholesome interest in nurturing reconstruction. The example was absurd, but Denison praised the "Colonel" for taking over a confiscated plantation and producing a marvelous crop of sugar by using black labor. Other speculators, some working in harmony with Andrew, emulated the "Colonel." Slaves attached to confiscated plantations obtained their freedom and worked for wages harvesting the crops. "I think there will not again, be any ground for complaint against Gen. Butler, for his toleration of speculators," Denison declared in a letter to Chase. Denison, however, was a staunch abolitionist and too impressed by Butler's emancipation policies to see the dirty work being performed outside the city.[27]

The activities of the Butler brothers created a poor impression on the soldiers who came to Louisiana to fight for the Union. Many of them had little to do, and some outside the city emulated their chieftain with their own enterprises. Sent to Donaldsonville to load three transports with sugar, one company of men forced their way into a mansion and carried off the owner's silver plate, whiskey, and all the ladies' clothing. The theft was observed by Lieutenant Francis A. Roe of the navy and reported through channels to Butler. The general had standing orders that any soldier molesting the property of peaceable citizens would be subject to punishment, and to put a good face on this incident, he issued additional orders threatening to hold the officers in charge liable and deduct the damages from their pay. Butler, however, did not like the navy snooping into his affairs and wrote Gideon Welles: "The acts of the troops in pillaging (if true) are without palliation or excuse; certainly no more to be justified than this improper, bombastic, and ridiculous rhodomontade of a sub-lieutenant of the Navy."[28]

Farragut, while standing off New Orleans in early December, also

---

Butler, 584, Parton whitewashed most of Butler's questionable affairs and claimed the auctions gave no man the slightest advantage over another.

27. Chase, *Diary and Correspondence*, 329.

28. General Orders No. 32, May 27, Roe to Morris, September 11, Butler to Welles, September 13, General Orders No. 74, September 19, 1862, ORA, XV, 445, 568–69, 573–74.

wrote the general, but on another subject. He discovered that the schooner *L. L. Davis*, a vessel laden with salt, cleared for the port of Matamoras, Mexico, but sailed across Lake Pontchartrain and delivered it to the Confederate post at Pontchitoula. The admiral did not know of Butler's possible involvement in the transaction when he wrote:

> While no one appreciates more highly than myself the energetic, perse-vering, and skilful merchant, I must confess that no one has a greater abhorrence and detestation of the unscrupulous speculator who takes advantage of every necessity of his fellow-beings, and, regardless of the consequences, by bribing and corruption forces his trade into the enemy's country, drawing down dishonor upon the cause as well as the country we serve, and upon us who are exerting every nerve to sustain our honor among nations, and even claim the respect of our enemies, however unwilling they may be to yield it. I have therefore determined to call to your attention the case of the Schooner "L. L. Davis," whose cargo is owned by one Mr. Wyer of New Orleans.[29]

Another letter, this one written on the same day by Denison, went to Chase, noting that "Col. Butler has three or four men in his employ who manage his business for him. The principal one is Mr. Wyer." When this information dribbled into Congress, Senator Garret Davis of Massachusetts accused the general of conspiring with his brother to seize abandoned property for private gain. Zachariah Chandler defended the general, not because he understood the situation but because Butler was a political ally.[30]

As he had done so many times before, Denison confronted Butler, who blithely concurred that *L. L. Davis* was no doubt a blockade run-ner. The general doubted if his brother had any hand in the business, but he promised to "investigate the matter thoroughly" and expel the guilty. Like so many times before, Denison believed the general and departed from the meeting happily deluded.[31]

Denison's reports, however, worried Chase, who on October 29 wrote the general: "So many and such seemingly well-founded charges against

29. *Butler Correspondence*, II, 526–27.

30. Chase, *Diary and Correspondence*, 338–39; *Butler Correspondence*, II, 528–29; Holzman, *Stormy Ben Butler*, 93.

31. Chase, *Diary and Correspondence*, 338–39.

your brother, Col. Butler, have reached me and other members of the administration, as well as the President, that I feel bound to say to you that in my judgment you owe it to yourself not to be responsible, even by toleration, for what he does. . . . It is said that Col. Butler's gains amount to between one and two million dollars." Chase closed by implying that it might be a good idea to send Andrew back to Massachusetts.[32]

Butler's reply read like a well-trimmed classic cover-up. Andrew, he declared, "has been no more successful than many others. I believe that every transaction has been legitimate mercantile operations." The general denied aiding him officially but admitted lending him capital and credit. He disputed the claim that his brother had netted $2 million, lowering his profit margins to "perhaps $200,000." With regard to Andrew's integrity, Butler invited Chase to interview members of the staff, men like Shepley, Weitzel, Kinsman, and others who undoubtedly played a major role in the conspiracy and would keep their mouths' shut. "I am willing," Butler declared, that my brother "abide by the result of the [investigation]." But the general wanted no inquiry and assured Chase that Andrew would close up his business and leave New Orleans, "so as to leave me entirely untrammeled to deal with the infernal brood of slandering speculators who have maligned me because I will not allow them to plunder the Government." If anybody in the Treasury Department had paused to investigate the numerous transactions floating through the Lowell accounts of Fisher Hildreth and the Boston accounts of Richard S. Fay, Jr., they would have found the Butler brothers deeply immersed in transactions involving huge sums of money—but nobody did.[33]

In mid-November, while Andrew Butler casually went through the motions of closing his affairs, Fisher Hildreth made plans to come to New Orleans. For what purpose is unclear, but Hildreth would not require much training to sustain the businesses established by the "Colonel." Whatever the reason, nothing materialized because Lincoln recalled the general in early December.[34]

32. *Butler Correspondence*, II, 422–23.

33. *Ibid.*, 424–25, 426, 464, 518–19; Chase, *Diary and Correspondence*, 329; Sandburg, *Abraham Lincoln*, II, 70.

34. *Butler Correspondence*, II, 464; General Orders No. 106, December 15, General Orders No. 107, December 17, 1862, ORA, XV, 610, 611.

How much money the Butlers took back to Massachusetts may never be known. Powerful politicians with intellectual gifts seldom get caught in their own conspiracies, and Butler remained insulated from direct involvement by relying on a shared loyalty with his brother. Nobody ever produced proof against him, and he refuted every attack upon his policies or practices. Andrew came to New Orleans with little money. The general's capital consisted of about $150,000. By 1868 Butler was worth $3 million. Andrew then died that year, leaving his own considerable estate to the general. Butler's fortune could not have been amassed on a general's salary, dividends from stockholdings, legal fees, or his reentry into national politics. This leaves but one source to account for the swiftly amassed fortune—New Orleans.[35]

Marion Southwood cultivated a horrible dislike for the Butler brothers, and in her recollections she printed one of the city's favorite but cautiously sung songs:

Two brothers came to New Orleans,
    Both were the name of "Butler."
The one was a major-general,
    The other merely a sutler.
The first made proclamations
    That were fearful to behold,
While the sutler dealt our rations
    And took his pay in gold.[36]

If the Butlers collaborated in schemes to trade with the enemy—even to the extent of supplying munitions, as some Confederates claimed— their crimes were against the government, not the South, which benefited from the trade. Such acts transcended simple corruption. Whether Ben Butler would risk the disgrace of treason to acquire wealth is still questionable, but Andrew Butler had no restraints beyond those imposed by his brother. Evidence suggests the existence of collusion, but the Joint Committee on the Conduct of the War exonerated

---

35. Parton, *General Butler*, 409; Butler Correspondence, II, 538; James Ford Rhodes, *History of the United States from the Compromise of 1850 to the Final Restoration of Home Rule in the South* (8 vols.; New York, 1902–1919), V, 312. Rhodes was especially harsh on Butler, and some of his claims cannot be supported.

36. Southwood, *"Beauty and Booty,"* 86.

the general. Butler relied on a simple argument. He did not confiscate property from the public—*the government did*. Many northerners, including some members of the presidential cabinet, praised his administration. Butler's recall had little to do with his questionable administrative practices or with his brother.[37]

From Lincoln's point of view there was a war to fight. He wanted Vicksburg captured and the entire Mississippi River secured. In this Butler failed, but for reasons having little to do with corruption, speculation, or trading with the enemy.

37. Caskey, *Secession and Restoration*, 68, 253.

II

The Campaigns
of Ben Butler

AT NEW ORLEANS, Butler concentrated on civilian matters, probably because he possessed none of the prerequisites of a great military strategist. He understood the importance of opening the Mississippi, but he did not have the manpower to entertain large-scale operations. The War Department ignored his requests for reinforcements because his campaigns had been marked by an ignorance of tactics. In the early stages of Butler's administration, Lincoln and Stanton were content to hold what Farragut captured, knowing that General Beauregard's Army of Tennessee—the only possible threat to Butler—lay near Corinth, Mississippi, stymied by a huge, indolent force under the command of Major General Henry W. Halleck. Because of the difficulty of attacking New Orleans by land, Butler never faced a serious threat, and after the turmoil of his first few weeks of occupation he had ample opportunity to expand his department slowly by conquest.[1]

Farragut's instructions from Welles, which dated back to January 20, ordered him to advance up the river after capturing New Orleans, taking the Confederacy's "defenses in the rear" until forming a junction with the Mississippi flotilla under Flag Officer Charles H. Davis, who in May, 1862, was standing above Memphis. On the evening of May 7, Commander James S. Palmer anchored the USS *Iroquois* off Baton Rouge and demanded the surrender of the city. Two days later he landed a force of sailors and marines and, finding no resistance, hoisted the Stars and Stripes. Farragut could not hold what he captured without infantry, so Butler detached part of General Williams'

1. At Corinth, Halleck had 110,000 men, Beauregard 66,000, and neither army demonstrated much activity. Faust, ed., *Historical Times Illustrated*, 486; Boatner, *Civil War Dictionary*, 176–77.

brigade to support the navy. With only 1,475 troops and four pieces of artillery, Williams could not be expected to safeguard what he occupied for very long, so he asked for his other three regiments and a battery of artillery.[2]

On May 10 Palmer continued upriver, anchoring off Natchez two days later. Mayor John Hunter surrendered the town, but Williams deposited no force to garrison it. Commander Stephen P. Lee led the rest of the squadron up to Vicksburg, and on May 18, joined by Williams' transports, demanded the surrender of the city. James L. Autrey, the town's military governor, replied, "I have to state that Mississippians don't know, and refuse to learn, how to surrender to an enemy. If Commodore Farragut or Brigadier-General Butler can teach them, let them come and try."[3]

The quick conquests of the middle Mississippi had come to an end. Heavy guns frowned down from the bluffs overlooking the great river, and Farragut anchored out of range. Williams had too few troops to attempt a lodgment on the eastern shore, so Farragut left six gunboats below Vicksburg and escorted Williams and his transports back to Baton Rouge to reprovision, garrison the arsenal, and pick up reinforcements. Farragut then steamed down to New Orleans to confer with Butler and ask for more men. The general considered the reversal a setback and promised to bring Williams' force to seven thousand troops if Porter would send up six to ten mortar vessels to bomb Vicksburg's heights.[4]

On June 3 Farragut requested Porter's mortar flotilla, but neither officer was enthusiastic about running up to Vicksburg with the river falling. With General Braxton Bragg's force operating in northern Mississippi, and with Halleck's army moving with excessive caution, Farragut had visions of becoming stranded and cut off by the Confed-

2. Welles to Farragut, January 20, Palmer to Farragut, May 9, Palmer to Bryan and Bryan to Palmer, May 8, Bryan to Palmer, May 9, 1862, *ORN*, XVIII, 7–8, 473–75; Williams' Report, May 29, 1862, *ORA*, XV, 22; *Butler Correspondence*, I, 535–36.

3. Palmer to Farragut, May 13, Lee and Williams to Vicksburg Authorities and Autrey to Lee, May 18, Farragut to Welles, May 30, 1862, *ORN*, XVIII, 489–90, 491, 519.

4. Williams' Report, May 29, 1862, *ORA*, XV, 22–24; Farragut to Welles, May 30, 1862, *ORN*, XVIII, 519–21; T. Williams, "Letters," 317; *Butler Correspondence*, I, 536, 539–40, 562–63.

erate army. Porter, who had been in the Gulf, immediately departed for the river with nineteen mortar boats, only to find Butler's promised towboats all occupied moving transports loaded with sugar, cotton, and other commodities for shipment east. Porter lost more than a week getting up to New Orleans and naturally suspected Butler of cultivating private interests at the expense of the navy. With each day lost, the Mississippi continued to fall, and Farragut's plans for a quick conquest of Vicksburg steadily trickled away.[5]

On June 21 Porter began shelling the batteries at Vicksburg. Farragut arrived with the rest of his fleet, and by June 25 Williams, with more than three thousand troops, prepared to move on Vicksburg. Farragut soon realized that Porter's mortars could not silence the enemy's guns and that to form a junction with Davis he would have to run by Vicksburg. An enormous horseshoe curve, known as De Soto Point, lay above the city and formed a long, narrow peninsula. Butler, who had looked at a map of the area, suggested that if the city could not be captured by conventional means, perhaps it could be taken by innovation. His instructions to Williams were confusing and largely dependent upon Farragut and Porter silencing the batteries, so instead of attempting a lodgment on the eastern shore, Williams exercised Butler's idea, landed on the west bank, and began to dig a canal across the lower end of De Soto Point, some three miles below Vicksburg. Butler had neither reconnoitered the area himself nor considered the intense heat or the rate of fall of the river. Williams' canal builders, reinforced by hundreds of blacks, soon discovered that the river level dropped faster than the ditch could be dug, and the diggers began to collapse before the eyes of their hard-driving general. Halleck refused to send reinforcements, so Farragut's squadron dimpled Vicksburg's bluffs with 25,000 shells, withdrew in late July, and brought the entire force back down the rapidly receding river.[6]

5. Farragut to Welles, May 30, June 3, Farragut to Porter, May 31, June 3, Porter to Farragut, June 3, 16, 1862, *ORN*, XVIII, 521, 558–59, 576, 577, 579–80; Lewis, *David Glasgow Farragut*, 80, 92.

6. Farragut to Welles, July 2, 4, 6, 11, 29, 1862, *ORN*, XVIII, 608–610, 624, 630–31, 677, XIX, 96–97; Butler to Williams, June 6, 16, Williams to Butler, July 17, Williams to Davis, July 26, Stanton to Halleck, July 14, Halleck to Stanton, July 15, 1862, *ORA*, XV, 25–26, 31–33, 518–19; Murray, *History of the Ninth Connecticut*, 108–112; *Butler Correspondence*, I, 562–63; T. Williams, "Letters," 322–23, 326. Williams'

Like Farragut, Butler expected cooperation from Halleck, but when the latter seemed content to occupy Corinth and operate on the defensive, Butler recalled Williams' command in anticipation of a clash at Baton Rouge. He also worried that with Williams in Halleck's department, the latter might detach Grant's command for operations against Vicksburg and demand that Williams be kept there. Butler cleverly condemned Halleck for a lack of cooperation, but he could not claim any success for himself.[7]

While Halleck loitered in Mississippi, Major General Earl Van Dorn, a West Point classmate of Williams', detached a small force under General John C. Breckinridge, a former political friend of Butler's, for an attack on Baton Rouge. If the town could be recaptured, Van Dorn considered operations to recover New Orleans a distinct possibility. Breckinridge spent his energy on a forced march to the state capital and on August 4–5 suffered a temporary setback. Williams lost his life defending the town, and Butler issued a grandiloquent report boasting of a great triumph, claiming that two thousand blueclads had routed six thousand grayclads. Breckinridge also claimed victory, and for good reason. Butler sent Weitzel to Baton Rouge to assess the situation. "We are not threatened at all here," Weitzel reported, "therefore this is the time to evacuate the city." He returned to headquarters and convinced Butler that it was more important to defend New Orleans than to hold Baton Rouge. Butler envisioned some "nineteen or twenty" Confederate regiments converging on Williams' replacement, Colonel Halbert E. Paine of the 4th Wisconsin, and foolishly ordered the withdrawal.[8]

---

canal would have been about six feet wide, five feet deep, and a mile and a quarter long near the base of the peninsula. Conventional wisdom held that once the canal was cut, the sweep of the river would open it, thereby enabling larger vessels to cross without coming under the fire of Vicksburg's batteries. As General Sherman discovered eight months later, the project had no hope of success because the river created a huge eddy near the canal's opening and quickly refilled it with mud.

7. Farragut to Halleck, June 28, Butler to Stanton, July 10, Butler to Halleck, July 26, 1862, ORA, XV, 514–15, 518, 530; *Butler Correspondence*, II, 82–83.

8. Weitzel to Davis, August 8, Butler to Stanton, August 16, Butler to Halleck, August 27, 1862, ORA, XV, 545, 552–53, 555–56; *Butler Correspondence*, II, 155, 172–73; Richard B. Irwin, "Military Operations in Louisiana in 1862," *B&L*, III, 583–84; George Denison to C. C. Denison, August 10, 1862, in Denison Papers. From each side about 2,500 men participated in the fight, and the casualties were about equal, 383 for the Union and 456 for the Confederacy.

Butler had not been to Baton Rouge since his visit on June 28, when he left a lasting impression on the town by warning that if England or France intervened, "I'll be d——m if I don't arm every negro in the South, and make them cut the throat of every man, woman, and child in it! I'll make them lay the whole country waste with fire and sword, and leave it desolate!" Whatever praise Williams deserved for defending Baton Rouge, Butler lost on August 20 by evacuating it. He ordered Colonel Paine to move the books of the libraries and a statue of George Washington to New Orleans before burning the town. Paine decided to not strike a match or to arm any slaves, and when he departed for New Orleans, Breckinridge, who had been fruitlessly waiting for support from the scuttled CSS *Arkansas*, had moved most of his force upriver to Port Hudson and no longer presented a threat. Butler then made a serious error by not combining his forces with Farragut's to dislodge the Confederates from their new position.[9]

Butler began to look like a general who would not fight—he had lost ground, not gained it—so he talked of taking Mobile or Galveston. Stanton would not send him troops, so he concentrated on a trivial expedition to the west. Major General Richard Taylor had begun to reinforce a small Confederate force in the Lafourche District, posing an obstacle to future Union operations upriver. Butler decided on a countermove and on October 24 General Weitzel, recently raised from lieutenant, invaded lower Louisiana—the parishes of Assumption, Lafourche, and Terrebonne—with four regiments of infantry (12th Connecticut, 1st Louisiana, 75th New York, 8th New Hampshire), two batteries (1st Maine, 6th Massachusetts), and four battalions of cavalry (Troops A, B, C, of the 1st Louisiana and Troop C, 2nd Massachusetts Battalion). In early May the Lafourche District could have been secured by no more than an infantry battalion, but the general was not a strategist.

Transports carried the brigade to Donaldsonville, where it disembarked on October 26, and Weitzel, after a nine-mile march, skirmished with Colonel William G. Vincent's regiment from Brigadier General

9. Paine to Breckinridge, August 14, Butler to Paine, August 19, 1862, ORA, XV, 551, 553; East, ed., *Sarah Morgan*, 139, 145, 225; Irwin, "Military Operations in Louisiana," *B&L*, III, 584; *Butler Correspondence*, II, 13.

Alfred Mouton's brigade. Overpowered, Vincent fell back to Labadieville, where Mouton promised reinforcements. Weitzel had divided his command, sending one regiment up the right bank of Lafourche Bayou and the other up the left bank. Mouton, to keep from being flanked, also divided his force, which was about half the size of Weitzel's command and consisted of Captain O. J. Semmes's six-gun battery, the 2nd Louisiana Cavalry, and the 33rd Louisiana Infantry. Two small regiments—the 18th and 24th Louisiana—defended Berwick Bay and Bayou Boeuf, along with Captain George Ralston's Battery H, 1st Mississippi Light Artillery, and Captain T. A. Faries' six-gun Pelican Battery of the Louisiana Light Artillery. Colonel Thomas E. Vick with about a thousand Louisiana militia held the railroad at Bayou des Allemands but was too far from Mouton's main force to be of any help.

On October 27, two miles above Labadieville, a sharp skirmish ensued at Georgia Landing. After a short but spirited engagement, Vincent's 1,392 troops fell back in confusion and attempted to connect with the other half of Mouton's command. Vincent considered his situation hopeless and began a slow withdrawal the next day. Weitzel entered Thibodaux on the afternoon of October 29 and found Mouton gone. The enemy had destroyed all the bridges and depots and retreated to Berwick Bay, reaching there the following day. Casualties were light, and Weitzel collected about 166 prisoners.[10]

Weitzel had anticipated Mouton's retreat toward Berwick Bay, and his original plans called for Lieutenant Commander Thomas McKean Buchanan to transport the 21st Indiana into the bay and trap the Confederates in a pincer while the 8th Vermont and the 1st Louisiana Native Guards marched out of Algiers to open the line of the Opelousas Railroad. This brought Weitzel's force to six thousand. Storms delayed the arrival of Buchanan's two transports, and Mouton slipped by safely. On November 3 Buchanan took the light-drafts four-

10. Weitzel's Report, October 25, 29, Mouton's Report, November 4, 1862, ORA, XV, 166–70, 176–78; *Butler Correspondence*, II, 13–16; Irwin, "Military Operations in Louisiana," *B&L*, III, 584; John M. Stanyan, *A History of the Eighth Regiment of New Hampshire Volunteers* (Concord, N.H., 1892), 139–41; Barnes F. Lathrop, "The Lafourche District in 1862: Invasion," *Journal of Louisiana History*, II (Spring 1961), 175–84; Richard Taylor, *Destruction and Reconstruction: Personal Experiences of the Late War* (New York, 1879), 112–13.

teen miles up Bayou Teche, only to find the Confederates safely posted behind obstructions blocking the bayou. Buchanan opened with his guns but suffered much damage in the ensuing artillery exchange. "I can do nothing," he reported, "until General Weitzel arrives." The general, however, remained at Thibodaux, content to safeguard that which he had captured rather than press on with his superior force.[11]

Butler expressed satisfaction with Weitzel's conquests—at best a badly synchronized third-class operation. He named the captured territory the District of the Lafourche and designated the general as military commander. Weitzel attempted to decline, declaring that he could not "command those negro regiments," the 1st Louisiana Native Guards. To Butler's assistant adjutant general he wrote: "The commanding general knows well my private opinions on this subject. What I stated to him privately, while on his staff, I now see before my eyes. Since the arrival of the negro regiments symptoms of servile insurrection are becoming apparent. . . . I cannot assume the command of such a force, and thus be responsible for its conduct." Like it or not, Weitzel remained in the Lafourche with the Native Guards.[12]

The issue of runaway slaves had troubled Butler since his arrival at New Orleans. They flooded the city, some in search of work, others in search of food and freedom. They were too numerous to declare contraband and too many to feed, as he had done at Fort Monroe, and since Lincoln had recently revoked Major General David Hunter's orders for military emancipation, Butler faced a crisis. He had also been warned by Lincoln that the administration was not prepared to announce a policy regarding blacks, so he was under orders to avoid creating insoluble problems or raising new issues. Planters lived in fear of a slave revolt, and with a growing influx of runaways, Butler looked for solutions. Earlier in his administration he had published lists of runaways and returned many of them to their masters. He soon

---

11. Butler's Reports, October 24, 27, November 2, Mouton's Report, November 4, Buchanan's Report, November 4, Fuller's Report, November 7, 1862, *ORA*, 159–61, 179–80, 183–85, 185–87; Lathrop, "The Lafourche District in 1862," 185–86; Mary F. Berry, "Negro Troops in Blue and Gray: The Louisiana Native Guards, 1861–1863," *Journal of Louisiana History*, VIII (Spring, 1967), 177–78.

12. Weitzel to Strong, November 5, Strong to Weitzel, November 6, 1862, *ORA*, XV, 164, 171–72; *Butler Correspondence*, II, 439.

learned that masters had merely turned their slaves loose to obtain subsistence, so he declared them voluntarily emancipated. To avoid an even greater influx of fugitives, he kept his declarations to himself.[13]

Butler explained his dilemma to Stanton and asked, "Now, what am I to do?" He voiced one option—remobilizing a regiment of free black troops that had been organized to defend New Orleans—but he expressed his doubts on the premise that blacks had acquired a great horror of firearms. "I am inclined to the opinion that John Brown was right in his idea of arming the negro with a pike or spear instead of a musket, if they are to be armed at all."[14]

As early as May 25 Butler had asked Stanton's permission to enlist five thousand able-bodied whites, all local residents looking for work. Stanton agreed, as long as the men were loyal and white. Butler offered a bounty of $100, to be paid after the war, and monthly wages of $13, and this enticed many men who had been paroled at Forts Jackson and St. Philip and who had no other source of income. When disease, resignations, and casualties reduced the ranks, he urged Confederate soldiers to desert and join the companies being formed at New Orleans. Butler brought his original regiments up to strength, added two new regiments, and mounted four companies of cavalry. When Andrew Butler first hired whites to harvest sugar crops, enlistments again fell because the "Colonel" offered higher wages than the army, forcing the general to consider other options.[15]

While Butler recruited whites, General Phelps, who placed John Brown on a level with the great martyrs of the Christian world, began recruiting fugitive slaves and forming them into companies. The influx of runaways had grown uncontrollably, one officer observing that "they

13. Caskey, *Secession and Restoration*, 53; Horowitz, "Ben Butler and the Negro," 173; Nash, *Stormy Petrel*, 165; David Donald, ed., *Inside Lincoln's Cabinet: The Civil War Diaries of Salmon P. Chase* (New York, 1954), 95–99.

14. Butler to Stanton, May 25, 1862, ORA, XV, 439–42; Weitzel to Butler, October 29, 1862, in Butler Papers, LC. John Brown, although he had 200 rifles and access to the Harpers Ferry arsenal, purchased 2,000 pikes to arm the slaves.

15. Butler to Stanton, May 25, Thomas to Butler, June 14, 1862, ORA, XV, 441, 493; Thomas to Butler, June 14, 1862, in Benjamin F. Butler Papers, Historic New Orleans Collection, Williams Research Center, New Orleans; *Butler Correspondence*, I, 494–95, 516–21; Winters, *Civil War in Louisiana*, 142–43.

are coming into camp by the hundreds and are a costly curse. They should be kept out or set at work, or freed or colonized, or sunk or something." Butler ordered Phelps to expel any unemployed blacks or whites from his command, but the commander of Fort Parapet ignored the directive and the influx continued. Phelps's rabid abolitionist views dismayed his command and eventually led to a conflict with Butler. If Phelps heard a slave had been punished on a plantation, he sent a detail to liberate him, and to keep his men busy, he would order them into the countryside to insult the planters and entice away their blacks. Finding three slaves confined in an outbuilding on a nearby plantation, a patrol released them and before returning to camp broke into the house and carried off the valuables. When Butler learned of Phelps's policy of liberation, he ordered the general to desist.[16]

A breach had been brewing between Phelps and Butler since their days on Ship Island. Phelps, who occupied the island in early December, had acted unilaterally and issued an extraordinary proclamation declaring slavery unconstitutional. Coming as it did from a barren island, everybody ignored it, and the navy refused to circulate the document. Phelps's declaration, however, put him on a collision course with Butler, who five months later demanded that fugitive slaves swarming into New Orleans be returned to their masters. Phelps ignored the order.[17]

Unknown to Butler or Lincoln, Phelps operated his own policy of emancipation and devoutly believed that as many as fifty black regiments could be recruited, armed, trained, and effectively utilized on southern battlefields. Butler remained unconvinced. Fugitive slaves made good laborers for repairing levees or widening drainage ditches, and he had already resisted appeals from northern abolitionists to enlist them in the Union army. When Phelps could no longer find jobs for washwomen, cooks, nurses, and laborers or provide facilities to house them, he resorted to desperate measures and surreptitiously

16. Butler to Stanton, May 25, Page to Butler, May 27, Haggerty to Phelps, May 28, Peck to Phelps, June 15, 1862, *ORA*, XV, 440, 446–47, 491; De Forest, *A Volunteer's Adventures*, 26–27; Russell, *My Diary, North and South*, 411.

17. Phelps's proclamation, December 4, McKean to Welles, December 27, 1861, *ORN*, XVII, 17, 18–21; Phelps's Report, December 5, 1861, *ORA*, VI, 465–68; Howard C. Westwood, "Benjamin Butler's Enlistment of Black Troops in New Orleans in 1862," *Journal of Louisiana History*, XXVI (Winter, 1985), 8–9.

organized the Union's first five companies of black infantry. Brigadier General Neal Dow, commanding Forts Jackson and St. Philip, also needed men, and Phelps sent him five hundred fugitives with the suggestion that they be given artillery training. Dow put them to work on the fortifications and reported that many of them would make good soldiers.[18]

Phelps, thinking he had discovered a unique solution to the fugitive problem, submitted requisitions to arm, clothe, and encamp three regiments of "Africans" to replace whites dying at the rate of two to three a day because they lived under "swampy and unhealthy" conditions. He believed the blacks would tolerate the foul climate better than men from New England. Astonished, Butler had visions of armed fugitives storming the countryside and fomenting servile insurrection. Furthermore, he had no authority to raise black regiments and ordered Phelps to use the fugitives to cut down trees, open a field of fire, and build an abatis. Phelps replied curtly, stating that while he was ready to prepare black regiments for defensive measures against assailants, he was not willing to become a "mere slave-driver." He tendered his resignation and in doing so shocked Butler, who appealed to Stanton for direction. Caught by surprise, Butler explained that only by presidential order or by act of Congress could black troops be recruited, and no such order had been passed. He denied Phelps's resignation, refused to grant a leave of absence, and demanded that the trees be cut. Dissatisfied with Butler's reply, Phelps sent his resignation to Washington but remained on duty at Camp Parapet near Carrollton. Lincoln accepted Phelps's resignation on August 21, and the following day Butler agreed that the troublesome general's effort to raise black regiments was, after all, basically sound. This was quite a reversal for a man who three years earlier stood in Boston's Faneuil Hall and declared blacks "the inferior race, as God has made it."[19]

Butler pressed Phelps to withdraw his resignation—as friends they

18. Butler to Stanton, August 2, Dow to Davis, July 18, 1862, ORA, XV, 523, 534; *Butler Correspondence*, I, 514, II, 131–34; John M. Stanyan, *A History of the Eighth Regiment of New Hampshire Volunteers* (Concord, N.H., 1892), 107; Benjamin Quarles, *The Negro in the Civil War* (Boston, 1953), 115; Neal Dow, *The Reminiscences of Neal Dow* (Portland, Maine, 1898), 672–73.

19. Butler to Stanton, August 2, Phelps to Davis, July 30, 31, Butler to Phelps, August 2, 5, 1862, ORA, XV, 534, 535, 536–37, 542–43; *Butler Correspondence*, I,

had been together since the beginning of the war. Phelps remained adamant. Weary of Butler's dictates, he registered his disgust for the military by giving his horse, epaulets, sash, and spurs to Weitzel, who had been promoted to brigadier general on Butler's recommendation. Some years later Butler wrote, "I loved General Phelps very much. He was a crank upon the slavery question . . . otherwise he was as good a soldier and commander as ever mounted a horse." Phelps, however, was more intractable than Butler realized. "He hates the Rebels bitterly," wrote one of his officers, "not so much because they are rebellious as because they are slaveholders." Phelps would not reconcile his differences with Butler, and Lincoln, after giving the issue careful study, ruled that slaves seeking freedom in Union camps need not to be returned to their owners, but he said nothing about arming them. Despondent, Butler confided to his wife, "The Government have sustained Phelps about the Negroes, and we shall have a negro insurrection here I fancy. If something is not done soon, God help us all."[20]

Butler studied the July Confiscation Act and decided that while Phelps's method of enlisting fugitive slaves might be illegal, the idea had merit. Besides, the city had been inundated with fugitives armed with clubs, razors, and shotguns. They clashed with police, and the *Picayune* reported the black invasion of the city unmanageable, noting that "they have become impudent, disobedient, and reckless." White laborers, mostly of German, French, or Irish extraction, had been enticed into civilian jobs by higher wages, and with no reinforcements in sight, Butler sought to alleviate the fugitive menace by finding some method to utilize the black population for military service. Fugitive slaves could not be enlisted, but no law existed preventing the recruitment of the city's ten thousand free blacks. The general even found two precedents—free blacks had served under Andrew Jackson in 1815, and in May, 1861, Governor Moore had permitted the forma-

---

613–15, II, 109–110, 125–27, 146–47, 207, 287; De Forest, *A Volunteer's Adventures,* 35–36; Stanton to Butler, August 23, 1862, in Butler Papers, LC; Horowitz, "Ben Butler and the Negro," 159, 174.

20. General Orders No. 139, September 24, 1862, *ORA,* XV, 622; Butler to wife, July 25, 1862, *Butler Correspondence,* II, 109; *Butler's Book,* 488; Nash, *Stormy Petrel,* 168; De Forest, *A Volunteer's Adventures,* 10.

tion of two regiments of Native Guards. By early 1862 Moore's black military organizations had grown to three thousand men, but when Lovell withdrew from the city, the Native Guards refused to leave. Some claimed they had been coerced to join the militia, others simply preferred to await the Union victory. Using his own brand of logic, Butler believed that if blacks had been willing to fight for a government founded on the continuance of slavery, why would they not fight for a government founded on the Declaration of Independence? He ordered the disbanded Native Guards to report to the Judah Touro Charity Building on the corner of Front and Levee Streets to be mustered into the service. One of Butler's biographers observed that the "arrival at so radical a solution to the manpower problem by a former Breckinridge Democrat was one of the ironies of the Civil War."[21]

On August 14 Butler decided to test the waters and wrote Stanton that without more troops he could neither support Farragut's effort to capture Vicksburg nor cooperate in an expedition against Mobile. He then exaggerated conditions at New Orleans by warning of a threatened attack on the city. "If it becomes at all imminent," he wrote, "I shall call on Africa to intervene, and I do not think I shall call in vain." He had already decided to expand the Native Guards and informed Stanton that "they are free; they have been used by our enemies, whose mouths are shut, and they will be loyal." Before Stanton could reply, Butler did very nearly what he had ordered Phelps not to do.[22]

When Butler first entered the city, officers from the Native Guards had offered their services. At the time he could find no work for them, doubted their fitness, and had no authority to officially enroll them.

---

21. *Butler Correspondence*, II, 209–211; Halleck to Butler, August 7, General Orders No. 63, August 22, 1863, ORA, XV, 544, 556–57; Muster Rolls, First Native Guards, Louisiana Militia, Confederate States of America, May 3, 1861, Record Group 109, War Records Division, National Archives; Chase, *Diary and Correspondence*, 312; George Denison to James Denison, November 14, 1862, in Denison Papers; New Orleans *Daily Picayune*, July 22, 1862; Trefousse, *Ben Butler*, 131; Parton, *General Butler*, 492–93, 516–17; Bragg, *Louisiana in the Confederacy*, 36; Berry, "Negro Troops in Blue and Gray," 169, 171–73.

22. Butler to Stanton, August 14, 1862, ORA, XV, 549. During mid-August and early September, Stanton's attention focused on the Union disaster at Second Manassas and Lee's invasion of Maryland, leaving Butler with no instructions to the contrary.

Nonetheless, he hired some of them to act as spies in the homes of their employers, noting that "in color, nay, also in conduct, they had much more the appearance of white gentlemen than some of those who have favored me with their presence claiming to be the 'chivalry of the South.'" On August 16, when the general offered a reward for guns, revolvers, and swords held without a permit, many of the Native Guards turned in the names of their employers, and with a bounty of three dollars for bowie knives and ten dollars for firearms, some of them pocketed a small bankroll.[23]

Once the process of enlistment began, nobody paid much attention to the antecedents of black volunteers. Any physically fit black who swore he was free entered the service. Field officers were white, line officers black, and more than half of the men enrolled in the first regiment were fugitive slaves. Butler quickly raised three regiments, the same number proposed by Phelps. West Point officers like Weitzel objected to commanding black regiments, so Butler temporarily assigned two of them elsewhere. He also raised two artillery batteries, not just because Phelps had suggested it but because it made sense. Before leaving for home, Phelps trained two of the regiments, and Butler deployed them mainly as railroad guards. After maligning Phelps for disobeying orders and organizing five companies of black infantry, Butler formed three black regiments without the sanction of the president or the War Department. When Phelps finally departed, a number of his officers believed that their commander had been bullied out of the service by Butler. Treasury agent Denison, however, praised the general for instigating a shrewd move: "By accepting a regiment which had already been in Confederate Service, he left no room for complaint (by the Rebels) that the government were arming the negroes."[24]

In an early September letter to Stanton, Butler pledged that within

23. Butler to Stanton, May 25, 1862, ORA, XV, 442; W. E. Burghardt Du Bois, *Black Reconstruction* (New York, 1935), 94; Parton, *General Butler*, 466; Dabney, "The Butler Regime in Louisiana," 514.

24. *Butler Correspondence*, II, 270–71, 323–24; Chase to Denison, September 8, 1862, in Denison Papers; Chase, *Diary and Correspondence*, 379; De Forest, *A Volunteer's Adventures*, 43; Wilson, *The Black Phalanx*, 195–99; Auvignac Dorville to Anatole de Ste. Gême, October 26, 1862, in Dorville Papers, Mss 100, Folder 396.

ten days he would have a regiment of one thousand Native Guards, "the darkest of whom is about the complexion of the late Mr. [Daniel] Webster." Lincoln spared Butler the embarrassment of explaining his unauthorized recruiting practices by issuing on September 24 the Emancipation Proclamation, granting freedom to all slaves "within any State or designated part of a State" in rebellion against the Union. The proclamation, which was to take effect on January 1, 1863, mentioned nothing about recruiting former slaves for military service, but Butler could now boast that his actions had the smell of legality because fugitives *would be* free and thereby eligible for military service. On September 27 the 1st Regiment of Native Guards entered the service as the first black unit officially mustered into the Union army, and Butler named an assistant provost marshal, Captain Spencer H. Stafford of Massachusetts, as its commander.[25]

The general defended his decision to recruit blacks, and when the French consul complained about a number of oranges pillaged from a plantation by "violent Negroes" of the 1st Native Guards, Butler lashed back. To counter slurs against the black race, he replied, "Their color and race is of the same hue and blood as your celebrated compatriot and author, Alexander Dumas, who, I believe, is treated with the utmost respect in Paris." Privately, though, Butler maintained the prejudicial belief that blacks tended to be more subservient than whites because of an inbred disposition to respond to the commands of their masters. With this in mind, he did not intend to let them fight, relegating them to garrison and fatigue duty in the department's unhealthy outposts.[26]

The general's recruiting strategies worked so well that soon after forming the 1st Regiment, another twenty companies enlisted. On October 12 the 2nd Regiment of Native Guards officially entered the service, followed by the 3rd Regiment six weeks later. Butler still had no answer from Washington approving his actions. Stanton ignored Butler's letters, and when Halleck became general in chief of the

25. Butler to Stanton, September [?], General Orders No. 139, September 24, 1862, *ORA*, XV, 559, 621–23; James G. Hollandsworth, Jr., *The Louisiana Native Guards: The Black Military Experience During the Civil War* (Baton Rouge, 1995), 17.

26. *Butler Correspondence*, II, 351–52, 360; *Butler's Book*, 494; De Forest, *A Volunteer's Adventures*, 50–51.

Union army, he temporized, writing on November 20, "The whole matter [is] left to the judgment and discretion of the department commander."[27]

Butler soon realized that he could never build enough regiments to absorb all the blacks filing into the city or onto the military posts defending it—nor could he feed them. As more plantations along the Lafourche became absorbed by Weitzel's command, Butler forced his brother to discontinue the practice of employing white harvesters in order to provide work for the blacks. Remembering the factory girls in his hometown of Lowell, he established a ten-hour workday, six days a week, at a wage of ten dollars a month for males and lesser amounts for women and children. The planter could deduct three dollars from their pay for clothing, but employers were responsible for providing the workers with food, housing, medical care, and humane treatment. Provost guards maintained order and protected the property of loyal planters. The system worked well and became one of the better policies of Butler's administration.[28]

What he did well, however, was not enough to overcome the rumors of extensive corruption that filtered almost daily into the White House. As for military accomplishments, Butler still held New Orleans, but he had accomplished little else. The national elections would soon be over—and the general could sense winds of change.

27. Butler's Testimony, February 2, 1862, *U.S. Senate Reports*, 37th Cong., 3rd Sess., No. 108, 357–58; Halleck to Butler, November 20, 1862, ORA, XV, 601.

28. General Orders No. 91, November 9, 1862, ORA, XV, 592–95; Chase, *Diary and Correspondence*, 330; Parton, *General Butler*, 522–24.

12

The Beast Bows Out

IN EARLY AUGUST, when Butler heard muffled rumors about another Massachusetts politician, he wrote his wife, "They have an absurd story here that [Major General Nathaniel P.] Banks is to be sent down to take my place. I wish to heaven he would come!" The general might not have been entirely honest about the coming of Banks, whom he hated. He resented Banks's political success and doubted his competitor's shabbily earned reputation as being the best general selected from public life.[1]

The rumor came as no surprise—Butler had heard it before and nothing had happened. Seward had mentioned it to the French minister, who mentioned it to the French consul, who in turn whispered it to his friends in New Orleans. Soon the city's fashionable gentry were placing bets at ten to one that Butler would be recalled before the end of the year. On September 1 the general had heard enough and wrote Halleck: "I learn by secession newspapers that I am to be relieved of this command. If that be so, might I ask that my successor be sent as early as possible, as my own health is not the strongest, and it would seem fair that he should take some part in the yellow-fever season." Two weeks later Halleck denied the rumor, blaming it on "a mere newspaper story, without foundation."[2]

Aware that he had accomplished little of military value, Butler then wrote Henry Wilson, a friend and senator from Massachusetts: "I beg you, as chairman of the Military Committee, to use your influence to have more troops sent here—Mass. troops especially." The general

1. *Butler Correspondence*, II, 149; Porter, "Journal of Occurrences," 373–74.
2. Butler to Halleck, September 1, Halleck to Butler, September 14, 1862, ORA, XV, 558, 572; Parton, *General Butler*, 599; *Butler's Book*, 526–29.

had his eye on Port Hudson, where the enemy had recently expanded and fortified an earthwork overlooking the Mississippi River. Butler, however, was about three months too late, having lost his best opportunity to flush out the Rebels in early August. His appeal to Wilson went unanswered until December 2, after the senator had spoken with Stanton, "who promised to do what he could to aid you and expressed his confidence in you, and his approval of your vigor and ability." The rhetoric might have made the general feel better had Stanton not—twenty-one days earlier—executed the order to replace him with Banks. When he discovered the subterfuge, Butler privately cried foul, asking himself if "lying, injustice, deceit, and tergiversation [could] farther go?"

Before Wilson's reply reached New Orleans, Butler learned from friends that Banks was actually en route to relieve him "upon the demand of Napoleon, because I was not friendly to France." Butler also noted that McClellan had been relieved from command of the Army of the Potomac and that the orders had been issued contemporaneously on the day following the national election. To Butler, the two orders reeked with political stench, and he wrote that "it might appear as if the Republican administration had determined to put out of command all generals who had heretofore been Democrats, and to supply true Republicans in their place." Butler never accepted corruption, mishandling of government funds, or military incompetence as a reason for his recall, and he incorrectly believed that Lincoln was still under the influence of the secretary of state when he grumbled, "Ah! Seward, that trick was too thin."[3]

Suspecting Seward of malfeasance, Butler wrote Lincoln on November 29, noting that Banks was being sent into the department with troops "upon an independent expedition and command":

> This seems to imply a want of confidence in the Commander of this Department, perhaps deserved, but still painful to me. In my judgment it will be prejudicial to the public service to attempt any expedition into Texas without making New Orleans a base of supplies and cooperation, to do this there must be but one head, and one Department.

3. *Butler Correspondence*, II, 465–66, 516–17; *Butler's Book*, 529–30; General Orders No. 184, November 8, Halleck to Banks, November 9, 1862, ORA, XV, 590–91.

... Why then am I left here when another is sent into the field in this department? If it is because of my disqualification for the service, in which I have as long an experience as any General in the United States Army now in the service (being the Senior in rank), I pray you say so, and so far from being aggrieved, I will return to my home, consoled by the reflection that I have at least done my duty as far as endeavor and application goes. I am only desirous of not being kept where I am not needed or desired.[4]

Butler was partially correct in blaming the secretary of state for his removal, although Lincoln would have made the change without any prodding. Seward claimed that he spent half of his time answering complaints from irate foreign ministers because of Butler's heavy-handed practices. There is no question that Lincoln's policy toward Great Britain and France was one of cautious appeasement, and the elimination of Butler's relentless attacks on European consuls would alleviate some of the pressure. Treasury Secretary Chase, after reading the general's letter to Lincoln, wrote Butler on December 14 with words of praise and reassurance: "Don't think that the appointment of General Banks will really harm you. It will not. Your retirement would, for it would be ascribed to wounded self-love. . . . Our friends in Congress are unanimous in your praise. Nobody finds fault except some honest people who really believe what has been said about your connection with trade." Chase's statement is fascinating because it implies that only *dishonest* people would doubt rumors accusing the general of improper trade practices. Charles Sumner, after a conversation with Lincoln, added another curious note. Writing from the Senate chamber, he said, "You shall not be forgotten," and then proceeded to inform the general that the French government had forbidden newspapers from mentioning his name.[5]

Butler's removal could be attributed to any of several issues pertaining to his administration—there were certainly enough to choose from—but his inadequacy as a military commander became one of

---

4. *Butler Correspondence*, II, 512–13.

5. Welles, *Diary*, I, 210; Niven, ed., *Chase Papers*, III, 336–37; Thornton Kirkland Lothrop, *William Henry Seward* (Boston, 1898), 373; *Butler Correspondence*, II, 520, 541–42; Dabney, "The Butler Regime in Louisiana," 524.

Lincoln's greatest concerns. Sending Banks to replace Butler improved little because the latter was no more adept at leading soldiers than Butler, whose original orders from McClellan emphasized the capture and occupation of New Orleans, Baton Rouge, Berwick Bay, and Fort Livingston. Had Butler not evacuated Baton Rouge, he would have accomplished the essence of his orders. McClellan spoke vaguely of capturing Mobile, Galveston, and Jackson, Mississippi—unreasonable objectives for a general with only fifteen thousand men. Guerrillas bothered Butler much more than Confederate regulars, and the swamps were always full of partisans looking to spill a little Yankee blood.[6]

Banks's orders read differently, and he brought with him some twenty thousand men. His role, to open the Mississippi, included gaining control of the Red River, and after that capturing Fort Morgan at the mouth of Mobile Bay and the city of Mobile. This was a large order for a man who was as deficient in planning and executing campaigns as Butler.[7]

Aside from military ineptness and rumors of rampant corruption, Lincoln held other reasons for relieving Butler. When his Emancipation Proclamation went into effect on New Year's Day, he wanted to lure Louisiana back into the Union in accordance with his own mild policy of reconstruction. Despite Butler's harsh methods, Union sentiment still existed in Louisiana, and with Banks in command the president hoped to strengthen the movement by enabling voters to elect two qualified Unionists to the House of Representatives. With Butler's record, Lincoln doubted whether the general could credibly administer emancipation, organize elections, or foster unionism after engendering so much hostility in the department. He also recognized the importance of stabilizing trade—Louisiana needed the products of the North at fair prices as much as the North needed cotton from Louisiana.[8]

6. McClellan to Butler, February 23, 1862, *ORA*, VI, 694–95; *Butler Correspondence*, I, 535; Keith to Butler, May 22, 1862, *ORA*, XV, 450–47.

7. Lincoln to Banks, November 22, 1862, *ORA*, Ser. 3, II, 862; Halleck to Banks, November 9, 1862, *ORA*, XV, 590–91.

8. *Butler Correspondence*, II, 570–71; Basler, ed., *Collected Works of Abraham Lincoln*, V, 350, 462–63, 504–505; Fred Harvey Harrington, *Fighting Politician: Major General N. P. Banks* (Philadelphia, 1948), 85–86. See also Caskey, *Secession and Restoration*, 55–67.

Butler, however, surprised him. In November he worked with Shepley in organizing elections in the First and Second Congressional Districts—people living in the outlying parishes below Canal Street going into the First District and everyone living above it going into the Second. Anyone could run who had taken the oath of allegiance and abided by the rules of Louisiana. By now, New Orleanians realized that for Union men "there were offices, employments, privileges, favors, honors, everything which a government can bestow. For rebels there was mere protection against personal violence—mere toleration of their presence." A number of candidates entered the race, some supporting slavery, some emancipation, and some entered the race at the eleventh hour. People went to the polls on December 3. The First District voted for Unionist Benjamin F. Flanders, a native of New Hampshire and a popular resident of New Orleans, and the Second District elected Democrat Michael Hahn, a Bavarian who had come to New Orleans at the age of ten and had actively stumped against secession. Voter turnout had been light, but both electees were staunch Unionists and strong advocates of Lincoln's policies. As a whole, New Orleans remained stubbornly Confederate, but the general gave the president exactly what he wanted by organizing a minority political machine to begin the process of civil reconstruction.[9]

On December 12, 1862, Butler received his first official notice of removal when Banks arrived with half of his command and presented his credentials in person. Banks brought no orders from the White House for Butler, who for six days suppressed his indignation and agonized over his future. He controlled his temper when Banks asked to retain the general's own handpicked administrative staff. Butler courteously agreed—at least until he better understood his role. When no cryptic explanation came from his superiors, he wrote Lincoln: "Having received no further orders, either to report to him [Banks] or otherwise, I have taken the liberty to suppose that I was permitted to return home, my services no longer being required here. I have given Gen'l. Banks all the information in my power, and more than he has asked in relation to the affairs of this Department." To a friend, Sarah

9. Parton, *General Butler*, 596; Caskey, *Secession and Restoration*, 64–65; Dabney, "The Butler Regime in Louisiana," 523–24.

Butler predicted, "We may go to Washington before returning home. . . . All is over for the present. . . . I shall soon see the children; that is a comfort amid the trouble."[10]

Knowing he had been relieved and not willing to serve under Banks, Butler on December 15 bid his soldiers good-bye, praising their good conduct for earning the "bravos of all nations" by bringing law and order to the Crescent City. Had the general asked, neither Seward nor the city's foreign consuls would have agreed with the "bravos." He also praised the troops for adding to the nation's treasury $500,000, which raises the question of where the other money went—the specie, the cotton, and all the other commodities stripped from the plantations and salt mines of southern Louisiana. "You have met double numbers of the enemy and defeated him in the field," Butler added effusively, but at Baton Rouge and the Lafourche the Federal force outnumbered the enemy by more than two to one. Butler's "Farewell, my comrades! Again, farewell!" made marvelous rhetoric but not much sense.[11]

The following day he met with his staff and formally relinquished command of the Department of the Gulf to General Banks. He then turned over all the public property in his possession—some $1 million worth—and spent the next few days briefing the new commander on civil and military affairs. Back in Washington, Gideon Welles noted in his *Diary*, "Information reaches us that General Butler has been superseded at New Orleans by General Banks. The wisdom of this change I question. I have not a very exalted opinion of the military qualities of either . . . and so told the President." Welles made another observation, writing that Banks "has not the energy, power, ability of Butler, nor, though of loose and fluctuating principles, will he be so reckless and unscrupulous." Welles, who took a balanced approach to every issue, assessed the change accurately.[12]

On December 24 Benjamin Butler delivered a parting address to the citizens of New Orleans, predicting that his name would be "indis-

---

10. General Orders No. 184, November 8, 1862, ORA, XV, 590; *Butler Correspondence*, II, 545, 547; *Butler's Book*, 529–30; Butler to Banks, December 16, 1862, in Butler Papers, LC; Memorandum of Conversation with General Butler, December 18, 1862, in Nathaniel P. Banks Papers, Essex Institute, Salem, Mass.

11. General Orders No. 106, December 15, 1862, ORA, XV, 610.

12. *Butler's Book*, 530–31; Welles, *Diary*, I, 209–210; Felix Grima to Victor Grima, December 17 [12?], 1862, in Grima Family Papers, Mss 99, Folder 59.

solubly connected" with the city. He extolled himself as a benevolent patriarch, lavishly praising his administration and adding a final platitude in defense of the Woman Order. He absolved himself of several executions—acts of treason deserved no less. It had been the good fortune of the Crescent City to have had Ben Butler and not somebody else:

> You might have been smoked to death in caverns, as were the Covenanters of Scotland by the command of a general of the royal house of England; or roasted, like the inhabitants of Algiers during the French campaign; your wives and daughters may have been given over to the ravisher, as were the unfortunate dames of Spain in the Peninsular War; or you might have been scalped and tomahawked, as our mothers were at Wyoming [Valley] by the savage allies of Great Britain in our own Revolution; . . . your sons might have been blown from the mouths of cannon, like the Sepoys of Delhi; and yet all this would have been within the rules of civilized warfare as practised by the most polished and hypocritical nations of Europe. For such acts the records of the doings of some inhabitants of your city toward the friends of the Union, before my coming, were a sufficient provocative and justification. But I have not so conducted [myself].

Compared with some of the most bloodthirsty scoundrels of the past, Butler's snapshot of his administration looked saintly. After all, he had fed the poor, cleaned the streets, flushed the sewers, stabilized currency, created employment, and organized elections. When measured against the lasting hatred of secessionists, though, his worthy deeds would not be long remembered.[13]

The general's "indissoluble connection" with the city began to manifest itself as he prepared to leave. An anonymous lady who claimed to have spoken to the general in private and through the press sent him a letter expressing her "loving (?) farewell" and informing him of the "true light with which your departure is viewed by us. Self-respect, however, prevented me from [seeing you off], as I feared contamination by even breathing the polluted air with which you are surrounded."

> Ever since you came among us, we have felt for you *hatred* so violent that no words can express it. We have always regarded you as a monster

13. *Butler Correspondence*, II, 554–57.

in whose composition the lowest of traits were concentrated; and "Butler the brute" will be handed down to posterity as a by-word, by which all true southerners will "remember *thee* monster, thou vilest of scum." . . . Not content with thieving and stealing from all sorts and conditions of men, you insulted our best citizens, and used language to our gentlemen such as they never heard, and such as *you* only are capable of uttering. . . . May you return to Lowell (the Yankee hole that gave you birth), and when your miserable wife decks herself off in her stolen finery, and appears with you in public, may every eye be turned, and every finger pointed to the "pair of Yankee thieves." . . . [M]ay the spirit of the glorious Mumford haunt you by night.

One of your She Adders[14]

For several months Jefferson Davis had been collecting complaints of "repeated atrocities and outrages" from citizens all over the South, and he was always looking for ways to steel the people's hearts with grim determination to win the war. Butler gave it to him. On December 24, the day of the general's departure, the Confederate president issued a lengthy proclamation enumerating Butler's crimes against the "entire population of the city of New Orleans," making special reference to the murder of Mumford, the contemptible Woman Order, the confiscation of millions in southern wealth, and the fomenting of insurrection by arming slaves. He declared the general a felon and ordered that he "no longer be considered or treated as a public enemy . . . but as an outlaw and common enemy of mankind," and that whoever caught him was to forego a trial and immediately execute him by hanging. Davis' anger extended to every officer in Butler's command, ordering that any of them, whenever captured, were not to be "considered as soldiers engaged in honorable warfare, but as robbers, and criminals, deserving death." Davis did not demand they be hanged but ordered them reserved for execution. Butler shrugged off the proclamation, writing that while it was filled with "simple lying abuse," Davis had issued it because the general had "armed the slaves," and

14. *Ibid.*, 548–59. Eugenia Levy Phillips had seen Butler's "She Adder" sign, as had many other women who had been called to his office, and she was at Ship Island when Alexander Walker wrote his lengthy letter to Jefferson Davis protesting Butler's methods. See Walker, "A Prisoner's Own Story," 5, 12.

that Davis simply wanted to discourage Union officers from commanding black troops.[15]

On the heels of Davis' proclamation, Richard Yeadon of Charleston, South Carolina, offered on January 1, 1863, ten thousand dollars to the person who captured and delivered "the said Benjamin F. Butler, dead or alive, to any proper Confederate authority." A local mother, living in the Darlington District of Charleston, wrote the Charleston *Courier*, "I propose to spin the thread to make the cord to execute the order of our noble president . . . when old Butler is caught, my daughter asks that she may be allowed to adjust it around his neck."[16]

During his tenure at New Orleans, Butler created new enemies at home—along with some appreciative business associates who organized a huge banquet in his honor. In an open letter to Butler, the *New Yorker* informed the public that the dinner had been "gotten up . . . by a few truckling scoundrels" who had conspired with the general and his brother to steal cotton, sugar, and other commodities and pocket the money. "The leading members of the Chamber of Commerce," wrote the editor, "refused to allow their rooms to be desecrated by any meeting to do honor to a man whose private character was so well-known before he had the opportunity to disgrace our country by his public acts." Now, rambled the editor, "you are to answer to the people of the North for your thieving; an account is coming out which may take down your bombastic vanity a degree, and another little account for which you try on all public occasions to excuse yourself, is the murder of Mumford, whom you call a drunken gambler,—the idea of a drunken sot like you calling another a 'drunken gambler.'" The diatribe ended with an open threat and closed with the warning: "Your rotten-hearted carcass must be deprived of vitality, your thieving soul of life, so prepare to meet your cohort, the Devil, who wants you more than this country does." Some people, North and South, sure hated the general.[17]

---

15. Davis' Proclamation, December 24, 1862, ORA, XV, 906–908; *Butler Correspondence*, II, 557–62; *Butler's Book*, 546; Coulter, *Confederate States of America*, 370–71.

16. *Butler's Book*, 547; Parton, *General Butler*, 612.

17. *Butler Correspondence*, II, 569.

Butler claimed to have landed at New Orleans with a military chest containing $75. Horace Greeley produced an accounting of Butler's administration, listing $345,000 turned over to the Treasury, $525,000 expended in feeding the poor, and $200,000 given to Banks's commissary and quartermaster. Through taxes, assessments, fines, and forfeitures, the general reported collections of $1,088,000. Millions, however, changed hands during the seven-month period, and where it all went can never be tracked.[18]

One instance extended well into Banks's administration—the incident of the "stolen spoons"—and as one researcher learned, the general's detractors continued to accuse him of the theft twenty-five years after his death. The case of the "stolen spoons" began on August 9, 1862, when Mrs. S. G. Ferguson, with a pass from Shepley, set out with her children to join her husband in Confederate Louisiana. Being permitted to carry only clothing and supplies, her belongings were searched at an outpost, where pickets discovered a large amount of silverware concealed on the floor of her buggy. Taken before the provost marshal, Mrs. Ferguson was convicted of smuggling and the silver was confiscated. She disavowed ownership, claiming the silver belonged to Mrs. M. Gillis, a Frenchwoman who lived at Bayou Goula near Baton Rouge. When John Gillis appeared before the provost marshal to claim the silver, Butler released Mrs. Ferguson from jail and sent Gillis to Ship Island for seventy-five days at hard labor for using a woman to conduct his smuggling operation. The spoons were signed into the customhouse, and Butler heard no more on the subject until December 17, when A. Villeneuve, a French citizen, claimed the property as his and produced receipts to prove he once owned it. Butler had just been recalled, so he referred the matter to Banks. When Banks failed to acknowledge Villeneuve's claim, the Frenchman appealed to Shepley, identifying the silverware and placing its value at two hundred dollars.

By then the silver had disappeared, having been delivered at different times to Colonel Stafford and, on Butler's departure, to Lieutenant David C. G. Field, the general's financial clerk. Field turned the silver over to Banks as part of the $1,088,000 collected by the department to the account of the government. Villeneuve appealed to the French

18. General Orders No. 106, December 15, 1862, *ORA*, XV, 610; Horace Greeley, *The American Conflict* (2 vols.; Hartford, 1866), II, 106.

consul, who forwarded copies of the growing file of documents to the French minister in Washington. On November 18, 1863, Seward, to his disgust, found himself embroiled in another controversy he attributed to Butler. He referred the matter to Stanton, who began an extensive search for Villeneuve's lost silver.

On March 12, 1864, the search reverted to Butler, who produced a receipt showing that Lieutenant Field had transferred the silver to Captain John W. McClure, Banks's assistant quartermaster. McClure could not recall the transaction, so Butler wrote the postmaster in New Orleans suggesting that the silverware was "doing duty on Banks' table." On April 29, 1864, the mystery ended when McClure suddenly recalled the silverware and admitted it had been in his possession, but, he said, "he sold it and accounted for it in his 'abstract.'" The other spoons, those confiscated from the Twiggs home, were purchased by Butler and sent to his mother. Ben Butler, who may forever be associated with New Orleans, confiscated two collections of silver "spoons," but he did not steal them.[19]

Butler was far too intelligent to get caught with his hand in the till, and nobody could ever prove that he blatantly stole from those he suppressed under martial law. He was also too shrewd an observer not to be aware of his brother's business practices, and a man of honor would not have waited for scandal unless he consciously chose to risk his reputation for the accumulation of personal wealth. According to historian James F. Rhodes, Butler went to New Orleans worth $150,000, and by 1868 his wealth had grown to an estimated $3 million. Three of those years he spent as a general, the other three as a politician and lawyer. By almost any standards of the 1860s, he could not have increased his net worth by $2,850,000 by simply practicing his two professions. Louisianians never doubted the source of Butler's millions.[20]

The general also had many admirers. On the morning of December 24, as his own 26th Massachusetts escorted Butler and his wife to the unarmed transport waiting at the wharf, hundreds of people bid him good-bye, among them Admiral Farragut. Working through the

19. Orcutt, "Ben Butler and the 'Stolen Spoons.'"
20. Rhodes, *History of the United States*, V, 312. Rhodes, after extensively researching Butler's rapid rise to wealth, became convinced the general was a scoundrel.

crowd, Butler shook every outstretched hand. Banks ignored the general's departure, but when the transport finally pulled from the wharf, *Hartford*, the admiral's flagship, fired a parting salute, followed by a major general's send-off from a shore battery.[21]

As the final echo from the guns grew silent, the crowd began to disperse. An aging black woman watched from the levee. She did not know the general, but she was wise in the ways of the world. She waved a final farewell and cried softly, "Good-bye, honey, you never stole nothing from me."[22]

21. *Butler's Book*, 532–33; Parton, *General Butler*, 602, 611–12.

22. Ficklin, "History of Reconstruction in Louisiana," 36 n. Also quoted in Holzman, *Stormy Ben Butler*, 258.

13

Aftermath

NEW ORLEANS GREETED the arrival of Banks with great enthusiasm. The handsome young commander quickly won the city's approval by rescinding many of Butler's standing orders. Banks discontinued the practice of charging fees for permits and of creating privileges and monopolies for special trade and interest groups. He allowed citizens to pass and trade freely within Union lines, and he encouraged slaves to remain on plantations to help with the harvests. On the day of Butler's departure the new commander evicted all Federal officers from houses "irregularly seized, occupied, or confiscated" and ordered the men to find quarters near their regiments. On Christmas Day he reopened all churches, and a day later he encouraged the people of the Southwest to join together in the reunification of America. To show his sincerity, Banks ordered the release of all political prisoners and discontinued Butler's practice of auctioning seized property. When Farragut suggested that Baton Rouge be reoccupied without delay, Banks detached ten thousand troops under Brigadier General Cuvier Grover and on December 17 intimidated the small garrison of Confederate defenders to a hasty withdrawal.[1]

After scorning Butler for seven months with the deepest hatred a woman could muster, Julia Le Grand praised Banks "so far" for his "equitable rule. . . . We know him as an enemy," she wrote, "but an honest and respectable one."[2]

---

1. Grover's Report, December 17, General Orders No. 113, December 20, Banks's Declaration, December 24, General Orders No. 117 and 118, December 24, General Orders No. 120, December 26, 1862, ORA, XV, 191–92, 615, 620, 623, 624–25. All of Banks's conciliatory orders are in Department of the Gulf, Letters Sent, Major General Banks, Book No. 4, War Records Division, NA.

2. Rowland and Croxwell, eds., *Journal of Julia Le Grand*, 55–56.

For Banks, the honeymoon lasted about two months. When he banished a boatload of dissidents to Secessia, hundreds of women and children gathered at the steamboat landing. They screamed and hollered, running to and fro waving handkerchiefs and shrieking their protests. There being no army regulations to cover the fracas, the soldiers attempted to stand their ground against the shoving and howling and hoped that the women would tire before they themselves did. Marion Southwood called it "The Pocket Handkerchief War," and it telegraphed a message to Banks that New Orleans remained contumacious and capable of defiance.[3]

By removing Butler, Lincoln did Seward a favor. One historian, after researching the general's ongoing disputes with New Orleans consuls, concluded that Banks proved the department could be governed "with almost equal efficiency and without the disturbances created by Butler's tactlessness. Never again during the Civil War did New Orleans appear in the correspondence exchanged between Spain and America."[4]

It had been an auspicious beginning for Banks, but a humiliating end for Butler, whose transport was met at the Narrows on the first day of January by a revenue cutter bearing a message from Lincoln inviting the general to come to Washington. The Army of the Potomac, led by Major General Ambrose Burnside, a West Point man, had recently suffered a bloody defeat at Fredericksburg. Under such circumstances, Lincoln felt awkward addressing the man he had so rudely dispossessed and whose support he now needed. The general's civil administration in Louisiana had won the praise of the Radical Republicans, and after Burnside's disaster, Lincoln could not afford to lose Butler's political influence.[5]

Back in Lowell the deposed general could become a greater menace than in the Gulf, and Lincoln strained the intellectual resources of the cabinet to contrive some new assignment to keep Butler happy. General Grant had just retreated from central Mississippi, and Major General William T. Sherman, acting under Grant's orders, had been repulsed at Chickasaw Bayou in a failed attempt to capture Vicksburg.

3. Southwood, *"Beauty and Booty,"* 279–81.

4. Egan, "Friction in New Orleans," 52.

5. *Butler's Book*, 389, 533; Lincoln to Butler, December 29, 1862, in Butler Papers, LC.

Lincoln considered placing Butler in command of the army in the Mississippi Valley, but he had recently promised an independent command to Major General John A. McClernand, a close political friend, and then decided it was wiser to keep the western army under Grant.[6]

When Butler reached Washington, Lincoln greeted him with great cordiality, but the general remained sour and unimpressed by the friendly reception. He circulated through the cabinet, demanding an explanation for his recall and asking for answers of how Jefferson Davis knew of his removal before he himself did. When nobody seemed willing to discuss the matter, Butler became surly, and Lincoln, boxed in a corner, finally suggested that the entire Mississippi Valley might be transferred to the angry general's command. Butler declined. He did not want Grant's army and demanded nothing less than his old department. Lincoln replied that such a move would unjustifiably disgrace Banks, and when the meeting ended, the president's offer stood. Butler stormed out of the White House feeling better, but still much annoyed. He then met with Stanton, who was still unsure of where the general stood on the slave issue. When Butler made it clear how ardently he favored emancipation, Stanton was surprised and later admitted to Sumner that he would not have consented to the recall had he understood the general's strong support of the proclamation. Before leaving Washington, Butler met separately with Halleck and Seward. Each blamed the other for the general's recall, and in a gesture of disgust, Butler departed for Lowell, convinced that both men had exposed themselves as pathetic liars.[7]

Butler journeyed home in triumph, stopping along the way to collect the praise of thousands who gathered to honor him. Jefferson Davis elevated the general's image by branding him a felon and ordering his execution. Secessionist gentlemen popularized him by offering large rewards for his head—dead or alive. Formal votes of thanks to the man who made the Rebels howl came from the House of Representatives, the state legislatures, and the city of New York. A grateful

6. Welles, *Diary*, I, 210; General Orders No. 210, December 18, 1862, *ORA*, Vol. XVII, Pt. 2, pp. 432–33.

7. *Butler's Book*, 534, 549–51, 568–70; Sumner to Butler, January 8, 1863, Memorandum, January 8, 1878, in Butler Papers, LC; Horowitz, "Ben Butler and the Negro," 183–84.

country, unhappy with recent Union defeats, elevated the general to new heights of popularity.[8]

Butler had not been home for a week before Lincoln realized the danger of having the rancorous politician rallying support at the expense of the White House. When the general appeared before the Joint Committee on the Conduct of the War, he testified that he had been given no reason for his recall. He then staged a brilliant defense of his administration in New Orleans and encouraged the formation of black regiments. Relying on his skills as a defense lawyer, he dispelled rumors of corruption, and Radical Republicans flocked to his defense.[9]

Against his better judgment—and the fondness he felt for Banks—Lincoln, on January 23, wrote Stanton, "I think General Butler should go to New Orleans again. He is unwilling to go unless he is restored to the command of the department." Lincoln wanted him out of the way so badly that he told Stanton to send him back to the Crescent City by February 1, but to not wound the feelings of General Banks. Knowing this would not be an easy task for Stanton, Lincoln drafted a carefully worded letter to Banks explaining his dilemma with Butler. For the present, Banks would retain command of the forces in the field but report to Butler. Lincoln did not send the letter. There were too many good reasons for keeping Butler out of the Gulf.[10]

Supporters of the populist movement put pressure on Lincoln to do something for their shabbily treated general, and with public sentiment building toward a crisis, Butler began to wear down the administration. Some members of the military suggested that he replace Stanton. A lady wrote Thaddeus Stevens recommending that all war appropriations be suspended until Seward was removed and Butler named secretary of state. From the custom office in the Crescent City, George Denison wrote, "Dear General: Come back to New Orleans." Lincoln had seen enough, and on January 28 he sent an urgent message to But-

8. *Butler Correspondence*, II, 557–63; *Butler's Book*, 547, 553–60; Butler to Etheridge, January 17, 1863, Warner to Butler, January 21, 23, 1863, in Butler Papers, LC.

9. T. Harry Williams, *Lincoln and the Radicals* (Madison, Wis., 1941), 223.

10. Basler, ed., *Collected Works of Abraham Lincoln*, VI, 73–74, 76–77; Lincoln to Stanton, January 23, 1863, ORA, LIII, 547.

ler: "Please come here immediately. Telegraph me about what time you will arrive."[11]

While waiting, Lincoln changed his mind. He did not trust the general's military competence, and by returning Butler to the Gulf he would dishonor Seward's intimations to European governments. Instead of a command, Lincoln offered Butler a special assignment, one that would take him back to the Mississippi but only to report on conditions there. The general declined. His sources, mainly Chase and Sumner, had informed him that he was to be reinstated to command of the Gulf with a greater force. That was what he wanted. He would not share power with Banks, whom he hated, so once again he departed from Washington leaving the unresolved burden of his assignment with Lincoln. No doubt Butler had other reasons for returning to New Orleans. If any irrefutable evidence of corruption existed anywhere, it would be there, and Banks would not hesitate to disclose it.[12]

Weeks passed into months. Butler remained politically active, captivated by the growing number of influential Republicans who spoke of his chances for the presidency. The notion appealed to the general. Enemies recognized the legitimacy of the threat and spoke loudly against the general's record of corruption. Butler searched for methods to improve his image, and by a stroke of good fortune author James Parton made a timely appearance, collaborated with the subject, and wrote *General Butler in New Orleans*, an immensely popular biography that extolled the virtues of the general, whitewashed his transgressions, and provided marvelous campaign publicity.[13]

The stain of his recall still rankled the general, and his tireless efforts at vindication became, for Lincoln, a constant annoyance. But-

11. *Butler Correspondence*, II, 589–90, 593; Amasa McCoy to Stevens, January 19, Denison to Butler, February 10, 1863, in Butler Papers, LC; Basler, ed., *Collected Works of Abraham Lincoln*, VI, 81.

12. Seward to Stanton, January 14, 1863, Banks Papers; Lincoln's draft order dated February 17, 1863, and Butler to A. J. Butler, February 18, 1863, in Butler Papers, LC; Basler, ed., *Collected Works of Abraham Lincoln*, VI, 100; *Butler Correspondence*, II, 570–71, 580, III, 13, 21–27; Niven, ed., *Chase Papers*, III, 388–89.

13. *Butler Correspondence*, III, 99–100; T. H. Williams, *Lincoln and the Radicals*, 272; M. Flower, *James Parton*, 62–72.

ler grumbled to Congress that he had been sent to New Orleans with about fourteen thousand men, never again to be reinforced from the North, but when Banks superseded him, he brought along an army of twenty thousand men. For several weeks the general heckled Congress and the administration for an acceptable military assignment and then rejected everything they offered. No wonder. He had friends like Chase lobbying for his reinstatement and waving letters from Denison in the administration's face condemning Banks's liberal policies and disappointing performance as a military commander. No offer satisfied Butler's ego, but after Gettysburg and the capitulation of Vicksburg Lincoln's presidency solidified and it was Butler who began to worry. He tried to make himself useful, sometimes succeeding and sometimes not. In late October, 1863, he finally consented to return to his old command at Fort Monroe, now the XVIII Army Corps. It had been expanded into the Department of Virginia and North Carolina and encompassed Norfolk, Portsmouth, Williamsburg, and several towns along the coast of North Carolina. The assignment appeased Butler and alleviated pressure on Lincoln, but for Grant it eventually led to problems of a military nature.[14]

In an April 29 letter to General Sherman, Halleck commented dourly, "It seems but little better than murder to give important commands to such men as Banks, Butler, McClernand, Sigel, and Lew. Wallace." Of the political generals drawing Halleck's scorn, only Butler had the opportunity to redeem himself. Having never been furnished enough troops to act on the offensive, he could now demonstrate his tactical skills without dependence upon the navy.[15]

Operating from his old headquarters at Fort Monroe, one of Butler's first acts was to visit the Federal prison camp at nearby Point Lookout.

---

14. *Butler Correspondence*, III, 118–19, 139–41; Niven, ed., *Chase Papers*, III, 393–94, 395–96, 404–405; General Orders No. 350, October 28, 1863, ORA, Vol. XXIX, Pt. 2, p. 397; Denison to A. J. Butler, October 9, 1863, in Butler Papers, LC; *Report of the Joint Committee on the Conduct of the War* (1863), III, 353–57.

15. Halleck to Sherman, April 29, 1864, ORA, XXXIV, 333. Banks had just been defeated during the Red River campaign; John A. McClernand had been deposed by Grant in May, 1863, at Vicksburg; Franz Sigel had been repulsed in May, 1864, by a weak Confederate force at New Market, Virginia; and Lewis Wallace, although he remained in command of the VIII Corps until the end of the war, never distinguished himself.

Tattered Confederates strained against the fences and greeted him with slurs:

"What will you take for your head?"

"You d——n lobster-eyed son of a b——h."

"Pay me the money you robbed me of in New Orleans."

"Why don't you fight men and not women?"

"How much are you worth, you Burglar?"[16]

Butler ignored the invectives, but the occasion set his mind at work. He enjoyed tinkering with policies, especially high-profile situations where the press could revile the administration for inaction or imperfect action. He had barely settled into his new headquarters when he decided to leap into the growing imbroglio over prisoner exchange. At the root of the impasse lay a contentious issue—an exchange of black troops for whites on a man-to-man basis. Butler believed he could reach a settlement, and nothing would rile Confederate prisoners more than knowledge that they had been exchanged for blacks. Stanton warned him against trying, but Butler forged ahead. He could not break the Confederate government's resistance to exchanging blacks, but he made good progress with the whites. This gave him encouragement, and he even managed to persuade Jefferson Davis to rescind his execution order, thereby enabling him to meet with Confederate negotiators. He did not like it when Grant, who had just been elevated to commander in chief of the Union army, vetoed his efforts and suspended all exchanges, white or black, except for invalids.[17]

Grant focused on one issue—bringing an end to the war. Having inherited Butler, he attempted to make the best of a bad situation, sending what soon became the Army of the James reinforcements and better officers. Butler had a way of mismanaging military campaigns, and four years in the army did little to improve his skills. In business transactions he excelled, and shortly after his arrival at Fort Monroe complaints of corruption, like those voiced during his administration at New Orleans, began to trickle into the White House. He realized,

16. Coulter, *Confederate States of America*, 370.

17. Butler to Stanton, Stanton to Butler, November 17, Butler to Stanton, November 18, 1863, ORA, Ser. 2, VI, 528, 532–34; Grant to Butler, April 14, 20, 1863, *ibid.*, Ser. 2, VII, 50, 76; *Butler Correspondence*, IV, 72, 83–84; *Butler's Book*, 592–93.

however, that the war was wearing down, and little time remained for him to make his mark as a military commander.[18]

Combined operations appealed to Butler. They had helped him at New Orleans, so why not again? Because the James River could be ascended by heavy navy vessels as far as the mouth of the Appomattox, some twenty-five miles by water below Richmond, Butler convinced Grant that the city could be taken by an amphibious operation. Grant had also studied a map and considered the idea himself, and now that Butler suggested it, he saw no harm in letting him try it. The landing site, a thirty-square-mile peninsula known as Bermuda Hundred, was by land sixteen miles south of the Confederate capital and nine miles north of Petersburg. By a lightning attack, the Army of the James could strike the Richmond and Petersburg and the Weldon Railroads, and in a giant pincer movement cooperate with the Army of the Potomac in assaulting Richmond.[19]

Grant began reinforcing Butler's army because he foresaw an opportunity to shorten the war, and knowing that the Army of the James might be required to fight for several days disconnected from the Army of the Potomac, he wanted it strong enough to withstand a Confederate counterattack. He added Major General Quincy A. Gillmore's X Army Corps, reinforced the XVIII Army Corps under Major General William F. Smith, added artillery and cavalry, and brought Butler's force to 35,916 men. Grant had some doubts about trusting Butler with an army of this size. He preferred the more experienced Smith, but after a conference with Butler he accepted the arrangement, wisely allowing Butler to believe that he was the sole author of the plan.[20]

On May 4 Butler received word from Grant that the two armies

18. Welles, *Diary*, II, 56, 81; *Butler Correspondence*, III, 282–84, 321–24, 450–60, 512–13, 450–60; Basler, ed., *Collected Works of Abraham Lincoln*, VII, 103, 135.

19. Ulysses S. Grant, *Personal Memoirs of U. S. Grant* (2 vols.; New York, 1885), II, 148; *Butler's Book*, 622–27.

20. Grant to Butler, April 2, 16, 18, 1864, ORA, XXXIII, 794–95, 885–86, 904; Organization of Army of the James, *ibid.*, Vol. XXXVI, Pt. 1, pp. 116–19; Grant, *Personal Memoirs*, II, 129–33; Andrew A. Humphreys, *The Virginia Campaign of '64 and '65: The Army of the Potomac and the Army of the James* (New York, 1883), 137; William Glenn Robertson, *Back Door to Richmond: The Bermuda Hundred Campaign, April–June, 1864* (Newark, Del., 1987), 18–19.

would commence simultaneous operations, and at daybreak on May 5 he departed from Hampton Roads with an endless string of transports accompanied by a squadron of warships from Rear Admiral Samuel Phillips Lee's North Atlantic command. Forty-eight hours later the huge flotilla landed at City Point and Bermuda Hundred, 150 miles upriver, and sent shock waves of consternation into the Confederate capital. The Army of Northern Virginia had siphoned off nearly every regiment to meet Grant's invasion, and there were less than 10,000 Confederate troops within fifty miles of Bermuda Hundred. About 1,000 men, mainly railroad guards, defended Petersburg, and another 4,000 clustered around Richmond.[21]

A rapid advance in force by the Army of the James would have gobbled up two railroads, the main turnpike to Richmond, and very likely the city itself. Instead, Butler quarreled with his two corps commanders for three days, made useless demonstrations that only induced the enemy to rush reinforcements, and set the men to work digging defensive works rather than pressing forward as he had promised Grant. General Beauregard marshaled a small force, attacked Butler, and drove the Army of the James into the entrenchments they had so hurriedly dug. In two weeks Butler shattered his best opportunity to succeed as a military commander, and he never regained the confidence of the army. Like his feeble attempts at conquest in Louisiana, he failed to assert command over his army and never strayed into the field to assess conditions for himself. Even had he done so, it is questionable whether he could have analyzed the situation. If he had simply adhered to the plan he had discussed with Grant, he may have gotten lucky and brought the war to an end.[22]

Grant could not understand what had happened to Butler's attack. He sent Brigadier General John G. Barnard from the Army of the

21. Grant to Butler, Apr. 28, 1864, *ORA,* XXXIII, 1009; Lemuel B. Norton's Report, Sept. 2, 1864, *ibid.,* Vol. XXXVI, Pt. 2, pp. 21–22; Alfred Roman, *The Military Operations of General Beauregard in the War Between the States* (2 vols.; New York, 1883), II, 196, 543–44.

22. George A. Bruce, "General Butler's Bermuda Campaign," and Alfred P. Rockwell, "The Tenth Army Corps in Virginia, May, 1864," *Papers of the Military Historical Society of Massachusetts,* vol. IX (Boston, 1912), 276–80, 310–22; Grant, *Personal Memoirs,* II, 148, 150–52; Trefousse, *Ben Butler,* 149–57.

Potomac to determine whether Butler could be relied upon in another joint operation. A few days later Barnard informed Grant that Butler had developed a marvelous defensive position. Using a map, he drew a line around Butler's army in the shape of a bottle, the neck representing Butler's entrenchments. Because the enemy had built works directly opposite, the Army of the James could not move. "He was perfectly safe against an attack," Grant glumly reflected, "but, as Barnard expressed it, the enemy had corked the bottle and with a small force could hold its cork in place."[23]

Command of the Army of the James played a bad trick on Butler—but one he probably deserved. During 1864, political supporters had mentioned him for the presidency, vice presidency, or perhaps a cabinet post, and for a while his prospects looked good. The fiasco at Bermuda Hundred changed all that, and James Parton's glowing biography praising Butler's administration at New Orleans failed to quell the onus of defeat. At one time Lincoln had cautiously considered enlisting Butler as his running mate, comparing him to "Jim Jett's brother . . . the damndest scoundrel that ever lived, but in the infinite mercy of providence, . . . also the damndest fool." Lincoln probably counted his blessings after the general declined, but it was a mistake Butler regretted for the rest of his life.[24]

After the Bermuda Hundred fiasco, Lincoln had sufficient justification for cashiering Butler, but it was an election year. Butler had cleverly shifted the responsibility for failure to his two subordinates, Smith and Gillmore. On July 1 Grant attempted to transfer him to "a department where there [were] no great battles to be fought, but a dissatisfied element to control." Remembering the turmoil of the general's reign in New Orleans, Halleck believed that wherever Butler went there would be havoc and suggested returning him to Fort Monroe in titular command of the department, but with Smith in charge of the troops in the field. Lincoln signed the order, and for the moment it appeared as if another political general had fallen—but not quite.[25]

The navy had another scheme under consideration, the capture of

23. Grant, *Personal Memoirs*, II, 151–52.

24. William Roscoe Thayer, *The Life and Letters of John Hay* (2 vols.; Boston, 1915), I, 144; *Butler Correspondence*, III, 515; *Butler's Book*, 633–35.

25. Grant to Halleck, July 1, Halleck to Grant, July 3, 1864, ORA, Vol. XL, Pt. 2,

Fort Fisher at the mouth of the Cape Fear River. For nearly four years the North Atlantic Squadron had been chasing blockade runners that sprinted up the river to deliver arms and supplies at Wilmington, North Carolina. In some respects the mouth of the river resembled the mouth of the Mississippi because it had two widely separated outlets, and Welles had to dedicate a large squadron to each of them. Fort Fisher, among the strongest fortifications in the world, guarded New Inlet and lay on a strip of sand facing the Atlantic Ocean on one side and the Cape Fear River on the other. To capture the enormous earthwork, Welles transferred David D. Porter, now an admiral, from command of the Mississippi Squadron and then asked General Grant for troops.[26]

The only troops Grant could spare were "bottled up" at Bermuda Hundred, so once again Butler and Porter—antagonists since the New Orleans expedition—came together on a collision course. Grant, however, intended to keep Butler at Fort Monroe and placed General Weitzel in charge of the army. Looking upon the capture of Fort Fisher as his last opportunity to gain military recognition, Butler imposed himself on Porter. The admiral attempted to lay all differences aside, and for a while their relationship remained tranquil.[27]

Butler and Porter shared one characteristic—both were innovators and experimenters—and when the general conceived a plan to topple Fort Fisher by filling a vessel with three hundred tons of powder and exploding it just offshore, Porter agreed to try it. Grant scorned the idea but relented, ordering Butler to tell Weitzel to make the landing, entrench, and by cooperating with Porter, whom he infinitely trusted, "reduce and capture" the works.[28]

To the surprise of both Grant and Porter, Butler decided to lead his troops. A soldier from New York shared their concern, writing, "Old Butler is here and will perhaps command the expedition—in order to assure its failure." The transports did not get started until mid-

---

pp. 558–59, 598; Grant to Halleck, July 6, General Orders No. 225, July 7, 1864, *ibid.*, Pt. 3, pp. 31, 59, 69.

26. Welles to Porter, September 22, 1864, *ORN*, XXI, 657; Welles, *Diary*, II, 127–29, 145–47.

27. Porter, *Incidents and Anecdotes*, 263–64; Hearn, *Admiral Porter*, 274.

28. Grant to Butler, December 6, 1864, *ORA*, Vol. XVII, Pt. 3, p. 835; *Butler's Book*, 775–76; Hearn, *Admiral Porter*, 277–78.

December, and to deceive the enemy, who already knew of the expedition, the general lost more time maneuvering at sea and then failed to meet Porter at the rendezvous. Butler then sailed for Fort Fisher without Porter, who steamed into Beaufort and had to wait for the weather to clear. Porter's squadron escorted the powder boat, but when it reached the rendezvous point off Fort Fisher, Butler, having brought insufficient supplies, had returned to Beaufort. Disgusted, Porter sent word to Beaufort that he would explode the powder boat that night and encouraged the general to return on the double. At 2:10 A.M. on December 23, the powder boat went up in a huge puff of smoke and barely disturbed the slumbering defenders of Fort Fisher. Midmorning, Porter opened with his entire squadron. Expecting to see Butler's transports at any hour, he kept up the bombardment all day, but the general did not arrive until late afternoon, and then with only part of his force.[29]

Butler's tardiness could have been forgiven if he had simply landed his force, entrenched as ordered by Grant, and laid siege to Fort Fisher. Instead, he landed a third of his force, retired after a reconnaissance, and stranded about a thousand men on the beach whom Porter rescued the following day. When Grant learned of the embarrassing debacle, he wrote Stanton asking that Butler be removed from active duty: "I am constrained to request the removal of General B. F. Butler from command of the Department of Virginia and North Carolina. I do this with reluctance, but the good of the service requires it. In my absence, General Butler necessarily commands, and there is a lack of confidence in his military ability, making him an unsafe commander for a large army. His administration of the affairs of this department is also objectionable."[30]

Lincoln no longer needed Butler and on January 7, 1865, relieved him of command. But this was not the end of it. Butler went to Washington and appeared before the Joint Committee on the Conduct of the War to plead his case. During the same span of time, Grant sent Major General Alfred H. Terry with a second force from the Army of

29. Porter's Report, December 26, 27, 1864, January 11, 1865, *ORN*, XI, 227–28, 253–60, 261–62; Butler to Grant, December 20, 27, 1864, January 3, 1865, *ORA*, Vol. XLII, Pt. 2, pp. 965–70. See also Hearn, *Admiral Porter*, 279–84.

30. Grant to Stanton, January 4, 1865, *ORA*, Vol. XLVI, Pt. 2, p. 29.

the James to cooperate with Porter in subduing Fort Fisher. While Butler was blaming Porter for the defeat and claiming that the fortress could not be taken without a prolonged siege, a newsboy came into committee chambers shouting, "Fort Fisher done took." Butler looked foolish, but his standing with the Radical Republicans saved him, and they allowed his tainted report to stand.[31]

Thus ended the military career of Benjamin F. Butler, but not his political career, and for both he owed much to Lincoln. Robert E. Lee surrendered to Grant on April 9, and five days later John Wilkes Booth assassinated the president. Lincoln's death inflamed the Radical Republicans against the war-torn South, and Butler discovered a new political niche—he joined the radicals. As he had bullied New Orleans, he now targeted the entire South for his style of reconstruction. When President Andrew Johnson attempted to follow Lincoln's policy of leniency, Butler remained loyal only until it became apparent that Johnson would neither appoint him military governor of a Confederate state nor ruthlessly punish the South for its transgressions. He resigned his commission as major general, and because he was not a member of Congress, he could not play a major role in the formation of the Joint Committee of Fifteen on Reconstruction.[32]

Andrew Johnson's disregard of Butler's power almost cost him the presidency. In 1866 Butler ran for Congress, pledging to impeach Johnson, and won easily. Keeping his pledge was not so easy. After taking his seat in Congress, Butler led a heated and fascinating debate that began on March 7, 1867, and ended on May 16, 1868, when the Senate defeated the primary articles of impeachment by one vote. Butler was stunned. He was on the verge of losing his greatest case, but not his tenacity. He singled out seven senators and imposed enormous pressure on them to change their vote in a second session scheduled for May 26, subjecting them to threats and hounding them with spies.

31. Halleck to Grant, January 7, Butler's Farewell Address, January 8, 1865, *ibid.*, 60, 70–71; William T. Sherman, *Memoirs of General W. T. Sherman* (2 vols.; New York, 1891), II, 242. *Report of the Joint Committee on the Conduct of the War*, 38th Cong., 2nd Sess. (3 vols.; Washington, D.C., 1865), II, i–viii.

32. *Butler Correspondence*, V, 641–42, 684; Butler to Johnson, October 25, 1865, Kelton to Butler, December 4, 1865, in Butler Papers, LC. The Joint Committee of Fifteen composed what became the Fourteenth Amendment.

He blamed Edmund G. Ross, a junior senator from Kansas, for the defeat, and a few days before the final vote, Butler said, "Tell the damned scoundrel that if he wants money there is a bushel of it here to be had." The final vote remained the same, and Butler, furious at losing, spent several months fruitlessly attempting to unearth evidence against the seven recusant senators.[33]

Johnson served out his term, and Butler, who had done everything in his power to prevent Grant's nomination, found himself in political shambles. His quarrel with the general began in late 1865 when Grant published his final report, dredging up Butler's ineptitudes in the field, and old epithets like Spoons Butler, Beast Butler, and Bottled-Up Butler surfaced all over again. Furious and determined to get even, Butler consulted James Parton and set him to work compiling scandalous evidence for a book to disgrace Grant. "I never forget nor forgive until reparation is made," Butler declared, "and in Grant's case it never can be."[34]

Butler worked hard on the book, but it was never published, and withholding the manuscript worked to his advantage. Soon after Grant's inauguration, Butler cleverly ingratiated himself and began to make himself useful. Once again immersed in issues concerning Reconstruction, he used his nimble intellect to discover ways he could influence Grant, and by 1870, although still a congressman, he had become the chief spokesman for the president. Historians who write of corruption in Grant's administration need look no further than Butler, who took good care of his friends and the friends of the president. Grant foolishly trusted his lieutenant, and Butler shrewdly jockeyed his own initiatives into executive policy. "The worst appointments made by the President were at Butler's suggestion," one editor wrote, and "the worst acts of Congress have been passed under Butler's whip and spur." The failure of Reconstruction, he added, "is due almost entirely to Butler." Not unlike his days in New Orleans, the retired general never seemed to know when to stop. By the end of Grant's

---

33. Schouler's Letter on the Nomination of Butler, October 25, 1866, in Butler Papers, LC; Edmund G. Ross, *History of the Impeachment of Andrew Johnson* (Santa Fe, 1896), 153; Trefousse, *Ben Butler*, 186–204.

34. Ulysses S. Grant, *Official Report of Lt.-Gen. U. S. Grant* (New York, 1865); Butler to Parton, January 15, 26, February 10, 1866, in Parton Papers; Butler to Rush C. Hawkins, May 1, 1866, in Butler Papers, LC.

second term, the public blamed Butler for the depression, the administration's poor record, and many of its scandals. Butler tried to hold his seat in Congress but failed, the opposition adding to his humility by lowering a bundle of large spoons behind his back as he stumped for votes before a large audience.[35]

No politician ever possessed more resilience than Butler. In 1876 his home district sent him back to Congress for another two years, but the general's relationship with the Republican party had cooled and the Democrats were back in power. Having picked the wrong horse, Butler recast his fortunes with the Democrats, and in 1882 they launched him into the governorship of Massachusetts. The general had become grossly fat and immensely wealthy, but neither had changed his ardor for a fight. In his inaugural address he presented his demands, and some of them rang like echoes from the past—a ten-hour workday, protection of laboring women and children, and reformation of the use of public funds for charities and poorhouses—remembrances, perhaps, of some of the good work done but long forgotten in New Orleans. Beast Butler no longer craved money, just power.[36]

In 1884 he failed miserably in his quest for the presidential nomination, and after that he never held public office. His fall from power came swiftly and decisively. When he died on the morning of January 11, 1893, he left a legacy of controversy that still fills the pages of American history.[37]

Twenty-five years after Butler's death, William D. Orcutt walked by the statehouse in Boston and noticed the "gilded dome to the grotesque statue of General Banks." He turned to his companion and asked why the state had failed to erect a statue to Butler.

"A statue to that thief and rascal!" his friend replied. "It would be a disgrace to Massachusetts."

"What did he steal?" Orcutt asked.

"Why, everything in sight—down at New Orleans."[38]

---

35. Springfield *Republican*, March 18, 1871, September 21, 1874, both quoted in Trefousse, *Ben Butler*, 222, 230.

36. *Address of His Excellency Benjamin F. Butler to the Two Branches of the Legislature of Massachusetts, January 4, 1883* (Boston, 1883).

37. New York *Times*, January 11, 12, 1893.

38. Orcutt, "Ben Butler and the 'Stolen Spoons,'" 66.

The citizens of New Orleans never knew how close they came to getting him back, and Grant may have ended the war sooner without him. Both hated and loved, Butler remains to this day a figure immensely amusing and much maligned. If not a genius, he was certainly a brilliant lawyer and a shrewd politician. During his seventy-four years he served great men, defended unsavory clients, and became a man of enormous wealth. His personal estate approached $7 million. The source of his fortune has remained a mystery, but much of it came from New Orleans—either directly during his administration or indirectly through the estate of his deceased brother. Nobody in the North much cared, except for a few Boston politicians who denied him a statue.[39]

Ben Butler would have wanted it that way—except for the statue.

39. Rhodes, *History of the United States*, V, 312.

BIBLIOGRAPHY

Manuscript Collections

Essex Institute, Salem, Mass.
    Banks, Nathaniel P. Papers.
Harvard University Library, Harvard University, Cambridge, Mass.
    Parton, James. Papers.
    Sumner, Charles. Papers.
Historic New Orleans Collection, Wallace Research Center, New Orleans, La.
    Butler, Benjamin F. Papers.
    Dorville, Auvignac. Papers. Mss 100, Folders 393–97.
    Grima, Felix, *et al.* Family Papers. Mss 99, Folders 58–59.
    Walton, Emma. Papers. Mss 135, Folders 15–16.
Library of Congress, Washington, D.C.
    Butler, Benjamin F. Papers.
    Cameron, Simon. Papers.
    Chase, Salmon P. Papers.
    Cushing, Caleb. Papers.
    Denison, George S. Papers.
    Fish, Hamilton. Papers.
    Phillips, Philip. Papers. Manuscript by Eugenia Levy Phillips, "A Southern Woman's Story of Her Imprisonment During the War of 1861 and 1862," and a manuscript by Philip Phillips, "A Summary of the Principal Events of My Life."
    Porter, David Dixon. Papers. "Private Journal of Occurrences During the Great War of the Rebellion, 1860–1865," 2 vols.
    Stanton, Edwin M. Papers.
Louisiana State Museum, New Orleans, La.
    Moss, George. Papers. Record Group 58.

Louisiana State University Libraries, Louisiana State University, Baton Rouge, La.

Louisiana and Lower Mississippi Valley Collections

Bush, Toxie L. "The Federal Occupation of New Orleans," Master's thesis, 1934.

Doyle, Elizabeth Joan. "Civilian Life in Occupied New Orleans." Ph.D. dissertation, 1955.

Flanders, Benjamin F. Papers.

"Historical Militia Data on Louisiana Militia."

Jarred, Simon G. Papers.

Solomon, Clara E. Diary, 1861–1862.

Walker, Alexander. "A Prisoner's Own Story."

Special Collections, Hill Library

Bradley, James Earl. Diary. File No. 1259.

Mercer, William Newton. Papers. File No. 1364.

Pierrepont, Edwards. Papers. File No. 2568.

Massachusetts Historical Society, Boston, Mass.

Andrew, John A. Papers.

National Archives, War Records Division, Washington, D.C.

War Department Records, Department of the Gulf

Banks, Nathaniel P. Book No. 4, Letters Sent.

Butler, Benjamin F. Book No. 1, Letters Sent.

Butler, Benjamin F. Letters Received.

War Department Records—Union

Department of the Gulf. Book No. 15, Special Field Orders.

Department of the Gulf. Book No. 26, General and Special Orders.

Department of the Gulf. Book No. 27, Special Orders.

Department of the Gulf. Book No. 28, Special Orders.

War Department Records—Confederate

Chapter VIII, Vol. CXLIV, Executive Communications, Louisiana State Troops, Letters Received.

Muster Rolls, First Native Guards, Louisiana Militia, May 3, 1861, Record Group 109.

New York Public Library

Welles, Gideon. Papers.

Tulane University, New Orleans, La.

Amistad Research Center

Butler, Benjamin F. Papers.

Harrod, Charles L. Papers.

Howard-Tilton Library

Gray, Helen. Manuscript, "The Three Clergymen of New Orleans and Gen. Benjamin F. Butler," in Suzanne Hiller Herrick Papers.
Harrod, Charles L. Journal.

Official Documents

Address of His Excellency Benjamin F. Butler to the Two Branches of the Legislature of Massachusetts, January 4, 1883. Boston, 1883.

Correspondence Between the War Department and General Lovell Relating to the Defense of New Orleans. Richmond, 1863.

General Orders from Headquarters Department of the Gulf, Issued by Major-General Butler from May 1, 1862–November 9, 1862. New Orleans, 1862.

Official Journal of the Proceedings of the Convention of the State of Louisiana, 1861. New Orleans, 1861.

Official Records of the Union and Confederate Armies, War of the Rebellion. 128 vols. Washington, D.C., 1987.

Official Records of the Union and Confederate Navies, War of the Rebellion. 30 vols. Washington, D.C., 1987.

Report of the Joint Committee on the Conduct of the War. 37th Cong., 3rd Sess. 3 vols. Washington, D.C., 1863.

Report of the Joint Committee on the Conduct of the War. 38th Cong., 2nd Sess. 3 vols. Washington, D.C., 1865.

Report of the Naval Engagements on the Mississippi Resulting in the Capture of Forts Jackson and St. Philip and the City of New Orleans and the Destruction of the Rebel Naval Flotilla. Washington, D.C., 1862.

U.S. Congress. *Papers Relating to Foreign Affairs, 1862.* 37th Cong., 3rd Sess. Washington, D.C., 1863.

————. House of Representatives. *Trade with Rebellious States.* 38th Cong., 2nd Sess. House Report No. 24. Washington, D.C., 1865.

U.S. Senate Reports. 37th Cong., 3rd Sess., No. 108. Washington, D.C., 1863.

Newspapers

Baltimore *American*
Boston *Bee*
Boston *Globe*
Boston *Herald*

New Orleans *Bee*
New Orleans *Commercial Bulletin*
New Orleans *Daily Crescent*
New Orleans *Daily Delta*
New Orleans *Daily Picayune*
New Orleans *True Delta*
New York *Herald*
New York *Post*
New York *Times*
New York *Tribune*
Washington *Chronicle*
Washington *National Intelligencer*
Washington *National Republican*
Washington *Post*

Other Primary Sources

Adams, Charles Francis, Jr. *Charles Francis Adams*. Boston, 1900.
Adams, Henry. *The Education of Henry Adams*. Boston, 1918.
Ashkenazi, Elliott, ed. *The Civil War Diary of Clara Solomon: Growing Up in New Orleans, 1861–1862*. Baton Rouge, 1995.
Basler, Roy P., ed. *The Collected Works of Abraham Lincoln*. 9 vols. New-Brunswick, N.J., 1953.
Bates, Edward. *The Diary of Edward Bates, 1859–1866*. Washington, D.C., 1933.
Beale, Howard K., ed. *The Diary of Edward Bates*. American Historical Association Report for 1930, Vol. IV. Washington, D.C., 1933.
Blair, Montgomery. "Opening the Mississippi." *The United Service: A Monthly Review of Military and Naval Affairs*, IV (January, 1881), 33–41.
Butler, Benjamin F. *Autobiography and Personal Reminiscences of Major General Benjamin F. Butler: Butler's Book*. Boston, 1892.
———. *Character and Results of the War*. Philadelphia, 1863.
Carpenter, George N. *History of the Eighth Regiment, Vermont Volunteers, 1861–1865*. Boston, 1886.
Chase, Salmon P. *Diary and Correspondence of Salmon P. Chase in Annual Report of the American Historical Association for the Year 1902*. Vol. II. Washington, D.C., 1903.
Chesnut, Mary Boykin. *A Diary from Dixie*. New York, 1906.

Corsan, W. C. *Two Months in the Confederate States.* Edited by Benjamin H. Trask. 1863; rpr. Baton Rouge, 1996.

Davis, Jefferson. *The Rise and Fall of the Confederate Government.* 2 vols. New York, 1881.

Dawson, Sarah Morgan. *A Confederate Girl's Diary.* Boston, 1913.

De Forest, John W. *A Volunteer's Adventures.* New Haven, 1946.

Dix, Morgan, ed. *Memoirs of John Adams Dix.* 2 vols. New York, 1883.

Donald, David, ed. *Inside Lincoln's Cabinet: The Civil War Diaries of Salmon P. Chase.* New York, 1954.

Dorsey, Sarah A. *Recollections of Henry Wadkins Allen.* New York, 1866.

Dow, Neal. *The Reminiscences of Neal Dow.* Portland, Maine, 1898.

East, Charles, ed. *Sarah Morgan: The Civil War Diary of a Southern Woman.* Athens, Ga., 1991.

Farragut, Loyall. *The Life of David Glasgow Farragut: First Admiral of the U.S. Navy.* New York, 1879.

Foltz, Charles S. *Surgeon of the Seas: The Life of Surgeon General Jonathan M. Foltz.* Indianapolis, 1931.

Gardner, Charles. *Gardner's New Orleans Directory for 1861.* New Orleans, 1861.

Grant, Ulysses S. *Official Report of Lt.-Gen. U. S. Grant.* New York, 1865.

———. *Personal Memoirs of U. S. Grant.* 2 vols. New York, 1885.

Greeley, Horace. *The American Conflict.* 2 vols. Hartford, 1864.

Gurowski, Adam. *Diary of Adam Gurowski.* 3 vols. Boston, 1862; New York, 1864.

Howe, Henry Warren Howe. *Passages from the Life of Henry Warren Howe, Consisting of Diary and Letters Written During the Civil War, 1861–1865.* Lowell, Mass., 1899.

Humphreys, Andrew A. *The Virginia Campaign of '64 and '65: The Army of the Potomac and the Army of the James.* New York, 1883.

Johnson, Robert U., and Clarence C. Buel, eds. *Battles and Leaders of the Civil War.* 4 vols. New York, 1884–88.

Jones, John Beauchamp. *A Rebel War Clerk's Diary.* 2 vols. Philadelphia, 1866.

Jones, Katherine M. *Heroines of Dixie: Confederate Women Tell Their Story of the War.* New York, 1955.

Lovell, Mansfield. *Correspondence Between the War Department and General Lovell Relating to the Defense of New Orleans.* Richmond, 1863.

Lufkin, Edwin B. *History of the Thirteenth Maine Regiment from Its Organization in 1861 to Its Muster-Out in 1865.* Bridgton, Maine, 1898.

Marshall, Jessie Ames, comp. *Private and Official Correspondence of Gen. Benjamin F. Butler During the Period of the Civil War*. 5 vols. Norwood, Mass., 1917.

McClellan, George B. *George B. McClellan's Own Story*. New York, 1887.

McClure, Alexander K. *Colonel Alexander K. McClure's Recollections of a Half Century*. Salem, 1912.

McGuire, Judith White [Brockenbrough]. *Diary of a Southern Refugee, During the War. By a Lady of Virginia*. New York, 1867.

Morgan, James Morris. *Recollections of a Rebel Reefer*. Boston, 1917.

Murray, Thomas Hamilton. *History of the Ninth Regiment, Connecticut Volunteer Infantry, "The Irish Regiment" in the War of the Rebellion, 1861–1865*. New Haven, 1903.

Nicolay, John G., and John Hay. *Abraham Lincoln: A History*. 10 vols. New York, 1914.

Niven, John, ed. *The Salmon P. Chase Papers*. 3 vols. Kent, Ohio, 1993–96.

Paine, Albert Bigelow. *A Sailor of Fortune: Personal Memoirs of Captain B. S. Osborn*. New York, 1906.

Papers of the Military Historical Society of Massachusetts. Vol. IX. Boston, 1912.

Pierrepont, Edwards. *A Review by Judge Pierrepont of Gen. Butler's Defense Before the House of Representatives, in Relation to the New Orleans Gold*. New York, 1865.

Porter, David Dixon. *Incidents and Anecdotes of the Civil War*. New York, 1885.

Puffer, Alfred F. "Our General." *Atlantic Monthly*, XII (July, 1863), 104–115.

Richardson, James D. *A Compilation of the Messages and Papers of the Confederacy, Including the Diplomatic Correspondence, 1861–1865*. 2 vols. Nashville, 1906.

Ross, Edmund G. *History of the Impeachment of Andrew Johnson*. Santa Fe, 1896.

Rouse, E. S. S. *The Bugle Blast; or, Spirit of the Conflict*. Philadelphia, 1864.

Rowland, Kate Mason, and M. L. Croxwell, eds. *The Journal of Julia Le Grand, New Orleans, 1862–1863*. Richmond, 1911.

Russell, William Howard. *My Diary, North and South*. Boston, 1863.

Seward, Frederick W. *Seward at Washington*. 3 vols. New York, 1891.

Sherman, William T. *Memoirs of General W. T. Sherman*. 2 vols. New York, 1891.

Smith, George G. *Leaves from a Soldier's Diary*. Putnam, Conn., 1906.

Southern Historical Society Papers. 52 vols. Millwood, N.Y., 1977.

Southwood, Marion. *"Beauty and Booty": The Watchword of New Orleans*. New York, 1867.

Sprague, Homer B. *History of the Thirteenth Infantry Regiment of Connecticut Volunteers, During the Great Rebellion.* Hartford, 1867.

Stanyan, John M. *A History of the Eighth Regiment of New Hampshire Volunteers.* Concord, N.H., 1892.

Stephens, Alexander H. *A Constitutional View of the Late War Between the States.* 2 vols. Philadelphia, 1868.

Swinton, William. *History of the Seventh Regiment, National Guard, State of New York, During the War of the Rebellion.* New York, 1870.

Taylor, Richard. *Destruction and Reconstruction: Personal Experiences of the Late War.* New York, 1879.

Thompson, Robert Means, and Richard Wainwright, eds. *Confidential Correspondence of Gustavus Vasa Fox.* 2 vols. New York, 1938.

Velazquez, Loreta Janeta. *The Woman in Battle: A Narrative of the Exploits, Adventures, and Travels of Madame Loreta Janeta Velazquez, Otherwise Known as Lieutenant Harry T. Buford, Confederate States Army.* Hartford, 1876.

Watson, William. *Life in the Confederate Army, Being the Observations and Experiences of an Alien in the South During the American Civil War.* New York, 1888.

Welles, Gideon. "Admiral Farragut and New Orleans, with an Account of the Origin and the First Three Naval Expeditions of the War." *The Galaxy: An Illustrated Magazine of Entertaining Reading,* XII (November, 1871), 673–82; (December, 1871), 817–32.

———. *The Diary of Gideon Welles.* Edited by John T. Morse. 3 vols. Boston, 1911.

Williams, B. A., ed. *Mary Boykin Chesnut: A Diary from Dixie.* Boston, 1949.

Williams, Thomas. "Letters of General Thomas Williams, 1862." *American Historical Review,* XIV (January, 1909), 307–38.

Woodward, C. Vann, ed. *Mary Chesnut's Civil War.* New Haven, 1981.

Secondary Sources

Asbury, Herbert. *The French Quarter: An Informal History of the New Orleans Underworld.* New York, 1989.

Bancroft, Frederic. *The Life of William H. Seward.* 2 vols. New York, 1900.

Baudier, Roger. *The Catholic Church in Louisiana.* New Orleans, 1939.

Berry, Mary F. "Negro Troops in Blue and Gray: The Louisiana Native Guards, 1861–1863." *Journal of Louisiana History,* VIII (Spring, 1967), 165–90.

Bland, T. A. *Life of Benjamin F. Butler.* Boston, 1879.

Boatner, Mark M. *The Civil War Dictionary.* New York, 1959.

Bonham, Milledge L., Jr. *The British Consuls in the Confederacy.* New York, 1911.

Bowen, James L. *Massachusetts in the War, 1861–1865.* Springfield, Mass., 1889.

Bragg, Jefferson Davis. *Louisiana in the Confederacy.* Baton Rouge, 1941.

Caskey, Willie Malvin. *Secession and Restoration in Louisiana.* Baton Rouge, 1938.

Coulter, E. Merton. *The Confederate States of America, 1861–1865.* Baton Rouge, 1950. Vol. VII of Coulter, *A History of the South.*

Crowley, Charles. *History of Lowell.* Boston, 1868.

Cutts, Cecil H. *Life and Public Services of General John Wolcott Phelps.* New York, 1887.

Dabney, Thomas Ewing. "The Butler Regime in Louisiana." *Louisiana Historical Quarterly,* XXVII (April, 1944), 487–526.

Dowdey, Clifford. *Experiment in Rebellion.* Garden City, N.Y., 1946.

Du Bois, W. E. Burghardt. *Black Reconstruction.* New York, 1935.

DuFour, Charles L. *The Night the War Was Lost.* New York, 1960.

Egan, Clifford L. "Friction in New Orleans: General Butler Versus the Spanish Consul." *Journal of Louisiana History,* IX (Winter, 1987), 43–52.

Everett, Donald E. "Ben Butler and the Louisiana Native Guards, 1861–1862." *Journal of Southern History,* XXIV (1958), 201–17.

Faust, Patricia L., ed. *Historical Times Illustrated: Encyclopedia of the Civil War.* New York, 1986.

Ficklin, John Rose. "History of Reconstruction in Louisiana." *Johns Hopkins University Studies in Historical and Political Science,* XXVII (1940), 9–33.

Flower, Frank Abial. *Edwin McMasters Stanton.* New York, 1904.

Flower, Milton. *James Parton: The Father of Modern Biography.* Durham, 1951.

Gorham, George C. *Life and Public Services of Edwin M. Stanton.* Boston, 1899.

Gragg, Rod. *Confederate Goliath: The Battle of Fort Fisher.* Baton Rouge, 1994.

Hart, Albert Bushnell. *Salmon Portland Chase.* Boston, 1899.

Hearn, Chester G. *Admiral David Dixon Porter: The Civil War Years.* Annapolis, 1996.

———. *The Capture of New Orleans, 1862.* Baton Rouge, 1995.

Helis, Thomas W. "Of Generals and Jurists: The Judicial System of New Orleans Under Union Occupation, May 1862–April 1865." *Journal of Louisiana History,* XXIX (Spring, 1988), 143–55.

Henry, Robert Selph. *The Story of Reconstruction*. Indianapolis, 1938.

Hesseltine, William B. *Lincoln and the War Governors*. New York, 1948.

Hollandsworth, James G., Jr. *The Louisiana Native Guards: The Black Military Experience During the Civil War*. Baton Rouge, 1995.

Holzman, Robert S. *Stormy Ben Butler*. New York, 1954.

Horowitz, Murray M. "Ben Butler and the Negro: 'Miracles Are Occurring.'" *Journal of Louisiana History*, XVII (Spring, 1976), 159–86.

Johnson, Howard Palmer. "New Orleans Under General Butler." *Louisiana Historical Quarterly*, XXIV (April, 1941), 434–536.

Kendall, John Smith. "Christ Church and General Butler." *Louisiana Historical Quarterly*, XXIII (October, 1940), 1241–57.

————. *History of New Orleans*. 3 vols. Chicago, 1922.

King, Grace. *New Orleans: The Place and the People*. New York, 1904.

Lang, James O. "Gloom Envelopes New Orleans: April 24 to May 2, 1862." *Journal of Louisiana History*, I (Summer, 1960), 281–99.

Lathrop, Barnes F. "The La Fourche District in 1862: Invasion." *Journal of Louisiana History*, II (Spring, 1961), 175–201.

Lewis, Charles Lee. *David Glasgow Farragut: Our First Admiral*. Annapolis, 1943.

Lonn, Ella. *Foreigners in the Confederacy*. Chapel Hill, N.C., 1940.

Lothrop, Thornton Kirkland. *William Henry Seward*. Boston, 1898.

Macartney, Clarence Edward. *Lincoln and His Generals*. Philadelphia, 1925.

McClure, Alexander K. *Abraham Lincoln and Men of War-Times*. Philadelphia, 1892.

McLaughlin, James Fairfax. *The American Cyclops: The Hero of New Orleans and Spoiler of Silver Spoons*. Baltimore, 1868.

Mahan, Alfred T. *Admiral Farragut*. New York, 1905.

Meneely, A. Howard. *The War Department, 1861: A Study in Mobilization and Administration*. New York, 1928.

Nash, Howard P., Jr. *Stormy Petrel: The Life and Times of General Benjamin F. Butler, 1818–1893*. Rutherford, N.J., 1969.

Nevins, Allan. *The Emergence of Lincoln*. 2 vols. New York, 1950.

Nichols, Roy Frank. *The Democratic Machine, 1850–1854*. 2 vols. New York, 1923.

Nicolay, John G., and John Hay. *Abraham Lincoln: A History*. 10 vols. New York, 1914.

Niven, John. *Gideon Welles: Lincoln's Secretary of the Navy*. New York, 1973.

Orcutt, William Dana. "Ben Butler and the 'Stolen Spoons.'" *North American Review*, CCVII (January, 1918), 66–80.

Owsley, Frank Lawrence. *King Cotton Diplomacy*. Chicago, 1931.

Parton, James. "Butler's Landing in New Orleans." *Journal of Louisiana History*, III (Spring, 1962), 146–48.

———. *General Butler in New Orleans*. New York, 1863.

Pearson, Henry Greenleaf. *The Life of John A. Andrew*. 2 vols. Boston, 1904.

Pomeroy, Marcus M. *Life and Public Services of Benjamin F. Butler, Major-General in the Army and Leader of the Republican Party*. New York, 1868.

Quarles, Benjamin. *The Negro in the Civil War*. Boston, 1953.

Reed, Emily Hazen. *Life of A. P. Dostie; or, The Conflict of New Orleans*. New York, 1868.

Reed, Rowena. *Combined Operations of the Civil War*. Lincoln, Nebr., 1993.

Rhodes, James Ford. *History of the United States from the Compromise of 1850 to the Final Restoration of Home Rule in the South*. 8 vols. New York, 1902–19.

Rightor, Henry, ed. *Standard History of New Orleans, Louisiana*. Chicago, 1900.

Roberts, A. Sellew. "The Federal Government and Confederate Cotton." *American Historical Review*, XXXII (1927), 262–75.

Robertson, William Glenn. *Back Door to Richmond: The Bermuda Hundred Campaign, April–June, 1864*. Newark, Del., 1987.

Roman, Alfred. *The Military Operations of General Beauregard in the War Between the States*. 2 vols. New York, 1883.

Sandburg, Carl. *Abraham Lincoln: The War Years*. 4 vols. New York, 1939.

Saxon, Lyle. *Fabulous New Orleans*. New York, 1928.

Schugg, Roger W. *Origins of Class Struggle in Louisiana: A Social History of White Farmers and Laborers During Slavery and After, 1840–1875*. Baton Rouge, 1939.

Sinclair, Harold. *The Port of New Orleans*. Garden City, N.Y., 1942.

Smith, William Ernest. *The Francis Preston Blair Family in Politics*. 2 vols. New York, 1933.

Steiner, Bernard Christian. *Life of Reverdy Johnson*. Baltimore, 1914.

Storey, Moorfield. *The Record of Benjamin F. Butler*. Boston, 1883.

Thayer, William Roscoe. *The Life and Letters of John Hay*. 2 vols. Boston, 1915.

Trefousse, Hans Louis. *Ben Butler: The South Called Him Beast*. New York, 1957.

Werlich, Robert. *Beast Butler: The Incredible Career of Major General Benjamin Franklin Butler*. Washington, D.C., 1962.

West, Richard S. "Admiral Farragut and General Butler." *U.S. Naval Institute Proceedings*, no. 640 (June, 1956), 635–43.

———. *Gideon Welles*. Indianapolis, 1943.

———. *Lincoln's Scapegoat General: A Life of Benjamin F. Butler*. Boston, 1965.

———. *The Second Admiral: The Life of David Dixon Porter, 1813–1891*. New York, 1937.

Westwood, Howard C. "Benjamin Butler's Enlistment of Black Troops in New Orleans in 1862." *Journal of Louisiana History*, XXVI (Winter, 1985), 5–22.

Williams, Kenneth P. *Lincoln Finds a General: A Military Study of the Civil War*. 3 vols. New York, 1949–52.

Williams, T. Harry. *Lincoln and His Generals*. New York, 1952.

———. *Lincoln and the Radicals*. Madison, Wis., 1941.

Wilson, Joseph T. *The Black Phalanx: A History of the Negro Soldiers of the United States in the Wars of 1775–1812, 1861–'65*. Hartford, 1888.

Winters, John D. *The Civil War in Louisiana*. Baton Rouge, 1979.

INDEX